THE SIGNIFICANCE OF SECTIONS IN
AMERICAN HISTORY

BY

FREDERICK JACKSON TURNER

WITH AN INTRODUCTION BY
MAX FARRAND

NEW YORK
HENRY HOLT AND COMPANY

INTRODUCTION

Professor Turner left among his papers a memorandum upon the gathering and reprinting of his several essays relating to sections in the United States. He evidently had in mind a companion volume to *The Frontier in American History*. Also among his papers are four pages written with his own hand that must have been an introduction to a lecture or series of lectures in 1924 showing a large number of maps. Two paragraphs from those pages will serve as the author's explanation of the place these essays had in the development of his own studies and thinking:

Looking back over my work as a university teacher, which ends this year, I find that the central interest of my study has been that of these maps of population advance—not as a student of a region, but of a process. From cave man to the occupation of the planet. Study of American advance required examination of the geographic, economic, social, diplomatic advances of the frontier, leading to a paper on "The Significance of the Frontier in American History," published 1893; to studies of the diplomatic contest for the Mississippi Valley; to examination of the sectional aspects of the advance into new geographic areas, which compelled me to study conditions in the various Atlantic Coast regions leading to migration, and into the effects of the newer regions upon these older ones, and to study the special geographic problems into which the various zones of advance brought new societies—the interaction of the various migrating stocks, each in its particular geographic province, adjusting to new social types, and the resulting play of sectional forces in American politics as the old and the new sections found in

[iii]

Congress and in party the need of adjustment or the impulse to conflict.

As a result, I have been led to a study of the various sections of the United States, both internally and in their mutual relations with each other and the federal government.

In accordance with the first memorandum, Professor Avery Craven and the writer have worked over the essays listed and have arranged them as we think Professor Turner might have done. The author was accustomed to keep copies of his printed articles, upon which he would make annotations in the margins, and sometimes he would file with these copies criticisms and suggestions that had occurred to him or he had received from others. Occasionally these notes embody specific corrections of the text; in most cases they are merely suggestions for possible elaboration or modification. The essays are reprinted here as they originally appeared; corrections have been made only when the author indicated them, and footnotes have been added relating to comments or notations if they seem to be of sufficient importance. For example, the article in the *Yale Review*, "The Children of the Pioneers," attracted considerable attention and evoked letters from various people who had suggestions to offer, and subsequently Turner himself noted many names of persons worthy of consideration. The article might be expanded almost indefinitely, but no attempt has been made to do so, for in its original form it represents a phase of the author's thinking at that time.

Professor Turner's former secretary, Mr. Merrill H. Crissey, has been of the greatest assistance in finding the material and in preparing it for reprinting. Grateful recognition is also given to the editors and publishers whose courteous permission has made possible the publication of this volume; specific acknowledgment is made in connection with each of the several essays. Perhaps attention should be called to three articles that were printed in the *Cyclopedia of American Government* (1914; edited by A. C. McLaughlin and A. B. Hart). They seemed hardly suitable for inclusion in this volume; yet they are valuable, concise summaries of the topics treated and contain, as did practically everything Turner wrote, statements and suggestions deserving consideration by anyone attempting to trace the development of ideas in the mind of one of America's constructive historical thinkers. "Greater New England in the Middle of the Nineteenth Century" (*Proceedings of the American Antiquarian Society,* 1919) is also omitted from this collection. The author did not include it in his list, probably because the substance is embodied in the chapter, from his forthcoming work, "The United States, 1830-1850: The Nation and Its Sections," that was printed in the first number of the *Huntington Library Bulletin* (May, 1931). It should, however, be taken into account as representing the stage of the author's study at that time.

MAX FARRAND

San Marino, California
May 27, 1932

CONTENTS

[vii]

MAPS

THE SIGNIFICANCE OF SECTIONS IN
AMERICAN HISTORY

CHAPTER I

PROBLEMS IN AMERICAN HISTORY [1]

A catalogue of specific problems which await solution in American history is, I am sure, not expected. Such a list would be altogether too large for the limits assigned to this paper, even if it were a desirable undertaking in itself. I prefer to discuss some larger lines of reconstruction of United States history, some points of view from which it may be approached, in the belief that such an estimate may be of service in presenting tests for determining the relative importance of our problems and in bringing into view some neglected fields of study and neglected methods of investigation.

In many ways the problems of American history differ from those of Old World history. The documents are, for the most part, recent, and exist in comparative abundance, although scattered and incompletely collected. Our problems with respect to material are therefore not primarily those of the technique of verification and criticism of scanty documents, but are chiefly those of garnering the scattered material, printed and written; making bibliographies and indexes; and, in general, rendering available for historical workers the sources for understanding our development. The American Historical Association (through its various committees), the Library of Congress, the Carnegie Institution, and other agencies, have already inaugu-

[1] Reprinted by permission from Congress of Arts and Science, Universal Exposition, St. Louis, 1904, Vol. II; published by Houghton, Mifflin and Company, 1906.

[3]

rated important work in finding and listing archives and manuscripts. But very much remains to be done in these respects, for material that would be of inestimable service to the historian is daily disappearing, and the existing material is inadequately known and used. The lack of systematic bibliographies of the documents in the various states of the Union, in the national archives and libraries, and in the foreign countries with which we have come in contact, or from which we have derived our origins, is much to be regretted. Comparatively moderate expenditures by historical societies and by the state and national governments to perfect their documentary collections and to make them known, would revolutionize our study and obviate the necessity of rewriting a great mass of our history. We are now using incomplete material when rich stores of documents casting new light upon our problems remain. The American historian is, I think, continually impressed with the unwisdom of reliance upon a partial collection of documents, although they may be examined with the minute and critical methods of the trained historical critic, when an abundance of material exists. In illustration, I may suggest that a large part of our early diplomatic history has been written from American printed material without the use of the archives of England, France, and Spain, and that speculation has too frequently taken the place of discussion of evidence actually in existence. This problem of materials is presented also in the neglect of our growing and practical people—more interested in making than in preserving history—to accumulate the records of its developments. In how few libraries are to be found complete collections of the early session laws of the various states, and particularly those of the group west of the Alleghenies! Indeed, how few of these states have themselves collected complete sets of their own public documents and newspapers. A whole era is thus becoming increasingly difficult to understand and to record. These problems of the preservation and organization of material are among the most pressing. Traveling missionaries of history who should explore the South and West, for example, listing and copying or bringing into secure and accessible libraries the materials in the form of newspapers, pamphlets, journals, correspondence, business records, etc., would do a work that posterity would recognize with gratitude.

Passing from this preliminary problem of the accumulation and listing of material, I desire next to raise the question, What is the special significance of American history? This should afford a test for determining the grand strategy of an attack upon its fundamental problems.

The especial contributions which students of American history are capable of making to the study of history in general are determined, it seems to me, by the peculiar importance of American history for understanding the processes of social development. Here we have a vast continent, originally a wilderness, at first very sparsely occupied by primitive peoples, opened by discovery to settlement by Europeans, who carry their institutions and ideas from the Old World to America. They are compelled to adjust old institutions to their new environment; to create new institutions to meet the new conditions; to evolve new ideas of life and new ethnic and social types by contact under these conditions; to rise steadily through successive stages of economic, political, and social development to a highly organized civilization; to become themselves colonists of new wildnerness areas beyond the first spheres of settlement; to deal again with the primitive peoples at their borders—in short, continuously to develop, almost under the actual observation of the present day, those social and industrial stages which, in the Old World, lie remote from the historian and can only be faintly understood by scanty records.[2] The factor of time in American history is insignificant when compared with the factors of space and social evolution. Loria has insisted that colonial society exhibits in social development material comparable in the study of society to that brought into view for the geologist's inspection by the upheavals of the earth's crust. These have elevated deep-lying strata of geological formations, so that it is possible from them to read the earlier pages of the history of the earth. But the idea is incompletely stated in this form, for the whole period of American history exhibits recurrences of the colonial society, modified by different frontier physiographic conditions, and by the character and intensity of industrial life of the society that throws off these new colonies. The process is still going on in those northern areas of prairies and plains in Canada, where we may pass, by railroad, from the youthful but highly organized manufacturing cities of the more densely peopled and still developing regions, through regions of increasingly scanty and primitive agricultural occupation, out to the waste of foothills, where the trail of the buffalo

[2] Discussed by the writer under the title, "Significance of the Frontier in American History," in the *Fifth Yearbook of the National Herbart Society*, and in *Report* of American Historical Association, 1893, p. 197. [Reprinted in *The Frontier in American History* (New York, 1920).]

seams the hillside, reaching to the far horizon line and showing the road which civilization will rapidly follow. It may frankly be conceded that the differences between the processes of social construction in Europe and in America are at least as important as the resemblances and analogies. But after all limitations are made, it remains true that the history of America offers a rich new field for the scientific study of social development, taken in the largest sense of the phrase.

The point which I wish to make, therefore, is that it is important to conceive of American history, first of all, as peculiarly rich in problems arising from the study of the evolution of society. Henry Adams has stated the matter in a somewhat less inclusive form in these words: "The scientific interest of American history centred in national character, and in the workings of a society destined to become vast, in which individuals were important chiefly as types. Although this kind of interest was different from that of European history, it was at least as important to the world. Should history ever become a true science, it must expect to establish its laws, not from the complicated story of rival European nationalities, but from the methodical evolution of a great democracy. North America was the most favorable field on the globe for the spread of a society so large, uniform, and isolated as to answer the purposes of science."

It is safe to say that the problems most important for consideration by historians of America are not those of the narrative of events or of the personality of leaders, but, rather, those which arise when American history is viewed as the record of the development of society in a wilderness environment; of the transformation of this society as it arose to higher cultural stages; of the spreading of it into new wildernesses by extension across the continent. In other words, we have to deal with the formation and expansion of the American people, the composition of the population, their institutions, their economic life, and their fundamental assumptions—what we may call the American spirit—and the relation of these to the different periods and conditions of American history.

If, then, the all-embracing problem in our history is the description and explanation of the progress of this society, at once developing and expanding, we shall find that within it are contained a multitude of subordinate problems. First, let us consider the phenomenon of our expanding society in reference to the fact that the vast spaces over which this forming people have spread are themselves a complex of physiographic sections. American sectionalism has been very inadequately dealt with by our historians. Impressed by the artificial political boundary lines of states, they have almost entirely given their attention either to national or to state history, or to the broad division of North and South, overlooking the fact that there are several natural, economic, and social sections that are fundamental in American historical development. As population extended itself, it flowed into various physiographic provinces, some of them comparable in size and resources, not only to the greater nations of Europe, but even to some of the great empires that have from time to time been formed by combinations of these nations. The American physical map may be regarded as a map of potential nations and empires, each to be conquered and colonized, each to rise through stages of development, each to achieve a certain social and industrial unity, each to possess certain fundamental assumptions, certain psychological traits, and each to interact with the others, and in combination to form that United States, the explanation of the development of which is the task of the historian.

The physiographers have recognized the existence of natural provinces and have mapped them under such names as the New England Plateaus, the Piedmont Plains, the Lake and Prairie Plains, the Gulf Plains, the Great Plains, etc. The Census Bureau has likewise attempted sectional divisions, on the basis of its maps of population, industrial conditions, resources, etc. Railroad managers realize and act upon the theory of such sections and study them with a thoroughness, an insight, and a power of constructive imagination that may well be imitated by the economists and historians. Sociologists, also, like Professor Giddings, have attempted to state a psychological classification of American sections. But as yet the historian has hardly begun the serious study of sectionalism, in the continent as a whole. And yet this is a fundamental fact in American history. We need studies designed to show what have been and are the natural, social, and economic divisions in the United States. We need to trace the colonization of these separate regions, the location, contributions, and influence of the various stocks that combined to produce their population. We should map the streams of migration of the settlers from the various sections into new provinces, and the areas of their settlement. Thus the composition of the sections will be revealed. We should study their economic evolution, their peculiar psychological traits, the leaders which they produced, their party history, their relations with other sections. Such a treatment would illuminate the history of the formation and character of the American people.

Perhaps I may be permitted to illustrate this idea somewhat. If the historian were to select the New England Plateaus as the province for his study, he would find that, after all the work that has been done in New England history, there remain some of the most fundamental problems for solution. Who is to trace for us the spread of population into the interior and north of New England during the second half of the seventeenth and the eighteenth century? Such a study, unfolding the economic and social aspects of the movement, the agrarian and religious causes at work, the modification of the people, the effects upon the social structure of New England, the party divisions and the institutions resultant, would give us important data for understanding that portion of New England which lies beyond the seaboard, and it would cast light upon the subsequent movement and contributions of this interior folk to New York and the Middle West. A detailed economic history of New England since the Revolution is sadly needed. It would bring out the relations of New England's physiography to her development; the pressure of population upon the hill regions; the transfer of economic interest from the sea to the water powers, from commerce to manufactures; the changing political attitude of the various portions of the section in response to the changing industrial interests; the economic, social, and religious conditions that led to the exodus from New England and the formation of a greater New England in the West. At present we do not know enough about this expansion of the New

England people—a movement certainly comparable in its importance, in its influence upon American history, to the much studied earlier colonization of the Puritans in New England proper. These later colonists carried New England men, institutions, and ideas into regions which far excelled the area from which they came, in size, in productiveness, and ultimately in political influence. The area of the northern counties of Illinois entered by New England settlers constitutes in itself a level region of solid fertility equal to the combined area of Massachusetts, Rhode Island, and Connecticut, with all their unproductive hills. The influence of New England upon the political history of the Middle West, and through it upon the nation, has been profound. Its effect in forming the social and moral ideas of the central region of the republic can hardly be overstated. But we really know but little about this colonization compared with the detailed information which historical investigators have given us about the location of the homes of the Pilgrims. We cannot even state with approximate correctness the periods when the various Western states received their largest numbers of New England settlers. Nor has the replacement of this New England stock in the parent region by immigration been adequately studied. We shall not understand the New England to today until we have a fuller account of the industrial, social, political, and religious effect of this transformation of New England by replacement of its labor population and by the revolution in its industrial life, with the accompaniments of social stratification, loss of homogeneity, and changed ideals in respect to democracy.

Not to dwell too long upon this region, let us turn

for a moment to indicate a few of the problems that arise when the South is considered from this same point of view. The term South as a sectional designation is misleading. Through a long period of our history the "Solid South" did not exist. We must bear in mind, not only the differences between the various states of the Southern seaboard, but also the more fundamental differences between the upcountry (the Piedmont region) and the Atlantic Plains. The interior of the South needs treatment as a unit. State historians of Virginia and the Carolinas, for example, recognize the fundamental contrasts in physiography, colonization, stock, and economic and social characteristics, between the lowlands and the uplands in their respective states. But as yet no one has attacked the problem of the settlement, development, and influence of the Piedmont Plains as a whole. This peninsula, as we may conceive it, thrust down through the Great Valley from Pennsylvania, between the mountains and the seaboard, the land that received the German, Scotch-Irish, and poorer white English settlers, developed, in the second half of the eighteenth century, an independent social, economic, and political character. It was a region of free labor upon small farms. It was devoted to cereals rather than to the great staple crops of the seaboard. In its social structure it was more like Pennsylvania than the Southern commonwealths with which it was politically connected. It struggled for just representation in the legislatures, and for adequate local self-government. The domestic history of the South is for many years the history of a contest between these eastern and western sections. When the cotton belt, with slavery as its labor element, spread across this

Piedmont area, the region became assimilated to the seaboard. The small farmers, raising crops by the labor of their own families, were compelled either to adjust themselves to the plantation economy, or to migrate. The process of this transformation and its effects constitute a problem not yet worked out in details. A migration of small farmers from the Piedmont across the Ohio and into the Gulf region followed. Many had moral and religious objections to slavery; many were unable to change their agricultural habits to meet the new conditions; many lacked the necessary capital for a slave plantation and preferred to accept the price of their lands offered by the planters, and to migrate to the public lands where they could continue their old industrial and social type of society. In this expansion of the South into the Ohio Valley and the Gulf Plains we have a colonization demanding study. Indeed, the whole industrial and social history of the South has been obscured by the emphasis placed on the political aspects of the slavery struggle. We need a history of the plantation in its various areas and at different periods. Such a study would give us the key to Southern history. The rise and fall of cotton values, the price of slaves, the agrarian history of the South, the relation of its political demands to these conditions, the distribution of rival political parties in the region— these and similar topics would come into prominence if the historian should select for treatment the Southern provinces of the Atlantic Plains, the Piedmont, and the Gulf Plains, their interaction, and the shifting center of political power between them.

It is unnecessary to point out that similar advantages would come from attempts to explain the evolution of the social structure of the Lake and Prairie Plains, the Great Plains, the Pacific Coast, etc. We should study the contact of whites and Indians; the history of the occupation of the public lands in these provinces; the movement into them of settlers from other sections; the industrial transformations of the provinces from primitive farming up to the complex economic conditions of today; the development and influence of railroad systems; the rise of cities; the rise of peculiar views of life in the respective sections. Such topics carry with them a rich freightage of problems, essential to explain our own history and capable of casting important light upon the evolution of society as a whole.

The problems of interprovincial relations need study also. The whole history of American politics needs to be interpreted in the terms of a contest between these economic and social sections. Periods when it seemed that there was no great issue dividing political parties will be found to abound in evidences—in the legislation of Congress, for example—that intense political struggles actually went on between the separate sections, combining and rearranging their forces as occasion showed the need. It is only when we get below the surface of national politics to consider the sectional party groupings, that we are able to discover the lines on which new party issues are forming and the significance of the utterances of the leaders of these rival sections. Again and again, we shall find the party candidates anxious to conciliate the conflicting interests of the different sections and attempting to "straddle" upon vital problems, which nevertheless continue to force themselves to the front. The outcome is determined by the combination of these rival sections for and against the proposition. Studied from this point of view, the careers of J. Q. Adams, Clay, Calhoun, and Jackson, as spokesmen of their areas (to take examples), acquire new meaning and significance. Even more obvious, perhaps, is the slavery struggle. When it is stated that, in one important aspect, that struggle was a conflict between the Lake and Prairie plainsmen, on the one side, and the Gulf plainsmen, on the other, for the control of the Mississippi Valley, the Civil War acquires new meaning. Lincoln, Grant, and Sherman were the outcome of the influences of the Middle West; Davis, Yancey, and A. S. Johnston came from the Cotton Kingdom of the Gulf Plains. We are forced to reëxamine the political strife with reference to the forces which conditioned the leaders of these rival sections. We are obliged to study such problems as the development of the industrial resources of the regions, both before and during the war.

The economic rivalries and industrial interrelations of the different sections of the country also are continuous factors in our history, and are more familiar to business men and to railroad managers than they are, as a rule, to the historian.

Passing, with these suggestions, from the problems that arise on breaking up our subject into provinces, let us next note that, for the explanation of the United States, we need historical investigation of a large number of topics as yet very imperfectly studied. It will be possible only to suggest some of the more important. First, let us inquire how far American historians have seriously attempted the study of the formation and development of our national character. The transition of the people of the United States from the conflicting ideals and traits of the colonial period to the present ideals of the nation, constitutes an important study in the evolution of the culture of the people, and, as yet, has been only imperfectly examined. We need to investigate the forces by which the composite nationality of the United States has been created, the process by which these different sections have been welded into such a degree of likeness that the United States now constitutes a measurably homogeneous people in certain important respects. We need to study the rise and growth of the intellectual character of the people, as shown in their literature and art, in connection with the social and economic conditions of the various periods of our history. In short, we need a natural history of the American spirit.

To take another topic, we need a political history of the United States which shall penetrate beneath the surface of the proceedings of national conventions to the study of the evolution of the organs of party action and of those underlying social and economic influences in the states and sections which explain party action. This matter has been indicated in connection with the importance of studying our history from the point of view of rival sections, but it is of sufficient importance to warrant separate consideration. We need to give a social and economic interpretation to the history of political parties in this country. In illustration, I may say that maps giving the location of Democratic counties and Republican counties in the states of the Old Northwest, through several decades of our history, show an astonishing coherence and persistence in area of these rival parties. Transition areas show close votes as a rule. This indicates that party grouping depends upon such social factors as nativity, persistence of traditions, economic conditions, etc., even more than upon leadership and reasoning. When such a study of our party development shall have been made, we shall be in a better position to comprehend the laws that determine party action in general, and an important contribution will have been made to the understanding of the development of society.

Another topic very inadequately treated is the agrarian history of the United States. To take one phase of it, we lack an extended history of the public domain in its economic and political influence. Fragments of these topics have been dealt with by able scholars, but we have no complete treatise on the subject. If, as I believe, the free lands of the United States have been the most important single factor in explaining our development, there should be increased attention to the land system. The history of land tenure and land values, the effects of the cheaper lands of the newly occupied regions upon the older settled country, the relation of cheap lands to wages and to society in general, need to be considered.

The subject of immigration has been hardly more than touched by the American historian. In spite of the fact that so vast a body of our population has been drawn since the later colonial days from non-English stocks, the history of the European conditions that brought these people to us, the process of transformation of the immigrants into American citizens, the effects which they produced upon American society and industrial life, are all too little known. We shall not understand the American people without giving much more attention to this important subject.

It is impossible to do more than name some of the long list of topics as yet inadequately treated. There is needed a study of our relations to the American Indian. No systematic study of this problem as a whole has been made, and yet it is an exceedingly important one in the history of American development, and one from which rich results may be expected. It is hardly necessary to say that such a study of the negro is needed. The history of the law in America remains to be written by the coöperative study of men trained to historical investigation as well as in the law. The history of religion and of the various churches in the United States has not yet been written as a phase of the general social development of the American people. It should be considered in its relation to American history as a whole, and it will be found that some of the most fundamental factors in our history require such a study for their explanation. Recently some important beginnings have been made at a history of labor in America. This has been one of the most important neglected fields in our history, and it is to be hoped that thorough investigation will be given to the rise of the laboring classes, the organization of labor, and its influence in American society. Somewhat connected with the same topic is the study of the development of democracy in the United States. As yet we know but imperfectly the stages in the development of the political power of the common people. A complete history of the franchise in this country and of the organization of the masses to impress their will upon legislation is a desideratum. A comparative study of the process of settlement of the United States would be another important contribution. If, with our own methods of the occupation of the frontier, we should compare those of other countries which have dealt with similar problems—such as Russia, Germany, and the English colonies in Canada, Australia, and Africa—we should undoubtedly find most fruitful results.

But I pass from the enumeration of these tempting problems of topical history—an enumeration which is merely begun, not at all completed—to suggest next that certain periods and areas of our history have been inadequately treated. The whole colonial history of the eighteenth century needs study. The Revolution and French and Indian wars of that period have withdrawn attention from the contemporaneous transformations in our economic, political, and social institutions. In some respects, this was the period of formation of the peculiarly American institutions in contrast to the English institutions that were imported. Then it was that the American people, psychologically considered, originated. But little attention has been given to the period, aside from its military aspect.

The generation that followed the Civil War has yet to read its history also. The time would seem to have come when the historians should bestow some of their attention upon the wonderful development of the nation since the Reconstruction period. How profoundly our whole life has changed in that period, it is unnecessary to say. The vast organizations of labor and capital; the tremendous increase in immigration whereby the American stock has been modified; the extraordinary growth of transportation facilities, and society with them; the concentration of industries; the spread of our commerce abroad, and the rise of the United States into the position of a world power; the new political issues—are but a few of the subjects as yet dealt with by the historian in only a cursory way.

From the lack of attention to our recent history, it follows that the area between the Mississippi and the Rocky Mountains—an empire in itself—is almost virgin soil for the historian. Nor is it a region without interest. It is doubtful whether, anywhere, more profitable work could be done than in the interpretation of the formation of society in this vast domain of the prairies.

Perhaps the first problem of all—one that I shall content myself with stating merely—is the problem of how to apportion the field of American history itself among the social sciences. The conception that history is past politics is now but little regarded, and the conception of history as the study designed to enable a people to understand itself, by understanding its origins and development in all the main departments of human life, is becoming the dominant one. But the history of the American people forces upon our attention the fact that no satisfactory undertsanding of the evolution of this people is possible without calling into coöperation many sciences and methods hitherto but little used by the American historian. Data drawn from studies of literature and art, politics, economics, sociology, psychology, biology, and physiography, all must be used. The method of the statistician as well as that of the critic of evidence is absolutely essential. There has been too little coöperation of these sciences, and the result is that great fields have been neglected. There are too many overlapping grounds left uncultivated owing to this independence of the sciences, too many problems that have been studied with inadequate apparatus, and without due regard to their complexity. I propose no solution of the difficulty; but it is important fairly to face it, and to realize that, without the combined effort of allied sciences, we shall reach no such results in the study of social development as have been achieved in the physical world by the attack of problems of natural science by the combined forces of physics, chemistry, and mathematics.

In short, American history should be studied as capable of making most illuminating contributions to the history of social development. All of the apparatus needed to solve the problems arising from this conception of the nature of American history should be used.

CHAPTER II

THE SIGNIFICANCE OF THE SECTION
IN AMERICAN HISTORY [1]

A generation ago I published in the *Proceedings* of this Society a paper, which I had read at the summer meeting of the American Historical Association, on "The Significance of the Frontier in American History." The Superintendent of the Census had just announced that a frontier line could no longer be traced, and had declared: "In the discussion of its extent, its westward movement, etc., it cannot therefore any longer have a place in the census reports."

The significance in American history of the advance of the frontier and of its disappearance is now generally recognized. This evening I wish to consider with you another fundamental factor in American history—namely, the Section. Arising from the facts of physical geography and the regional settlement of different peoples and types of society on the Atlantic Coast, there was a sectionalism from the beginning. But soon this became involved and modified by the fact that these societies were expanding into the interior, following the frontier, and that their sectionalism took special forms in the presence of the growing West. Today we are substantially a settled nation without the overwhelming influence that accompanied the westward spread of population. Urban concentration, chiefly in the East, has reversed the movement to a considerable

[1] Reprinted by permission from *The Wisconsin Magazine of History,* March, 1925.

extent. We are more like Europe, and our sections are becoming more and more the American version of the European nation.

First let us consider the influence of the frontier and the West upon American sections. Until our own day, as I urged in that paper, the United States was always beginning over on its outer edge as it advanced into the wilderness. Therefore, the United States was both a developed and a primitive society. The West was a migrating region, a stage of society rather than a place. Each region reached in the process of expansion from the coast had its frontier experience, was for a time "the West," and when the frontier passed on to new regions, it left behind, in the older areas, memories, traditions, an inherited attitude toward life, that persisted long after the frontier had passed by. But while the influence of the frontier permeated East as well as West, by survival of the pioneer psychology and by the reaction of the Western ideals and life upon the East, it was in the newer regions, in the area called the West at any given time, that frontier traits and conceptions were most in evidence. This "West" was more than "the frontier" of popular speech. It included also the more populous transitional zone adjacent, which was still influenced by pioneer traditions and where economic society had more in common with the newer than with the older regions.

This "West," wherever found at different years, thought of itself and of the nation in different ways from those of the East. It needed capital; it was a debtor region, while the East had the capital and was a creditor section. The West was rural, agricultural, while the East was becoming more and more urban and

3

industrial. Living under conditions where the family
was the self-sufficing economic unit, where the complications of more densely settled society did not exist,
without accumulated inherited wealth, the frontier
regions stressed the rights of man, while the statesmen
who voiced the interests of the East stressed the rights
of property.

The West believed in the rule of the majority, in
what John Randolph, the representative of the Virginia
tidewater aristocracy, called "King Numbers." The
East feared an unchecked democracy, which might overturn minority rights, destroy established institutions, and
attack vested interests. The buoyant, optimistic, and
sometimes reckless and extravagant spirit of innovation
was the very life of the West. In the East innovation
was a term of reproach. It always "stalked" like an
evil spirit. The East represented accumulated experience, the traditions of the family living generation after
generation in a single location and under a similar
environment, as President Thwing, of Western Reserve
University, has aptly put it. But out in the newer West,
through most of its history, men lived in at least two
or three states in the course of their migrations. Of
the hundred and twenty-four members of the first Wisconsin constitutional convention in 1846, the average
was three states for each member. Four had moved
eight times. Sixteen had lived in five or more different
states, or foreign countries and states; six had lived in
seven or more.

The West demanded cheap or free lands on which to
base a democratic farming population. The ruling
interests in the East feared that such a policy would
decrease land values at home and diminish the value

of lands which its capitalists had purchased for speculation in the interior. It feared that cheap lands in the West would draw Eastern farmers into the wilderness; would break down the bonds of regular society; would prevent effective control of the discontented; would drain the labor supply away from the growing industrial towns, and thus raise wages.

The West opened a refuge from the rule of established classes, from the subordination of youth to age, from the sway of established and revered institutions. Writing in 1694, when the frontier lay at the borders of Boston Bay, the Reverend Cotton Mather asked: "Do our *Old* People any of them *Go Out* from the Institutions of God, swarming into New Settlements where they and their Untaught Families are like *to Perish for Lack of Vision?*" To their cost, he said, such men have "got unto the *Wrong side of the Hedge*" and "the Angel of the Lord becomes their enemy."

No doubt all this makes too sharply contrasted a picture. But from the beginning East and West have shown a sectional attitude. The interior of the colonies on the Atlantic was disrespectful of the coast, and the coast looked down upon the upland folk. The "Men of the Western World" when they crossed the Alleghenies became self-conscious and even rebellious against the rule of the East. In the thirties the tidewater aristocracy was conquered by the Jacksonian Democracy of the interior.

And so one could go on through the story of the antimonopolists, the Grangers, the Populists, the Insurgents, the Progressives, the Farmers' *Bloc,* and the La Follette movement, to illustrate the persistence of the sectionalism of the West, or of considerable parts of it, against the East.

Perhaps Eastern apprehension was never more clearly stated than by Gouverneur Morris, of Pennsylvania, in the Constitutional Convention of 1787. "The busy haunts of men, not the remote wilderness," said he, are "the proper school of political talents. If the western people get the power into their hands they will ruin the Atlantic interests. The back members are always averse to the best measures." He would so fix the ratio of representation that the number of representatives from the Atlantic States should always be larger than the number from the Western States. This, he argued, would not be unjust "as the Western settlers would previously know the conditions on which they were to possess their lands." So influential was his argument that the convention struck out the provision in the draft which guaranteed equality with the old states to the states thereafter to be admitted to the Union. But on the motion that the representatives from new states should not exceed those from the Old Thirteen, the affirmative vote was cast by Massachusetts, Connecticut, Delaware, and Maryland; Pennsylvania was divided; and the motion was defeated by the votes of the Southern States plus New Jersey.

To the average American, to most American historians, and to most of the writers of our school textbooks (if one can trust the indexes to their books), the word *section* applies only to the struggle of South against North on the questions of slavery, state sovereignty, and, eventually, disunion.

But the Civil War was only the most drastic and most tragic of sectional manifestations, and in no small degree the form which it took depended upon the fact that rival societies, free and slave, were marching side by side into the unoccupied lands of the West, each attempting to dominate the back country, the hinterland, working out agreements from time to time, something like the diplomatic treaties of European nations, defining spheres of influence, and awarding mandates, such as in the Missouri Compromise, the Compromise of 1850, and the Kansas-Nebraska Act. Each Atlantic section was, in truth, engaged in a struggle for power; and power was to be gained by drawing upon the growing West. In the Virginia ratification convention of 1787 William Grayson, by no means the most radical of the members, said: "I look upon this as a contest for empire. . . . If the Mississippi be shut up, emigrations will be stopped entirely. There will be no new states formed on the Western Waters. . . . This contest of the Mississippi involves the great national contest; that is whether one part of this continent shall govern the other. The Northern States have the majority and will endeavor to retain it." Similar conceptions abound in the utterances of North Atlantic statesmen. "It has been said," declared Morris in 1787, "that North Carolina, South Carolina and Georgia only, will in a little time have a majority of the people of America. They must in that case include the great interior country and everything is to be apprehended from their getting power into their hands."

If time permitted, it would be possible to illustrate by such utterances all through our history to very recent times how the Eastern sections regarded the West, with its advancing frontier, as the raw material for power. To New England, until her own children began to occupy the prairies ("reserved by God," as her pioneers declared, "for a pious and industrious people"), this aspect of the West threatened to enable the South perpetually to rule the nation. The first great migration, the most extensive in the area covered, flowed into the interior from the Southern upland. Some of the extreme leaders of the New England Federalists did not so much desire to break away from the South as to deprive that section of the three-fifths representation for its slaves, and either to permit the Western states to leave the Union or to see them won by England. Then the Old Thirteen could be united under conditions which would check the expansion of the South and would leave New England in control.

Writing in 1786 Rufus King, of New York, later senator and minister to England, while admitting that it was impolitic at the time wholly to give up the Western settlers, declared that very few men who had examined the subject would refuse their assent "to the opinion that every Citizen of the Atlantic States, who emigrates to the westward of the Alleghany is a total loss to our confederacy."

"Nature," he said, "has severed the two countries by a vast and extensive chain of mountains, interest and convenience will keep them separate, and the feeble policy of our disjointed Government will not be able to unite them. For these reasons I have ever been opposed to encouragements of western emigrants. The States situated on the Atlantic are not sufficiently populous, and losing our men is losing our greatest source of wealth."

Of course the immediate complaint in New England and New York was against the South itself, its Jeffersonian principles (so obnoxious to New England Puritanism), its slavery, its pro-French sympathies. But all these gained much of their force by the conviction that the West was a reservoir from which the South would continue to draw its power. Among the proposals of the Hartford Convention was that no new state should be admitted into the Union without the concurrence of two-thirds of both houses of Congress. Had this proposed amendment been made, the New England States with two other states in the Senate could have blocked the West from future statehood. The report warned the old states against "an overwhelming Western influence" and predicted that "finally the Western States, multiplied in numbers and augmented in population will control the interests of the whole." Nathan Dane, after whom Dane County in this state is named, furnished the argument for this proposed amendment by his elaborate tabulations and schedules. He pointed out that in the commercial states capital was invested in commerce, and in the slaveholding states in Western lands. When "Kentucky, Ohio and Tennessee were raised up by this interest & admitted into the Union, then the balance was, materially, affected. The non-commercial states pressed the admission of Louisiana and turned the balance against the Northeast." "It clearly follows," he reasoned, "that if a bare majority in Congress can admit new States into the union (all interior ones as they must be) at pleasure, in these immense Western regions, the balance of the union as once fairly contemplated, must soon be destroyed."

But Jackson defeated the British at New Orleans. The Mississippi Valley remained within the Union, Louisiana's interests became affiliated with the commercial states in many ways, and New England people poured so rapidly into the West that New England found in the northern half of the Valley the basis for a new alliance and new power as disturbing to the slave-holding South as the Southern and Western connection had been to New England.

By the middle of the century the South was alarmed at the Western power much in the way that New England had been. "I have very great fears," wrote Justice Campbell, later of the federal Supreme Court, from Mobile to Calhoun in 1847, "that the existing territories of the United States will prove too much for our government. The wild and turbulent conduct of the members upon the Oregon question and their rapacity and greediness in all matters connected with the appropriation of the revenues induces great doubt of the propriety of introducing new States in the Union so fast as we do." Of the legislators from the Western states he said: "Their notions are freer, their impulses stronger, their wills less restrained. I do not wish to increase the number till the New States already admitted to the Union become civilized."

On the other hand, it must be clearly borne in mind that as the West grew in power of population and in numbers of new senators, it resented the conception that it was merely an emanation from a rival North and South; that it was the dependency of one or another of the Eastern sections; that it was to be so limited and controlled as to maintain an equilibrium in the Senate between North and South. It took the attitude of a section itself.

From the beginning the men who went West looked to the future when the people beyond the Alleghenies should rule the nation. Dr. Manasseh Cutler, the active promoter of the Ohio Company of Associates, which made the first considerable permanent settlement in the Old Northwest Territory, wrote in 1787 a *Description of Ohio*. Though himself the minister at Ipswich, in the heart of that stronghold of conservatism, the "Essex Junto," he declared that on the Ohio would be "the seat of empire" for the whole Union. Within twenty years, he predicted, there would be more people on the western side of the Allegheny watershed than in the East, and he congratulated these people that "in order to begin right there will be no wrong habits to combat and no inveterate systems to overturn—there will be no rubbish to remove before you lay the foundations." Evidently it did not take long to produce the Western point of view!

In the Senate in 1837 Benton, of Missouri, scorned the proposals of Calhoun regarding the disposition of the public domain, and boasted that after the census of 1840 had shown the weight of the West it would be so highly bid for that it would write its own bill. Perhaps the debate over the Compromise of 1850 brings out the self-assertive Western attitude in these years most clearly. Calhoun had argued that the equilibrium between North and South was being destroyed by the increase in free states made out of the Western territories. But Stephen A. Douglas, of Illinois, spoke for the West when he attacked the Southern statesman for the error of thinking of the West as property of the older sections. "What share had the South in the territories," he asked, "or the North, or any other geographical division unknown to the Constitution? I answer none—none at all." And Douglas calculated that if its right to self-determination were admitted, the West would form at least seventeen new free states, and that therefore the theory of equilibrium was a hopeless one.

It was not only the slavery struggle that revealed the Eastern conception of the West as merely the field of contest for power between the rival Atlantic sections, and the West's counter assertion of its own substantive rights. The same thing was shown in many different fields. For example, rival Eastern cities and states, the centers of power in their respective sections, engaged in contests for the commercial control of the Mississippi Valley by transportation lines. The contests between rival European powers for the control of the Bagdad railway, the thrust of Germany toward the rich hinterlands made up of the Balkans and India, and the project of "Central Europe" in the history of the World War, have a resemblance to these American sectional contests for the still more valuable hinterland of the Mississippi Valley. American sections did not go to war over their trade and transportation interests. Nevertheless, they recognized that there were such interests. A Southern writer in *DeBow's Review* in 1847 declared:

"A contest has been going on between the North and South not limited to slavery or no slavery—to abolition or no abolition, nor to the politics of either whigs or democrats as such, but a contest for the wealth and commerce of the great valley of the Mississippi—a contest tendered by our Northern brethren, whether the growing commerce of the great West shall be thrown upon New Orleans or given to the Atlantic cities."

[32]

SIGNIFICANCE OF THE SECTION

Shortly after this, in 1851, the *Western Journal* of St. Louis published articles lamenting that "the Western States are subjected to the relation of Provinces of the East" and that New Orleans was giving way to New York as their commercial city. Since (so the argument ran) exports can never build up a commercial city, the mouth of the Mississippi must be so improved that imports would enter the Valley by way of New Orleans. "Then," said the writer, "a line of cities will arise on the banks of the Mississippi that will far eclipse those on the Atlantic coast."

The middle of the century saw an extension of this sectional contest for economic power derived from the growing West; but it was the railroad trunk lines rather than the canals that occupied the foreground. The goal became the ports of the Pacific. The Memphis convention of 1845 and the Chicago convention of 1847 illustrate how interior cities were now repeating the rivalry for Western trade which had earlier been seen on the Atlantic Coast. The contests between New Orleans, Memphis, St. Louis, and Chicago influenced the Kansas-Nebraska Act, and the later strategy of the struggle for position between the Pacific railroads.

Throughout our history, then, there has been this sectionalism of West and East, and this Eastern conception of the West as recruiting ground merely for the rival Atlantic Coast sections. Nation-wide parties have had their Eastern and Western wings, often differing radically, and yet able by party loyalty and by adjustments and sacrifices to hold together. Such a struggle as the slavery contest can only be understood by bearing in mind that it was not merely a contest of North against South, but that its form and its causes were fundamentally shaped by the dynamic factor of expanding sections, of a West to be won.

This migratory sectionalism has not always been obvious, but it was none the less real and important. Year after year new Wests had been formed. Wildernesses equal in area to the greater European nations had been turned into farms in single decades.

But now the era of the frontier advance has ended. The vast public domain, so far as it is suited to agriculture, is taken up. The competent experts of the Department of Agriculture now tell us that "the nation reached and passed the apogee of agricultural land supply in proportion to population about 1890, and that we have entered a period which will necessarily be marked by a continually increasing scarcity of land." The price of lands has risen as the supply of free lands declined. Iowa farm lands mounted from an average of thirty dollars per acre in 1890 to over two hundred dollars in 1920.

Shortly after 1890, men began to speak less confidently of the inexhaustible forest supply. The reclamation act early in the twentieth century began a new era in governmental conservation and governmental economic activity. The Conservation Congress met in 1908, three centuries after the Jamestown settlers sank their axes into the edge of the American forest. The purpose of the congress was to consider the menace of forest exhaustion, the waste of soil fertility and of mineral resources, the reclamation of the deserts, the drainage of the swamps. Now we are told by high authority that we shall feel the pinch of timber shortage in less than fifteen years. The free lands are no longer free; the boundless resources are no longer boundless.

Already the urban population exceeds the rural population of the United States.

But this does not mean that the Eastern industrial type of urban life will necessarily spread across the whole nation, for food must come from somewhere, and the same expert authorities that predict that within about fifty years the United States itself will be unable to feed its population by its home supply, also conclude that the deficient food supply will not be available from outside the nation, because the same phenomenon of the encroachment of population upon food is in evidence throughout the world. Already Europe as a whole depends upon importation for its food supply. Its large population in proportion to its area and resources cannot be made the basis for estimates of what is possible in the United States, for Europe's large population was made possible by these imports from the United States as well as from other nations.

If the prediction be true, or if anything like it be true, then there must remain in the United States large rural farming interests and sections. The natural advantages of certain regions for farming, or for forestry, or for pasturage will arrest the tendency of the Eastern industrial type of society to flow across the continent and thus to produce a consolidated, homogeneous nation free from sections. At the same time that the nation settles down to the conditions of an occupied land, there will be emphasized the sectional differences arising from unlike geographic regions.[2]

To President Coolidge, as a speech of his in November last shows, the prospect is of a nation importing its

[2] Or rival industrial sections, if, by improvement in agricultural machinery and organization, fewer men are required in the farming needed for national food supply and raw materials.

SIGNIFICANCE OF THE SECTION

supplies of food and resources, facing "the problem of maintaining a prosperous, self-reliant, confident agriculture in a country preponderantly commercial and industrial." Whether our destiny is to become a nation in which agriculture is subordinate, or one in which it is an equal partner with urban industrial interests, it seems clear that there will be sectional expression of the differences between these interests; for in certain geographic provinces agriculture will be entirely subordinate to manufacture, as in others such industry will be insignificant as compared with farming.

Unlike such countries as France and Germany,[3] the United States has the problem of the clash of economic interests closely associated with regional geography on a huge scale. Over areas equal to all France or to all Germany, either the agricultural or the manufacturing types are here in decided ascendency. Economic interests are sectionalized. The sections occupied by a rural population are of course far inferior in numbers of voters to the sections of urban industrial life. The map is deceptive in this respect, for Greater New York City, which would be a point on the map, has almost as many people as live in all the vast spaces of the Mountain and Pacific States. The population of the New England States and the Middle States of the North Atlantic division is over thirty millions, while the combined population of Wisconsin, Minnesota, North and South Dakota, Montana, Wyoming, Idaho, Washington, and Oregon is less than ten millions. On the map these states take an imposing space, but owing to physical geography a large portion will always remain sparsely settled. Nevertheless, New England and the

[3] There are, of course, *regional* economic clashes there.

[36]

Middle States together have only eighteen senators, while the states of the section which I have just named have also eighteen senators. New York State alone has a larger population than this northwestern zone of states; but this wealthy and populous state has only two senators as against the eighteen senators of the other region.

On a map constructed so as to give to each state a space proportioned to its population, or to its income tax, instead of to its dimensions in square miles, the Western lands would shrink in their map space in a startling fashion.[4] But in the Senate is exhibited the outcome of the tendencies which statesmen like Gouverneur Morris saw so clearly—namely, the great power of the newer states by their equal representation in the Senate and their ability to take property by taxation from the wealthier section and to distribute it according to numbers, or even according to deficiencies, throughout the Union as a unit. Obviously, there is here the certainty of a sectional clash of interests not unlike those which led to Calhoun's South Carolina Exposition.

Sectionalism will hereafter be shaped by such new forces. We have become a nation comparable to all Europe in area, with settled geographic provinces which equal great European nations. We are in this sense an empire, a federation of sections, a union of potential nations. It is well to look at the result of our leap to power since the ending of the frontier, in order to appreciate our problems arising from size and varied sections.

We raise three-fourths of the world's corn, over a

4 See P. White, *Market Analysis*, p. 322.

third of its swine, over half its cotton, and over one-fifth its wheat. Out of the virgin wilderness we have built such industrial power that we now produce two-thirds of the pig iron of the world, over twice the steel tonnage of England, Germany, and France combined. We mine nearly half the world's coal. We have fully half the gold coin and bullion of the world, and in 1920 our national wealth exceeded the combined wealth of the United Kingdom, France, and Germany. In the World War President Wilson gave the word that sent two million Americans across the seas to turn the scale in that titanic conflict. We are forced to think of ourselves continentally and to compare ourselves with all Europe. Why, with so vast a territory, with so many geographic provinces, equal in area, in natural resources, and in natural variety to the lands of the great nations of Europe, did we not become another Europe? What tendencies have we developed that resembled those of Europe in the course of our history? Are there tendencies toward the transformation of our great sections into types similar to European nations?

It was evident at the outset of a study of the frontier movement that the American people were not passing into a monotonously uniform space. Rather, even in the colonial period, they were entering successive different geographic provinces; they were pouring their plastic pioneer life into geographic moulds. They would modify these moulds, they would have progressive revelations of the capacities of the geographic provinces which they won and settled and developed; but even the task of dealing constructively with the different regions would work its effects upon their traits.

Not a uniform surface, but a kind of checkerboard

of differing environments, lay before them in their settlement. There would be the interplay of the migrating stocks and the new geographic provinces. The outcome would be a combination of the two factors, land and people, the creation of differing societies in the different sections. European nations were discovered, conquered, colonized, and developed so far back in history that the process of nation-making is obscure. Not so with section-making in the United States. The process has gone on almost under our own observation. But by the bondage to the modern map, as John Fiske put it, much American history has been obscured. Our constitutional forms, in contrast with the realities, provide for a federation of states. Our historians have dealt chiefly with local history, state history, national history, and but little with sectional history. Our students of government have been more aware of the legal relations of states and nation than with the actual groupings of states into sections, and with the actions of these sections beneath the political surface. State sovereignty, for example, has in fact never been a vital issue except when a whole section stood behind the challenging state. This is what gave the protest reality.

One of the most interesting features of recent geographical studies is the emphasis placed upon regional geography and human geography. Europe has given more attention to such studies in human geography than has the United States. Perhaps this is because European nations have been forced to consider the geographical aspects of the self-determination of nations and the rearrangement of the map by the treaty which seemed to close the World War. Perhaps in the hard realities of that war the military staffs and the scientists who had to deal with the problem of supplies of food and of raw material were compelled to give attention to the subject. But even before and after this war, the increasing pressure of population upon the means of life compelled in Europe the study of the natural regions, their resources and peoples, and their relations to each other. Now the conditions which I have been attempting to make clear in the United States are forcing us to face the same problem. We, like European nations, are approaching a saturation of population.

That sectionalism which is based on geographical regions has been in evidence from the early colonial period, but it has been obscured and modified by the influence of the unoccupied West. The states have been declining and are likely to continue to diminish in importance in our politics; but the groups of states called sections are likely to become more significant as the state declines. A study of votes in the federal House and Senate from the beginning of our national history reveals the fact that party voting has more often broken down than maintained itself, on fundamental issues; that when these votes are mapped or tabulated by the congressional districts or states from which those who cast them came, instead of by alphabetical arrangement, a persistent sectional pattern emerges.

There has been in the earlier periods the sharp clash between New England and the South, with the Middle States divided and unstable, constituting a buffer zone and often holding the balance of power. Then, as population spread westward, the greater parties were composed of sectional wings. Normally, in the Republican party there came to be a fairly solid conservative

New England, a mixed and uncertain Middle Region, and a more radical North Central wing, ready in the shaping of legislation to join the Democrats in a kind of sectional *bloc* (even before the days of the *bloc*) to oppose the conservative and dominant Eastern wing. As time went on, the East North Central States came into closer connection with the Eastern wing, and in the West North Central lay the areas of radical dissent and of third-party movements. Legislation was determined less by party than by sectional voting. Bills were shaped for final passage by compromises between wings or by alliances between sections. The maps of presidential elections showing majorities by counties look like maps of North against South; but there was always a concealed East and West which temporarily laid aside their differences.

I think it not too much to say that in party conventions as well as in Congress the outcome of deliberations bears a striking resemblance to treaties between sections, suggestive of treaties between European nations in diplomatic congresses. But over an area equal to all Europe we found it possible to legislate, and we tempered asperities and avoided wars by a process of sectional give-and-take. Whether we shall continue to preserve our national, our intersectional, party organization in the sharper sectional conflicts of interest that are likely to accompany the settling down of population, the completer revelation of the influence of physical geography, remains to be seen.

As an illustration of the newer forms of sectionalism, take the movement for the Great Lakes-St. Lawrence deep waterway. Middle Western leaders are arguing that there is "in the heart of the continent a large area beyond the radius of logical rail haul for the movement of bulk commodities to either seacoast." "Nature," runs the argument, "which has indicated the extent of the area which sends its surplus to the Atlantic seaboard and to the Gulf and to the Pacific ports, has provided the American continent with one potential seacoast not yet utilized. Upon the map of economic divides indicated by geography—the Atlantic seaboard, the Gulf territory, and the Pacific slope—there is, as it were, an economic desert a thousand miles east and west, five hundred miles north and south beyond the radius of logical rail haul to either coast." The desire to give an outlet to what is called this "landlocked commerce to the coast," leads to the demand for "a fourth economic divide based upon the Great Lakes as linked with the ocean, giving to the coast of the Great Lakes access to marine commerce" and permitting the erection of each rail system upon the sea base.[5]

When ex-Senator Townsend, of Michigan, was running for reëlection, a Detroit daily reported: "The East is opposed to him because of his leadership in the waterways movement, but the entire West from Ohio to Idaho is looking hopefully and earnestly to Michigan to give him the largest majority he has ever received. The east and the west will be 'listening in' election night —the east hoping for a reduced Townsend vote, the west hoping fervently that his vote will be a knockout blow to the eastern opposition to the St. Lawrence waterway."

I quote this to take the opportunity to point out that

[5] *The Sea Base: Relation of Marine to National Transportation System and of Lakes to Ocean Route to Continental Traffic,* published by Great Lakes-St. Lawrence Tidewater Association (Duluth, Minn., 1923). For an argument in favor of the New York route, see John B. Baldwin, *Our Dardanelles* (Honolulu, 1924).

SIGNIFICANCE OF THE SECTION

sweeping statements like these exaggerate the sectional
feeling. As a matter of fact, of course, very few Eastern voters knew much about Townsend, and, East and
West, most of the radio fans were listening in to the
vaudeville or the football game or the real prize fight.

But while Duluth writers press the importance of
what they call this "frustrated seaway," New York
writers protest that the outlet should be through an
enlarged Erie Canal if there is to be such a water route
at all, and it is argued that the projected St. Lawrence
route would be "Our Dardanelles," liable to be closed
against the West by Canadian or British government
whenever disagreements invited this mode of coercion.
In New England, meantime, there are fears that Boston
would be injured as a port, besides the loss of her
advantages by sea-borne commerce to the Pacific Coast.
A few years ago Mayor Curley, of Boston, indignantly
declared that such a waterway "would obliterate New
England absolutely."

I read, the other day, editorials in the *Chicago Tribune*
which made the decision of the Supreme Court against
the claim of the sanitary district to divert water from
Lake Michigan, without the permission of the Secretary
of War, the occasion for this language: "It is time for
Chicago, Illinois, and the entire Mississippi Valley to
rise in revolt against a tyranny which now threatens its
very existence. . . . This is neither a conquered country
nor a colony but an integral part of a nation, and as
such entitled to the same consideration afforded to New
England and New York." The editorial goes on to
demand action to prevent the houses of Congress from
organizing, etc. In another editorial of that issue, under
the caption "The West is West, but the East is Lon-

don," it is said: "It is natural that the East should turn to London for London policy is Atlantic policy"; and the editor speaks of "London and its provinces in Montreal, Boston, New York and Washington."

No doubt this language is not to be taken with entire seriousness, but it is vigorous enough. It proposes revolt, and paralysis of government; and it, in effect, reads a rather substantial "chunk" of America out of the Union. Allowing for New England's restraint in speech, mildly similar utterances can be found in the press of that section whenever its interests seem threatened by West or South.[6] When Senator John Taylor, of Virginia, informed Jefferson that the Northeast felt that union with the South was doomed to fail, that philosophic statesman replied in words that are worthy of extended quotation as illustrating both a tolerant spirit and an amusing impression of New England:

"It is true that we are completely under the saddle of Massachusetts and Connecticut and that they ride us very hard, cruelly insulting our feelings, as well as exhausting our strength and substance. Their natural friends, the three other eastern states, join them from a sort of family pride, and they have the art to divide certain other parts of the Union so as to make use of them to govern the whole." But, "seeing," said Jefferson, "that an association of men who will not quarrel with one another is a thing which never existed . . . seeing we must have somebody to quarrel with, I had rather keep our New England associates for that purpose than to see our bickerings transferred to others. They are circumscribed within such narrow bounds, and their population is so full, that their numbers will ever

[6] See Chapter 12.

[44]

be in the minority, and they are marked, like the Jews, with such perversity of character, as to constitute from that circumstance the natural division of our parties." It will be observed that although he does not extol New England he does not read her out of the Union. The significant fact is that sectional self-consciousness and sensitiveness is likely to be increased as time goes on and crystallized sections feel the full influence of their geographic peculiarities, their special interests, and their developed ideals, in a closed and static nation.

There is a sense in which sectionalism is inevitable and desirable. There is and always has been a sectional geography in America based fundamentally upon geographic regions. There is a geography of political habit, a geography of opinion, of material interests, of racial stocks, of physical fitness, of social traits, of literature, of the distribution of men of ability, even of religious denominations. Professor Josiah Royce defined a "province" or section, in the sense in which I am using the word, as "any one part of a national domain which is geographically and socially sufficiently unified to have a true consciousness of its own ideals and customs and to possess a sense of its distinction from other parts of the country." It was the opinion of this eminent philosopher that the world needs now more than ever before the vigorous development of a highly organized provincial life to serve as a check upon mob psychology on a national scale, and to furnish that variety which is essential to vital growth and originality. With this I agree. But I wish also to urge here, as I have elsewhere, that there is always the danger that the province or section shall think of itself naïvely as the nation, that New England shall think that America

[45]

is merely New England writ large, or the Middle West shall think that America is really the Middle West writ large, and then proceed to denounce the sections that do not perceive the accuracy of this view as wicked or ignorant and un-American. This kind of nationalism is a sectional mirage, but it is common, and has been common to all the sections, in their unconscious attitude if not in clear expression. It involves the assumption of a superiority of culture, of *Kultur,* to which good morals require that the nation as a whole must yield.

We must frankly face the fact that in this vast and heterogeneous nation, this sister of all Europe, regional geography is a fundamental fact; that the American peace has been achieved by restraining sectional selfishness and assertiveness and by coming to agreements rather than to reciprocal denunciation or to blows.

In the past we have held our sections together, partly because while the undeveloped West was open there was a safety valve, a region for hopeful restoration; partly because there were national political parties, calling out national party allegiance and loyalty over all sections and at the same time yielding somewhat under stress to sectional demands. Party was like an elastic band.

But there would often have been serious danger, such as showed itself when parties became definitely sectionalized just before the Civil War, had it not been the fact that popular party majorities over most of the sections are much closer than is usually supposed. The party held its tenure of power by a narrow margin and must use its power temperately or risk defeat. It must conciliate sectional differences within itself.

Not only the narrowness of normal party majorities,

county by county over the nation, but also the existence, within each of the large sections, of smaller sections or regions which did not agree with the views of their section as a whole, constituted a check both upon party despotism and upon sectional arrogance and exploitation of other sections.

In every state of the Union there are geographic regions, chiefly, but not exclusively, those determined by the ancient forces of geology, which divide the state into the lesser sections. These subsections within the states often cross state lines and connect with like areas in neighboring states and even in different sections of the larger type. Many states have now been made the subject of monographic studies of their internal sections shown in party politics, in economic interests, in social types, in cultural matters such as education, literature, and religion. I have prepared such maps of the United States for the year 1850.[7] For example, the map by counties showing the distribution of white illiteracy so closely resembles the map of the physiographic regions that the one might almost be taken for the other. Much the same is true for the map of farm values by counties. I have also mapped the Whig and Democratic counties in the presidential elections from 1836 to 1852 and combined them in a map, which shows that certain regions, certain groups of counties, were almost always Whig and others normally Democratic through all these years. Then I have had the photographer super-impose these maps one upon another. As a result it is shown that the rough, the poorer lands, the illiterate counties were for the most part the Democratic coun-

---

[7] [Several of these maps will be published in Professor Turner's forth-coming volume, *The United States, 1830-1850: The Nation and Its Sections.*]

ties; while the fertile basins—like the richer wheat areas
of the Old Northwest; the limestone islands about
Lexington, Kentucky, and Nashville, Tennessee; the
Black Belt of the Gulf States, the center of the cotton
and slavery interests, the abode of the wealthy and
educated great slaveholding planters—were Whig.
The Whigs tended to be strong in the areas of the
greater rivers and commercial centers and routes, and
in the counties with the better record in the matter of
illiteracy.

Now I am not saying that Democracy and illiteracy
and poor soils are necessarily connected. One of the
interesting results of the study is to show that there
were exceptions that prevent any such exclusively physical explanations. In North Carolina, for example,
very notable Whig areas were in the most illiterate,
rough, mountainous counties of that state, where the
poor whites were antagonistic to the wealthy slaveholding Democratic planters of the eastern counties. Certain
regions, like western New York and the Western
Reserve of Ohio, show not so much the influence of
physical geography as of the fact that they were
colonized by New Englanders and carried on the interest in vested rights which distinguished the Puritan
stock.

In short, the studies show that generalizations which
make physical geography or economic interests alone
the compelling explanation of political groupings are
mistaken. There are also the factors of ideals and
psychology, the inherited intellectual habits, derived
from the stock from which the voters sprang. Sometimes these ideals carry the voters into lines that
contradict their economic interests. But as a rule there

has been such a connection of the stock, the geographic conditions, the economic interests, and the conceptions of right and wrong, that all have played upon each other to the same end.

Next I wish to emphasize the fact that these regional subdivisions are persistent. Often they remain politically the same for several generations. Probably the mass of voters inherit their party and their political ideas. Habit rather than reasoning is the fundamental factor in determining political affiliation of the mass of voters, and there is a geography, a habitat, of political habit.

There is the same geography of culture, though I am not able in the time that remains to develop this. For example, in a recent map of short-story areas (of what the author calls local-color areas) almost exactly the same regions are shown as appear on the maps which I have mentioned.

There is, then, a sectionalism of the regions within the larger divisions, a sectionalism of minority areas, sometimes protesting against the policies of the larger section in which they lie and finding more in common with similar regions outside of this section. Herein lies a limitation upon the larger section in case it attempts a drastic and subversive policy toward other sections. As Professor Holcombe has pointed out, in this kind of nation, in this vast congeries of sections, voters cannot hope to have a choice between parties any one of which will stand for all the measures which they oppose. The most they can reasonably hope for, he thinks, "is the formation of a party, resting upon a combination of sectional interests which are capable of coöperation in national politics without too much jealousy and friction, and including that particular interest with which they are themselves most closely associated. No sectional interest is strong enough, alone and unaided, to control the federal government, and no major party can be formed with a fair prospect of domination in national politics which does not contain more or less incongruous elements."

With this I agree, and indeed have long been on record to this effect. It emphasizes the need for tolerance, for coöperation, for mutual sacrifices by the leaders of the various sections. Statesmanship in this nation consists, not only in representing the special interests of the leader's own section, but in finding a formula that will bring the different regions together in a common policy. The greatest statesmen have always had this goal before them. If there were time I should like to quote the striking confirmation of this in writings of even such men as John Quincy Adams, Van Buren, and Calhoun, who are ordinarily thought of as rather definitely sectional. Each formulated plans for concessions to the various sections whereby a national pattern could emerge.

The significance of the section in American history is that it is the faint image of a European nation and that we need to reëxamine our history in the light of this fact. Our politics and our society have been shaped by sectional complexity and interplay not unlike what goes on between European nations. The greater sections are the result of the joint influence of the geologists' physiographic provinces and the colonizing stocks that entered them. The result is found in popular speech in which New England, the Middle States, the South, the Middle West, etc., are as common names as Massachusetts or Wisconsin. The Census divisions are more definite and official designations. Of course, the boundary lines are not definite and fixed. Neither are those of European nations. These larger sections have taken their characteristic and peculiar attitudes in American civilization in general.

We have furnished to Europe the example of a continental federation of sections over an area equal to Europe itself, and by substituting discussion and concession and compromised legislation for force, we have shown the possibility of international political parties, international legislative bodies, and international peace. Our party system and our variety in regional geography have helped to preserve the American peace. By having our combination of sections represented in a national legislative body, by possessing what may be called a League of Sections, comparable to a League of Nations, if it included political parties and a legislative body, we have enabled these minority sections to defend their interests and yet avoid the use of force.

The thing to be avoided, if the lessons of history are followed, is the insistence upon the particular interests and ideals of the section in which we live, without sympathetic comprehension of the ideals, the interests, and the rights of other sections. We must shape our national action to the fact of a vast and varied Union of unlike sections.

CHAPTER III

THE ORIGIN OF GENET'S PROJECTED ATTACK ON LOUISIANA AND THE FLORIDAS [1]

From the point of view of the foreign relations and particularly of the maintenance and expansion of the territorial basis of the United States, the decade from 1793 to 1803 was a critical period in American history. To one who appreciates the importance of the possession of the Mississippi Valley, and its approaches, in the history and destiny of the United States, these years are alive with interest. It was in this decade that Wayne's victory turned the tide against the Indians in the Northwest, and Jay's treaty relieved it of English occupation; then it was that Spain's intrigues with Indian scalping parties and Kentucky malcontents, her claims in the Southwest, and her closure of the Mississippi to the products of the West, came to an end. At the close of the decade the nation, having thus secured its flanks, took its gigantic march across the Mississippi by the Louisiana Purchase.

One of the gravest of the dangers of this period, however, has not received the attention which its importance warrants. The mission of Genet has been chiefly considered as a matter of his own personality, in the effects which his enthusiasm and his democratic societies produced upon party crystallization, and in regard to his demands for money and the use which he

[1] Reprinted by permission from *The American Historical Review*, July, 1898.

made of our ports.[2] His picturesque effrontery in lecturing the government and his threatened appeal from Washington to the people, have perhaps concealed from us the most important feature of his mission—namely, the desire of the French Republic to form connections with the frontiersmen of America and to seize Louisiana, the Floridas, and Canada as a part of the same enthusiastic crusade for liberty that carried the French armies across the European frontiers in the early days of the Revolution. In this case France reckoned upon the active support or the connivance of the American people, and particularly upon the irate Kentuckians, to aid her in repelling the hated Spaniard from the approaches to the Mississippi and perhaps from both Americas. It was an attractive program. The enthusiasm for revolutionary France, and the Western resentment against the power that closed the Mississippi, made it possible that this fierce young French Republic, strong with the zeal of the Revolution, might be able to succeed the decadent Spanish monarchy on the Gulf of Mexico, and hold the gratitude and friendship of the men of the West. What this transfer under such conditions might have meant, European history in the years that soon followed may enable us to guess. But in the way of this outcome stood George Washington. By throwing the weight of a vigorous policy and his powerful influence in favor of strict adherence to the duty of neutrality, he blocked the plan of France and performed one of the greatest of his services to America.

It is not strange that France in her revolutionary

[2] Dr. von Holst, *Constitutional History of the United States*, I, 113-120, has used DeWitt, *Thomas Jefferson*, to put the main purpose of France in a clearer light; but he does not go at any length into the Western intrigue.

renaissance, and when war was about to be declared
upon England and Spain, should have turned her eyes
toward the remains of her colonial glory in Canada and
Louisiana. Indeed, it is one of the significant elements
in her policy during the War of Independence that she
never lost sight of the weakness of Spain, or of the
advisability of keeping the United States a dependent
ally, restricted within the limits of the Alleghenies. Her
statesmen were well aware of the looseness of the federal bond in the Confederation and of the disaffection
of the West. Memoirs for the recovery of Louisiana
were framed for presentation to the government of the
Old Régime. In 1787 Lord Dorchester sent home from
Canada a copy of a memoir[3] presented to the French
minister in the United States and by him forwarded to
his court. The object of its author was to induce France
to retake Louisiana. He argued that separation was
the inevitable destiny of the West. "Unity," he said,
"is broken by the Mountains. Those beyond seek for a
new support and they offer to the power which will
welcome them, advantages which will before long efface
those which America, as it now is, could promise. These
may be seen at a glance, from the Appalaches to the
mountains of New Mexico, and from the Lakes of
Canada to the mouth of the Mississippi. Here is a zone
of the globe capable of containing fifty million inhabitants, situated in a continuous plain, inclosed in the same
compass, of which all the parts have a close connection,
a common and indivisible point of trade and navigation.
In a few years will be born a new policy, and it is a
colony not yet perceived which will hatch the germ. It

[3] *Report on Canadian Archives*, 1890, pp. 108-117. See also Report of Historical Manuscripts Commission, in the *Report of the American Historical
Association*, 1896, pp. 946, 947.

requires a protector; the first who will stretch out his arms to it will have made the greatest acquisition that could be desired in this New World. Fortunate my country if she does not let this moment escape, one of those not presented twice."

This discontent of the West and the weakness of the ties that bound it to the coast had also been shown in proposals by malcontents to England [4] and to Spain. General Wilkinson, the most consummate artist in treason that the nation ever possessed, received Spanish money for his efforts to carry Kentucky from the Union, and even George Rogers Clark, the conqueror of the Illinois country in the famous campaign of 1778 and 1779, had desired in 1788 to take service under Spain in return for a liberal land grant. Clark was disgusted with the neglect which Virginia and the United States gave to his claims. His friend and adviser in this period was Dr. James O'Fallon, a Revolutionary soldier, who later married Clark's youngest sister. One of the

[4] Professor J. F. Jameson has called my attention to an interesting proposition of this period made to the British authorities.

In a letter of Phineas Bond, British consul in Philadelphia, written to the foreign secretary, the Duke of Leeds, and dated January 3, 1791, he says: "In case of a rupture with Spain, my Lord, it may become an object of consideration with Government how far the Spanish settlements on the Mississippi near the mouth of that river might be accessible to [a] force collected near the Ohio and conveyed down the rivers in craft calculated for that purpose. Perhaps it might be deemed too hazardous an undertaking to engage in an enterprise of this sort without the concurrence of the United States, nor could such a concurrence be expected but upon [the basis] of stipulations reciprocally beneficial yet it may [be] expedient to observe, my Lord, that the western settl[ements] have constantly murmured at the restrictions laid upon their exports, thro' the medium of the Mississippi, by the Court of Spain. It is but reasonable to suppose . . . [they] would favor nay co-operate in any measure that m[ight] tend to secure them a free trade which the uninterr[upted] passage of the Mississippi would effectually establish.

"The settlers, my Lord, upon the whole frontier of the United States are a hardy race of men. Adventurers by profession, and ready to seize every opportunity of profit or employment. I could not presume, my Lord, to delineate the plan of such an enterprize tho' I can not restrain a suggestion which may be improved by others more conversant with subjects of this nature." Compare England's intrigue with Miranda in John Adams' administration.

5

famous Yazoo land companies[5] which purchased from Georgia a part of her Western claims, was the South Carolina Yazoo Company, of which the active agent was this Dr. O'Fallon. Since the colony was to be located in the region of the present Vicksburg, in territory claimed by Spain, O'Fallon attempted to conciliate that power by assuring Governor Miro that the colonists had been led to "consent to be the slaves of Spain, under the appearance of a free and independent colony, forming a rampart for the adjoining Spanish territories and establishing with them an eternal reciprocal alliance, offensive and defensive." In this proposed separation from the Union, it was rumored that George Rogers Clark had been selected as chief in command of the battalion which O'Fallon organized. In 1790 "it was expected in Lexington that General Scott would take five hundred families to the settlement and that Wilkinson and Sevier would follow, each with a thousand fighting men and their families. General McDowell accompanies the Frankliners from the Long Island, where they are to embark with 300 from the back parts of North Carolina and 200 with Capt. Alston from Cumberland." Washington's proclamation and the prospect of the use of force, together with Spanish opposition, put an end to the project; but the reports about the expedition reveal unmistakable symptoms. The frontiersmen were about to advance. Their produce was useless if the Mississippi were closed. They were weary of the incessant Indian war on their borders. The federal government discouraged their attacks on the savages and appeared indifferent to the

[5] Haskins, "Yazoo Land Companies," *Papers of the American Historical Association*, V, 403, 405, 406.

closing of navigation by Spain. To the frontiersmen the essential thing was relief from this intolerable situation. The new government had not yet approved its value to them; the future of a united nation extending from Atlantic to Pacific appealed less to their imagination than did the pressing need of themselves possessing the portals of the great valley which they occupied. There appeared to be two solutions of the difficulty: either to come to an agreement with Spain, which would open the Mississippi, stop the Indian raids and furnish them with liberal land grants, or to fight their way out. In either case Spain would not long have withstood this hardy backwood stock. While thus the West seethed with intrigues, with projects of colonization in Spanish territory, and with yearnings for war, there came the reports of the wars of the French Revolution and perhaps intimations of the policy of France with respect to the Spanish dependencies in America.[6]

It is, therefore, not at all surprising that at Christmas time, in 1792, General Clark and Dr. O'Fallon concerted a plan for an attack on Louisiana under the French flag. This proposition, together with a private letter from O'Fallon to his friend Thomas Paine, then a member of the Convention, would seem to have reached France before Genet sailed.[7] In the meantime,

[6] Sorel, *L'Europe et la Révolution Française*, III, 157; Jefferson, *Writings*, ed. Ford, I, 216.

[7] At least that careful Western student, Dr. Lyman C. Draper, in a note to the George Rogers Clark Manuscripts, in the State Historical Society of Wisconsin, mentions that Paine wrote in answer to O'Fallon, from Passy, February 17, 1793, conveying the idea that Clark's application had gone through the medium of the French minister to the United States and that the proposal had been laid before the Provisory Executive Council of the Republic. However this may have been, Clark, as we shall see later, learning of Genet's mission, wrote to him (February 2, 1793), and this letter was received by the minister on his arrival in this country; and with his answer (July 12), Genet forwarded Paine's reply to Dr. O'Fallon's letter. Conway, *Life of Paine*, II,

and entirely independently, the French government was devoting attention to the project of operations in America. Brissot de Warville, one of the leaders of the Girondins, or Brissotins, was a warm admirer of America. In 1788 he had traveled in the United States, and he brought the fruits of his observations into his *Nouveau Voyage dans les États-Unis* (Paris, 1791). He had noted the discontent of the Westerners over Spain's closure of the Mississippi. "They are determined," he wrote, "to open it with good will or by force; and it would not be in the power of Congress to moderate their ardor. Men who have shook off the yoke of Great Britain, and who are masters of the Ohio and the Mississippi, cannot conceive that the insolence of a handful of Spaniards can think of shutting rivers and seas against a hundred thousand free Americans. The slightest quarrel will be sufficient to throw them into a flame; and if ever the Americans shall march toward New Orleans, it will infallibly fall into their hands." Brissot pressed for the war with Austria, and as the current of the revolution hastened towards a general European conflict, he became more and more interested in the problems of foreign relations. Saint Just afterward declared, in his report on the proscribed Girondin deputies (July 9, 1793), that "the attention of Brissot extended to the other hemisphere, Brissot ruled the Council." It was partly due to his influence that Lebrun was made minister of foreign relations in the summer of 1792. Another intimate friend of Brissot was Clavière, the Genevese banker, who became minister of finance in the spring

<hr>

156; *Report of the American Historical Association*, 1896, pp. 967, n. 2, 986, 987, 996, 1007.

of the same year. He had accompanied Brissot in one of his journeys through America, and was, with him, the author of the works, *De la France et des États-Unis* (London, 1787) and *Commerce of America with Europe*. Otto, chief secretary of a division of Lebrun's office, had been private secretary to Luzerne, during his American mission, and was later chargé d'affaires in the United States, from which he returned in 1792. Otto declared, in 1797, that Brissot, who had unlimited influence in the diplomatic circle, proposed Genet as minister to the United States.[8] Thus the innermost circles of the Girondist authorities were strongly affected by American influence.

Lebrun was now considering the probability of a war with Spain; Miranda, who had visited the United States soon after the War of Independence, and whose South American exploits were to make him famous, had come to confer with him about the project of a revolution in the Spanish colonies. Brissot desired to make use of Miranda, aided by over 30,000 San Domingo troops. But more moderate plans were chosen. Lebrun decided to send Genet to the United States, with a secret mission to foment the revolution (Lebrun to Dumouriez, November 6, 1792).[9] Jefferson afterwards noted that Colonel W. S. Smith,[10]

[8] Archives des Affaires Étrangères, États-Unis, Vol. 47, folio 401.

[9] Sorel, *L'Europe et la Révolution Française*, II, 157; *Atlantic Monthly*, May, 1860, p. 589.

[10] The Minister of Public Contributions reports to the Provisory Executive Council, January 4, 1793: "I have given information to the citizen Genet of the offers made by Col. Smith, of New York, to procure the republic not only the reimbursement of what remains due from the United States, although not yet payable, but also the application of it, either to supplies for the army, or wheat flour and salted provisions in augmentation of our internal supplies." This proposal was approved by the council, in a letter to Colonel Smith, November 7, 1792; and the minister notes that by the time of his report (considered on January 4, 1793) Smith had gone to England. *American State Papers, Foreign Relations*, I, 144. Jefferson's minute of the interview with

who left Paris November 9, 1792, reported that they were sending Genet here, and that "the ministers told him they meant to begin the attack [on the Spanish colonies] at the mouth of the Mississippi, and to sweep along the bay of Mexico, southwardly, and that they would have no objections to our incorporating into our government the two Floridas." Dumouriez wrote to Lebrun (November 30, 1792) that "once masters of Holland we shall be strong enough to crush England, particularly by interesting the United States in sustaining our colonies, and in executing a superb project of General Miranda." [11]

A vast and startling project, indeed! sweeping into a single system the campaigns of France in Europe, the discontented frontiersmen of the Mississippi Valley, and the revolutionary unrest that was before long to give independence to Spanish America. The historical possibilities of the great design are overwhelming.

Around Brissot and his party leaders in the fall of 1792 and the spring of 1793, there were also gathered a group of well-known Americans. Among them was the famous Thomas Paine, keen of scent for revolutionary breezes, whose relations with his old-time friend in the American War for Independence, Dr. O'Fallon, we have already mentioned; and here, too, was Joel Barlow, the poet, whose *Vision of Columbus* lives, at least in the history of American literature, and

---

Col. Smith was dated February 20, 1793 (Jefferson, *Writings,* I, 216). Col. W. S. Smith was the son-in-law of John Adams. He had been aide-de-camp to Washington, and secretary of legation under Adams in London, where he was on intimate terms with Miranda. His connection with the Miranda project of 1798, when Great Britain took somewhat the rôle towards Spanish America that France now essayed, is well known. See John Adams, *Works,* I, 679; VIII, X, *passim; Edinburgh Review,* XIII, 277 ff. Col. Smith may have given Jefferson an understanding of the inception of the plan.

[11] Sorel, III, 175,

the promoter, whose notorious Scioto Land Company lives in the history of American settlement. Brissot aided him in this land scheme, which lured unfortunate French emigrants to Gallipolis, and, later, Barlow was the translator of Brissot's *Travels*.[12] Both Paine [13] and Barlow were enjoying their recent honors as naturalized citizens of France. Gilbert Imlay was another of the group—that soldier of the American Revolution, and of fortune, who had brought his Kentucky observations into the *Topographical Description of the Western Territories of America* (London, 1792). He was living with Mary Wollstonecraft, afterwards the mother of Shelley's wife (Mary Godwin), and his perfidy is embalmed in her *Letters to Imlay*. In Paine's home, an old mansion of Madame de Pompadour, we find, a little later, gatherings in which the Brissots, Bonneville, Barlow, Imlay, Mary Wollstonecraft, and the Rolands met. Less influential, perhaps, but active also, in promoting the interest of the government in American affairs was Stephen Sayre, a native of Long Island, New York, who after graduating at Princeton had become a banker in London, and later, sheriff. His enthusiasm for the War of Independence ruined his fortunes in London and he attached himself for a time to Franklin and to Arthur Lee. At this time we find him, with Beaupoils, a French officer who had served in Poland, engaged in promoting the plan of an expedition against Louisiana. Lyonnet, a Frenchman who had lived in New Orleans, and who had influence with the Gironde leaders, contributed valuable information concerning the discontented set-

---

[12] See Barlow's proposal in 1793 to take the contract for the conquest of Louisiana himself, on a business basis. *American Historical Review*, III, 508.
[13] Conway, *Life of Paine*, II, 64.

tlers in the old capital of Louisiana. Such were the influences at work in Paris at the period when George Rogers Clark, at the Falls of the Ohio, was brooding over the wrongs imposed on him by the Virginia legislature [14] and considering plans for expatriation and the reduction of Louisiana.

It was in the summer of 1792 that there returned to Paris, fresh from his Russian mission, that ruddy, bustling brother of Madame Campan, the friend and companion of Marie Antoinette. Genet had been destined for Holland, but, as we have seen, he was determined upon in November for the United States, when Lebrun and Dumouriez were embracing all Spanish America in their designs. Genet himself seems afterwards to have desired it to be understood that the friendly relations which his family bore to the Queen had led to his selection as agent to carry out the plan of some of the Girondists for deporting Louis to the United States and thus avoiding execution by exile. Mr. Moncure D. Conway quotes from Genet's papers in his possession this interesting statement: "Roux Facillac, who had been very intimate in my father's family at Versailles, met me one morning and wished me to spend the evening at Lebrun's, where I had been invited. He accompanied me there and we met Brissot, Guadet, Leonnet [Lyonnet?], Ducos, Fauchet, Thomas Paine and most of the Gironde leaders . . . Tom Paine, who did not pretend to understand French, took no part in the conversation, and sat quietly sipping his claret. 'Ask Paine, Genet,' said Brissot, 'what effect the execution of Capet would have in America?'

[14] Clark learned of the failure of his claims in the Virginia courts and legislature in November, 1792. 53 Clark MSS., 81.

Paine replied to my inquiry by simply saying, 'bad, very bad.' The next day Paine presented to the convention his celebrated letter demanding in the name of Liberty and the people of the United States that Louis should be sent to the United States. . . . 'Genet,' continued Lebrun, 'how would you like to go to the United States and take Capet and his family with you?' " [15]

This anecdote is interesting as showing the kind of gatherings in progress at this time, though it bears internal evidence of apparent inaccuracy, at least, since Paine's speech was made on the fifteenth of January, 1793, and Genet's instructions had been first made out in December, although they were supplemented by additional instructions on January 17.[16]

Genet's instructions [17] recite that, at the moment when he is sent to the United States, a rupture with England and Spain is imminent. He is, therefore, to endeavor to secure a treaty establishing a close concert for the extension of the empire of liberty, guaranteeing the sovereignty of the peoples, and punishing the powers which have an exclusive commercial and colonial system, by declaring that the vessels of these powers shall not be received in the ports of the contracting nations. This compact, it was urged, would conduce rapidly to the freeing of Spanish America, to the opening of the navigation of the Mississippi to the inhabitants of Kentucky, "to the deliverance of our ancient brothers of Louisiana from the tyrannic yoke of Spain,

---

[15] Conway, *Writings of Thomas Paine*, IV, p. xii.

[16] On the sixteenth of January, Clavière wrote two letters to Jefferson regarding Genet's mission. Jefferson Correspondence, Department of State, Series 2, Vol. 16, No. 88; *Bulletin of Bureau of Rolls*, No. 8, p. 119.

[17] *Report of American Historical Association*, 1896, pp. 957, 960; Aulard, *Recueil des Actes du Comité de Salut Public*, I, 361, 393 n., 478.

and perhaps to the uniting to the American constellation of the fair star of Canada." In case, however, the course of the United States is wavering and timid, and if they do not determine to make common cause with France, Genet is to take all measures which his position permits, to propagate the principles of the French Revolution in Louisiana and in the other provinces of America adjoining the United States. The Kentuckians, who had long burned with the desire for the navigation of the Mississippi, it was noted, would probably second Genet's efforts without compromising Congress. Genet was accordingly authorized to keep agents in Kentucky, and to send them to Louisiana. He was also to make the expenditures which he judged necessary for the execution of this project. Blank brevets of officers up to the rank of captain, for bestowal on Indian chiefs, were entrusted to him.

Delays in getting to sea kept him at the harbor of Rochefort [18] until about the last week of February, 1793.[19] Between the date of Lebrun's letter to Dumouriez (November 6, 1792), on the day of the victory of Jemmapes (announcing the purpose to attack the Spanish colonies), and the time of Genet's departure, important events had occurred. The declaration by the French people of their readiness to wage war for all peoples upon their kings [20] had been followed by the execution of Louis.[21] Four days later the Executive Council assigned to Brissot a report on the possibility of an expedition against the Spanish depend-

[18] Near La Rochelle.
[19] Genet to Lebrun, April 16, 1793. Archives, États-Unis, Vol. 27, folio 217, and appendix to DeWitt, *Thomas Jefferson* (Paris, 1861); Hamilton, *Republic*, V, 247.
[20] November 19, 1792.
[21] January 21, 1793.

encies.[22] On the thirtieth of January, the council had ordered that Genet's departure be hastened.[23] War was declared against England on the first of February, and the declaration of war against Spain [24] was inevitable. The new minister to the United States left France, fired with the enthusiasm and the great designs of the days of Dumouriez.

It was forty-eight days before Genet, driven out of his course by adverse winds, reached Charleston.[25] In the meantime the foreign office was receiving plans from the Americans in Paris for effecting the reduction of Louisiana by the aid of the Kentucky riflemen. Several of these plans were in the hands of the government before the date of Genet's departure. His instructions and later actions in America are therefore to be read in the light of this fact.

One of the earliest as well as one of the most interesting of the communications is an anonymous draft, endorsed 1792.[26] The writer says that he had hoped, in vain, to interest the old French government in the recovery of Louisiana, and he refers to a memoir containing his views, the result of researches during five years. Putting aside as chimerical the Miranda idea of revolutionizing the more southern regions of Spanish America, he urges the Louisiana project as easy to carry out, owing to the weakness of the garrisons (not over 1500 men, he believed) and the temper of the French inhabitants. He also points out the value of the conquest as a diversion which would alarm Spain into devoting troops to the defense of her other Ameri-

[22] Aulard, *Recueil*, II, 10; III, 82.
[23] *Ibid.*, II, 27.
[24] Made March 9, 1793.
[25] April 8, 1793.
[26] *Report of American Historical Association*, 1896, p. 945

can frontiers, and as a means of checking Spanish privateers. The measures for inaugurating this movement were, in the opinion of the writer, secretly to send three or four French military men, including Lyonnet, to Philadelphia; to send an emissary by way of Philadelphia to New Orleans; to give to Genet the powers concerning the employment of these commissioners and charge him with the responsibility of the expedition; and to send revolutionary agents to Kentucky, to the colonies of Marietta and Scioto and Cumberland, promising the free navigation of the Mississippi. He would give to the expedition the guise of a filibustering raid in order to avoid compromising the government of Kentucky, and he advised that General Wilkinson (!) be made the commander-in-chief. The emissaries were to assemble five hundred men at different points on the Ohio, brought together by hope of booty and of confiscated Spanish lands. To cover these proceedings they were to take the appearance of an expedition against the Indians. The commander-in-chief should be empowered to make a treaty of alliance between France and Louisiana. The total expense he reckoned at 400,000 livres. Taking up the important question of the relation of this expedition to the United States, the author puts the questions: whether the leaders of the Republic should be acquainted with the plans; whether Louisiana ought to be united to France or to the United States; and how to avoid compromising the neutrality of the United States. Ten years before, he says, America would have welcomed the independence of Louisiana as infinitely desirable, for then they had the enthusiasm of liberty; but the enjoyment of it has made them calmer, and they no longer regard liberty

[66]

like lovers, but like married persons; reflection guides them, but it cools them. He then develops the argument that nature has destined a separation of the West, and that Congress is reluctant to secure the navigation of the Mississippi from Spain, lest this separation be facilitated. While, therefore, Genet ought adroitly to sound the disposition of the leaders of the government regarding the union of Louisiana with the United States, the envoy should speak of this merely as desirable, and should dispose them to receive with satisfaction the news of French success. By attributing the expedition to the disquietude of French settlers on the Scioto, Genet would enable the government to disavow the expedition and save the neutrality of the United States. The orders of Congress to courts of justice to act against the leaders of the invasion, on the remote frontiers, were not to be feared. He reaches the conclusion that the expedition should ignore the United States, and that the coöperating force should be found in Kentucky and along the Ohio; and he names among those whose aid is desirable, Wilkinson, Tardiveau (the brother of the late commandant of Kaskaskia), and Brackenridge. He leaves the future relations of Louisiana to be settled by the situation of France after the peace, but he expresses his opposition to uniting it to the United States.

In the same year, Captain Imlay contributed observations, in which he enforced the commercial and strategic importance of Louisiana to France and her West Indian islands.[27] The expedition could, in his opinion, be carried out by France for 750,000 livres, but Imlay adds

---

[27] *Report of American Historical Association,* 1896, p. 953; *American Historical Review,* III, 491.

that if this is too considerable an expenditure, Genet should be left to his discretion to find men in the West to undertake the expedition at their own cost and risk. This he declares to be entirely possible if they are assured that France will furnish assistance.[28]

From these plans and instructions prior to Genet's departure, it is evident that, whatever Genet's impetuosity and maladroitness may have done to damage the French project, he cannot be charged with having undertaken an unauthorized expedition. The essential features of the plan he attempted to carry out were those of the government and its advisers. His mistakes were of method rather than of object.[29] Nevertheless, Genet was not without warnings from the Minister of Foreign Affairs.[30] Lebrun distinctly cautioned him that the cold character of Americans only warms by degrees, and that the negotiations with the government must be secret. He was advised to have entire confidence in the sentiments of the President and Jefferson, Butler and Madison. His instructions, furthermore, enjoined upon him to follow scrupulously the forms established for official communications between the government and the agents of foreign states, and to give no offense with regard to provisions of the Constitution of the United States. But he was advised to exert an influence on public sentiment, and he was informed that the indirect ways were more useful than the official approaches. The difficulty with these requirements lay,

[28] Imlay mentions a report on the expedition presented to the Executive Committee by Lebrun; and the value of Imlay's advice regarding the expedition is vouched for by Brissot. *American Historical Review*, III, 503.

[29] Lebrun to Genet, March 10, 1793; DeWitt, *Jefferson*, p. 517. Lebrun was opposed to the United States securing the freedom of the Mississippi by negotiation.

[30] Lebrun to Genet, February 24, 1793; Archives, États-Unis, Vol. 37, fol. 132.

not merely in Genet's impetuous character, and the party conflicts in America; it lay also in the fact that, as the event proved, Washington pursued a genuine and vigorous policy of neutrality, and thus Genet had to choose between abandonment of his project and a conflict with the authorities. The President neither consented to aid France, nor to engage in an intrigue which provided for avowing neutrality, while permitting the frontier to follow the flag of France. The people, moreover, in the last resort, were loyal to Washington.

The plans submitted to the French authorities increased in number and detail in the early days of March, when that nation declared war against Spain. Among others, the former resident of New Orleans, Lyonnet, presented elaborate expositions of the advantages of Louisiana and the condition of the Spanish posts along the Mississippi. He believed that Louisiana should be joined to the United States. Six persons, he thought, should be sent to Philadelphia to proceed to Kentucky on the pretext of buying lands, but really to arrange matters in the West. He recommended Tardiveau as able to suggest useful men in Kentucky, and he wrote: "At the head of these filibusters of the woods, must be placed General [Clark], who in the late war took Vincennes, among other posts. His name alone is worth hosts, and there is no American who has not confidence in him." Among the expenses, he notes that much must be spent for drink, "for the Americans only talk of war when vis-à-vis with a bowl." [31]

On the fourth of March, Sayre and Beaupoils, already mentioned, together with Pereyrat, offered to

[31] Archives, Louisiane et Florides, 1792 à 1803, Vol. 7, Docs. 4 and 5; Espagne, Vol. 635, Docs. 316, 317; Vol. 636, folios 37, 101, 205; *American Historical Review*, III, 496-505.

Lebrun a plan,[32] the substance of which they had communicated to Dumouriez, probably in the early summer of 1792, while he was still minister of foreign affairs. Referring, doubtless, to the Miranda project, they declare that, in the present juncture, a fleet and a formidable army cannot properly be devoted to the expedition, but they present a plan which would also have the ultimate aim of seizing Mexico and creating a revolt in South America.[33] The uprising in Louisiana, which their project was designed to effect, would afford a beginning for such further designs, in harmony with the larger proposals, as might be deemed expedient by the government; and it would in itself compel Spain to send vessels and troops to America to intercept a general revolt of the Spanish provinces. In Kentucky, they declared, were a large part of Washington's officers and soldiers, and the desire for the freedom of the Mississippi, and the hope of glory and profit from such an expedition against Spain, would attract them. A few boats, batteries and munitions, together with supplies for two months for 3000 men, were needed. The boats could be built at the Falls of the Ohio. The French of Louisiana would embrace the opportunity to revolt; but if the taking of New Orleans was not deemed important, the tributaries of the Mississippi would open a way to Mexico, and the Panuco Indians, lately ill-treated by Spain, could be counted on to aid. An important consideration, in the opinion of the memorialists, was that such an expedition, made without the consent of the United States, would lead inevitably to an attitude on the part of England and Spain which

[32] *Report of American Historical Association*, 1896, p. 954.
[33] Compare *ibid.*, p. 945, and *American Historical Review*, III, 496.

would force the United States to take part with France, particularly since the Americans knew that the English were the authors of the Indian war then in progress in the United States. An expenditure of 280,000 livres, exclusive of artillery and ammunition, would suffice for the expedition, and the agent of the Republic could draw upon the treasury of the United States to meet these expenses; the modesty of this sum would conceal the secret.

While these plans were offered to Lebrun, a project for the formation of a committee to arrange for the expedition was also considered. For membership in this the proposition suggested: Joel Barlow, "a true friend of liberty, a philosopher, and pure in his morals," who might have, under Genet, the general direction of the matter, as well as the management of the funds; Sayre, who (owing, perhaps, to his London sojourn) should be well watched; and Beaupoils and Lyonnet. These four were to be sent to Philadelphia to begin the formation of the committee, having first concerted their plans with Otto. This project also provided that a part of the money due from the United States to France should be devoted to the enterprise. It was expected that these men would prepare the revolt of the Spanish colonies, which Miranda would complete, and they were to act in concert with a Mexican who had written to Clavière regarding the expedition.

Some contemporary comments [34] upon several of these plans (made apparently by one of the French authorities) declare that Mexico and the Spanish colonies should not be thought of again. And, in fact, in the United States as well as in France, the larger aspects

[34] *Report of American Historical Association,* 1896, p. 945, n. 3.

of the original design seem at least to have been left to await the outcome of the operations in Louisiana and the Floridas.

But in France domestic and foreign troubles followed fast in the weeks that succeeded the declaration of war against Spain. The loss of Belgium, the defection of Dumouriez, the revolt in La Vendée, the formation of the Committee of Public Safety, and the struggle between the Girondins and the Mountain, culminated in the downfall of the Girondins on the second of June, 1793. Genet had, therefore, hardly reached Philadelphia and begun active operations, when his party friends were in prison or in flight. That awful summer, with civil war, military reverses, a dozen countries in arms against France, and the reign of terror in her midst, was no time for attention to remote or widely extended plans of conquest in another hemisphere, even if the Jacobins had desired to sustain Genet. The interest in the expedition turns, therefore, to the United States.

At Charleston, Genet at once communicated the plan that had been drawn up to Governor Moultrie, the well-known Revolutionary leader. Genet and the consul, Mangourit, both report that a complete confidence existed between them and "this venerable veteran, the sincere friend of our Revolution." Genet informed Lebrun in his first dispatch [35] that Moultrie had rendered all the good offices in his power, permitting him to arm privateers, and furnishing him useful information on various parts of his instructions. Moultrie favored combined action by the United States, and

[35] April 16, 1793. Archives, États-Unis, Vol. 37, fol. 217; DeWitt, *Thomas Jefferson*, Appendix.

was impressed by the advantage that the freedom of
Louisiana would afford in checking the Indian attacks
instigated by Spain,[36] and in opening the Mississippi.
Mangourit impressed upon him the idea that all that
France would gain from the expedition would be the
weakening of the enemy, while the substantial advantages would be with the United States.[37] A few days
later the consul visited Savannah to talk with General
Mackintosh and others afterward engaged in the expedition against Florida. So far from concealing the
purpose of this visit from Moultrie, he induced that
obliging official to grant him letters of introduction.
Throughout his correspondence, Mangourit shows a
steady confidence in Moultrie's good will, even after
the latter became dissatisfied with Genet, and officially
proclaimed the policy of neutrality for South Carolina.[38]
Moultrie's private secretary, Freneau, was said to be
a brother of Jefferson's translating clerk, the editor of
the *National Gazette*.

Thus Genet's brief visit to Charleston had sufficed to
set in action the Florida side of the intrigue, which he
left in the hands of the energetic Mangourit. While
the minister was traveling by land to Philadelphia,
amid the jubilations of the democratic admirers of
France, Washington and his cabinet were considering
the attitude of the United States toward neutrality and
our treaty with France. As early as the twentieth of
February, 1793, as we have seen,[39] Jefferson had
received from Colonel Smith intimations of the French
project and of Genet's mission. On the seventeenth

---

[36] *Report of American Historical Association*, 1896, p. 987.
[37] Archives, États-Unis, Supp. Vol. 5, Doc. 9 (1790-1813), Mangourit to
Genet, April 24, 1793.
[38] *American State Papers, Indian Affairs*, I, 310.
[39] Jefferson, *Writings*, I, 216; *Works*, ed. Washington, III, 534.

of January, Clavière had written to him of the minister's coming, and on the twenty-third of March, Jefferson, with Washington's approval, had drafted instructions [40] for Carmichael and Short, our commissioners to Spain. These instructions mention the desire of France to offer independence to the Spanish-American colonies, beginning with those on the Mississippi, and that she would not object to our receiving those of the east side into our confederacy. The proper course, Jefferson observed, was to keep ourselves free to act according to circumstances and not to guarantee the Spanish colonies. The idea of providing for a guaranty of Louisiana on condition of the cession of the Floridas was abandoned, because when it was originally thought of we apprehended it would be seized by Great Britain, who would thus completely encircle us with her colonies and fleets. "This danger," he adds, "is now removed by the concert between Great Britain and Spain; and the times will soon enough give independence, and consequently free commerce to our neighbors, without our risking the involving of ourselves in a war for them."

The proclamation issued by Washington on the twenty-second of April required the pursuance of a conduct friendly and impartial toward the belligerent powers. Jefferson, while acquiescing as a matter of expediency,[41] nevertheless regarded the proclamation as pusillanimous.[42] Large masses of the people of Philadelphia were bitterly opposed to the President's policy, and rioting was imminent at the very seat of government. This was, then, the situation at the open-

[40] Jefferson, *Writings*, VI, 206.
[41] Jefferson to Madison, June 23, 1793; *Works*, III, 591.
[42] Jefferson to Madison, May 19, 1793; *Works*, III, 562.

ing of Genet's mission. The Democratic-Republican forces of the country desired a liberal construction of our treaty obligations with France, and the most friendly relations, if not positive alliance, with her. The fomentation of Indian attacks upon our southwestern frontier by Spain, to say nothing of her stubborn attitude regarding the Mississippi, had led the government to serious protests in the fall of 1792, and by the early summer of 1793 war seemed inevitable.[43] Washington asked of Knox,[44] in the middle of June, information regarding the Spanish strength in Florida, to provide for the event of embroilment; and Jefferson wrote Monroe at the end of that month that war with Spain was absolutely inevitable.[45] As early as the autumn [46] of 1792 Jefferson had expressed his apprehension that Spain and England had a common understanding on the frontiers of the United States; and the declaration of war by England and Spain against France, together with the complaints of English intrigues among the Indians by our settlers on the Northwest, did not tend to lessen the apprehension. In short, Genet's opportunity was an ideal one.

But almost from the first he alienated the President and even rendered the support of his friends difficult. He found Washington cold and impassive. He asked in vain that the United States should anticipate the payment of their debt to France (about $2,300,000) and he engaged, in conformity with his instructions, to accept certificates to be expended among the various states for supplies and munitions of war. These were to be

[43] Jefferson to Carmichael and Short, October 14, 1792; *Works*, III, 474.
[44] Washington to Jefferson, June 14, 1793; Washington's *Writings*, XII, 297.
[45] Jefferson, *Works*, IV, 6.
[46] Jefferson to Washington, September 9, 1792; *Works*, III, 459.

devoted, in part, to the provisioning of the French islands; but it needs no penetration to perceive that the plan was admirably suited to cover all kinds of expenditures from this fund among the frontiersmen for the purposes of the expedition. The federal government declined the proposition, and Genet soon practically abandoned his effort to win the administration, and turned to intrigues.

On his arrival he found awaiting him the letter of George Rogers Clark, written February 2, 1793, from the Falls of the Ohio.[47] In this letter the frontier leader recounted his services, his investigations into Spanish defenses in the Mississippi Valley, his possession of friends in those places, and his relations to the Indians. He declared that with four hundred men he could expel the Spaniards from upper Louisiana, and with eight hundred execute the same operation upon New Orleans. He asked naval assistance of two or three frigates and three thousand pounds sterling for the expedition.[48] Genet also received, a few days after his arrival at Philadelphia, two memoirs from André Michaux,[49] the French botanist, to whom Jefferson had in January of that year given instructions in behalf of

[47] *Report of American Historical Association,* 1896, pp. 967, 971.

[48] Another draft, in the Clark MSS. (*ibid.,* p. 967), dated February 5 or 3 (for the date shows emendation), proposed to raise fifteen hundred men out of Kentucky, Cumberland, the Holston settlements, and the Illinois. As many more French of the Spanish settlements would flock to his standard. With the first he could take Louisiana, beginning with St. Louis, and with further aid he could take Pensacola and, if Santa Fe and the rest of New Mexico were desired, he knew their avenues; and all of Spanish America with its mines would follow. He planned to expatriate himself: "My country has proved notoriously ungrateful for my services and so forgetful of those successful and almost unexampled enterprizes which gave it the whole of its territory on this side of the great mountains, as in this, my very prime of life, to have neglected me." Compare also the unsigned memoir in *Report of the American Historical Association,* 1896, p. 972.

[49] *Proceedings of American Philosophical Society,* 1889, Michaux's Journal, with biographical introduction, and bibliographical references.

the American Philosophical Society for the transcon-
tinental exploration which he proposed.[50] But while
Genet was holding his first conference with Jefferson,
Michaux was engaged in drawing up his observations
on the French colonies in America, for a different kind
of exploration.

The month of June was a busy one for the French
minister. Finding Michaux' exploring tour a convenient cover for his own designs, he selected him as
his agent to go to Kentucky, and he conferred with
John Brown, the Kentucky congressman,[51] who gave
Michaux letters of introduction to Governor Shelby, of
Kentucky, and to George Rogers Clark. Genet wrote
to Lebrun, on the nineteenth of this month,[52] that in
spite of "old Washington," who "had hindered his
progress in a thousand ways," he had won popular
enthusiasm, and was secretly pressing for the calling of
Congress, where he expected a majority. In the meantime, he is provisioning the Antilles, exciting the
Canadians,[53] arming the Kentuckians, and preparing an
expedition by sea to second their descent upon New
Orleans. The week before this letter, he had received
a memorial from DePauw, a Kentucky merchant,[54]
familiar by his trading voyages down the Mississippi
with the forts held by Spain on the route, and who had
just come from New Orleans. DePauw related in a

[50] Compare Jefferson to George Rogers Clark, December 4, 1783 (52 Clark
MSS., 93, printed in *American Historical Review*, III. 673), proposing the
exploration to him, and see Turner, "Indian Trade in Wisconsin," in *Johns
Hopkins University Studies*, IX, p. 18 ff.
[51] *Report of American Historical Association*, 1896, pp. 982, 983.
[52] Archives, États-Unis, Vol. 37, fol. 431.
[53] On the French intrigues in Canada see *Report on Canadian Archives*,
1891, 1894, and Dorchester's proclamation of November 26, 1793, in *Philadelphia Gazette*, March 6, 1794.
[54] *Report of American Historical Association*, 1896, pp. 977, 1002, 1102.
Charles De Pauw is said (*Representative Men of Indiana*) to have come out
with LaFayette. His grandson was the benefactor of DePauw University.

paper written about 1808 that, on the twentieth of April, 1793, he had taken part in a French dinner party in New Orleans, at which plans for a descent on New Orleans from Kentucky were concocted.[55] The correspondence of Governor Carondelet, of New Orleans, with his government [56] shows that French intrigues were then in progress in that city, and that he had reason to fear an insurrection. Indeed, in the July following, Carondelet reported the expulsion of sixty-eight French suspects from New Orleans, and he was inquiring into mysterious gatherings, outside the city.[57] He wrote: "It is whispered by some that in a few months the French will be here. For my part I can affirm that if (which may God forbid) the arms of Spain and of her allies were to suffer any drawback, or if some four frigates were to present themselves here with 1200 French troops there would arise a faction in this city in favor of the Convention which would cause great havoc and perhaps the loss of the province. My small garrison and the faithful vassals of the king are resolved to achieve impossibilities and to die arms in hand; but unless the 300 men lacking to this regiment are sent from Spain by the end of the year we shall lose even this honorable consolation, since for the protection of the most necessary posts and for avoiding a surprise, the men remaining are hardly sufficient, . . . while those previously received are of such a bad character that the prisons are continually filled and but for the adoption of extreme penalties against the delin-

[55] He says that Colonel John "Blane," of Lincoln, and John Speed, of Bullet, County, Kentucky, were present. *Report of American Historical Association*, 1896, p. 1103.

[56] *Ibid.*, p. 974.

[57] Draper Collection, 42 Clark MSS., 1.

quents in these circumstances, two-thirds of the regiment would be in prison, and we should remain without any troops. To these important reasons must be added the fears inspired in us by the very disquieting movements of the Americans settled in the West, against whom I cannot oppose sufficient forces in case of any hostility from them." [58] He states further that, owing to the withdrawal of the troops that had come from Havana, the New Orleans garrison scarcely amounted to 700 men, and 920 were employed in twenty-one detachments distributed over more than 600 leagues.

This apprehension of the governor of Louisiana and West Florida was amply confirmed by the statements of DePauw and other informants in regard to the weakness of the Spanish posts and the ease of taking them.[59] Most of the plans against New Orleans proposed to leave St. Louis unassailed, to be taken after the lower river was secured. Below the confluence of the Ohio with the Mississippi, the first post was that of New Madrid, or L'Anse à la Graisse, where a captain and twenty to forty men, with ten cannon, were reported. The fort, it was thought, could easily be taken, or passed in the night. Chickasaw Bluff, or Écores à Margot, was as yet unoccupied by a fort, but the Spaniards suspected the Americans of the design of securing that point. Walnut Hills, or Nogales (now Vicksburg), the site of O'Fallon's projected Yazoo colony, was begun in 1790 to resist that project. It

[58] Carondelet to Alcudia, July 3, 1793; *Report of American Historical Association*, 1896, p. 996.
[59] See *American Historical Review*, III, 497; and *Report of American Historical Association*, 1896, p. 972. Carondelet's description of his posts and preparations for defence in 1793 and 1794 is in *American Historical Review*, II, 475. General Collot, in the service of France, visited these posts in 1796, and his description of them, with an excellent atlas, giving plans of each, is in his *Journey in North America*.

was believed to be commanded by neighboring hills, however, and since its garrison of about 100 men were chiefly Frenchmen, its numerous artillery was less to be feared. Below Walnut Hills, as Carondelet admitted, there was nothing to prevent the enemy from reaching the capital. The French settlers were ripe for revolt, and Natches, dominated on all sides, and with American settlers about it, would fall an easy prey. The forts of Manchac and Baton Rouge were in ruins. New Orleans was expected to revolt against the Spanish rule; and a French fleet blockading the mouth of the river would coöperate with the frontiersmen. Such, in outline, were the plans proposed for the Kentucky side of the expedition. Mangourit was himself engaged in preparing for a descent on St. Augustine from South Carolina and Georgia, with a fleet and 1500 frontiersmen, while another expedition, of 2000 backwoodsmen from the southern upcountry, was to descend the Tennessee to unite its forces with George Rogers Clark.

After his interviews with Michaux, Brown, and DePauw, the matter was sufficiently advanced for Genet to sound Jefferson; for if the Secretary of State and leader of the Democratic party could be actively enlisted in the design, its success seemed certain. From what has already been said, it is clear that as early as February, 1793, Jefferson understood that it was the intention of France to free Louisiana. He was opposed to the form, at least, of the proclamation of neutrality, and he expected war with Spain. On the fifth of July Genet unfolded to him, "not as Secretary of State, but as Mr. Jefferson," the outline of his Kentucky project,[60]

[60] *Report of American Historical Association*, 1896, p. 948; Jefferson, *Writings*, I, 235.

as embodied in his instructions to Michaux. He also
read his proposed address to the Canadians. Jefferson's
minute of the conversation indicates that he understood
that the expedition was to rendezvous out of the territories of the United States (he supposed in Louisiana),
and that Louisiana was to be established as an independent state connected in commerce with France and
the United States. "I told him," said Jefferson, "that
his enticing officers and souldiers from Kentucky to go
against Spain, was really putting a halter about their
necks, for that they would assuredly be hung if they
commenced hostilities against a nation at peace with the
United States. That leaving out that article I did not
care what insurrections might be excited in Louisiana."
Jefferson adds that he gave Michaux a letter of introduction to Governor Shelby, of Kentucky, changing the
original draft at the desire of Genet, so that it intro-
duced him, not only as a man of science, but also as having the good opinion of Genet, and commended him to
the notice, councils, and good offices of Shelby. "His
character here persuades me," wrote the Secretary,
"that they will be worthily bestowed on him, and that
your further knowledge of him will justify the liberty I
take of making him known to you." This letter, innocent
enough in appearance, was, doubtless by design, left
with the date of June 28, antedating the second conversation with Genet. It is further elucidated by the letter
of this minister to his government, on the twenty-fifth
of July. "Mr. Jefferson," he declares, "seemed to me
to be quickly sensible of the utility of the project, but
he told me that the United States had begun negotiations with Spain on the subject of the demand that the
Americans be given an entrepôt below New Orleans

and while this negotiation was not broken off, the delicacy of the United States did not permit them to take part in our operations; nevertheless he made me understand that he thought that a little spontaneous irruption in New Orleans could advance the matter, and he put me into connection with several deputies of Kentucky and notably with Mr. Brown." [61]

Jefferson's attitude toward the French design is interesting, since his own presidency was rendered illustrious by the acquisition of Louisiana for the United States. "There is on the globe one single spot," he wrote in 1802, "the possessor of which is our natural and habitual enemy. It is New Orleans. The day that France takes possession of New Orleans fixes the sentence which is to restrain her within her low water mark. . . . From that day we must marry ourselves to the British fleet and nation." [62]

But Jefferson's position in 1793 is less easy to explain, partly because it is doubtful how far he understood the ulterior designs of France to hold Louisiana and detach the West; partly because the policy of aggressive territorial acquisition by that power was the work of the succeeding years, and Jefferson's own nationalism was to a considerable degree the work of his presidency; and partly, also, because his views of Genet's personality changed rapidly. Genet himself wrote in the succeeding autumn [63] that, in the beginning, Jefferson seemed disposed to second his views, and gave him useful ideas of the men in position; nevertheless, he says that he noted in his official declarations a sort of

[61] Genet then recounts the assistance given him by the latter in advice and influence. *Report of American Historical Association*, 1896, p. 982, n. 2.

[62] Jefferson to Livingston, April 18, 1802.

[63] Genet to Minister, October 7, 1793; Archives, États-Unis, Vol. 38, fol. 402.

reserve which convinced him that Jefferson was aiming
to keep in place, whatever happened, and he finally
found himself deserted by him. Jefferson, on the other
hand, came to know that Genet's desire was to force
the Americans into war on the side of France, contrary
to his professions, and that he did not promise everything and ask nothing, as he had at first supposed. The
truth seems to be that, in the beginning, Jefferson
believed that motives of policy coincided with his
friendliness for France, and that in the probable event
of war against Spain the freedom of Louisiana by
French assistance was not to be rejected. He was not
yet dispossessed of his illusions with respect to French
disinterestedness. By a protest against the use of
Kentucky to violate our neutrality, he saved his official
conscience, at least; but he did not break with Genet.
He wrote the letter of introduction for Michaux,[64]
and he was left in a position to "watch events." Genet's
actions, however, soon compelled Jefferson to abandon
him. Even before this interview, Jefferson wrote
Monroe that he did not augur well of the mode of
conduct of the new French minister, and he was aiming
to disabuse him of the idea that he had an appeal from
President and Congress to the people. The affair of
the "Little Democrat," immediately after the interview,
led Jefferson to declare: "his conduct is indefensible
by the most furious Jacobin. I only wish our countrymen may distinguish between him and his nation." [65]

[64] Later he seemed desirous to conceal the significance of this letter. See
Report of American Historical Association, 1896, p. 933.

[65] Jefferson, *Works,* IV, 19. Genet wrote on the twelfth of August that
he would publish his correspondence with Jefferson, "a man endowed with good
qualities but weak enough to sign what he does not think and defend officially
measures which he condemns in conversation and anonymous writings."
Archives, États-Unis, Vol. 38, fol. 182; De Witt, *Jefferson,* p. 530.

And, indeed, the Jacobinical forces themselves, which had come into power in France in June, did not desire to defend him. Soon Deforgues' letter [66] was on its way, in which the new Minister of Foreign Relations, foreseeing the tendency of his course, pointed out in severe terms that he was instructed "to treat with the *government* and not with *a portion of the people,*" and not to exercise *proconsular* powers in *a friendly* nation. Referring to the criticisms on Washington in Genet's dispatches, he says: "Deceived by a false popularity you have alienated from yourself the only man who could be for us the organ of the American people." He sneers at Genet's professions of having already armed the Kentuckians and Canadians, and awaits the developments of these measures, but observes that an expedition by sea prepared at Philadelphia against New Orleans would openly violate American neutrality and render Genet odious to the government; and finally he charges him to gain the confidence of the President and Congress. Genet, in the thick of party contests, took little heed of the warning, and rushed boldly on to meet his fate by the appeal to the people against Washington.

It is not the purpose of the present paper to relate the progress of the preparations for the expedition that followed.[67] The downfall of the Girondins led naturally to the disavowal and recall of Genet. Soon after arriving, Fauchet, his successor, issued a proclamation (March 6, 1794) terminating the expedition. It came when Clark and his friends were actively preparing for

[66] July 30, 1793. Archives, États-Unis, Vol. 38, fol. 107; De Witt, *Jefferson,* p. 525.

[67] See *American Historical Review,* III, 490; Report of American Historical *Association,* 1896, p. 930, and the documents published in the same *Report* for 1897, on the expedition in the Carolinas and Georgia.

the descent of the Mississippi, and when troops were already gathered at the St. Mary's and along the frontier of Georgia for an attack on St. Augustine. Had the proclamation been delayed, the attempt would certainly have been begun. What the result of such an attempt would have been, with the Spaniards fully informed, the military forces of the United States under orders to oppose it, and the leading friends of Genet already alienated, need not be considered here.

The very extensiveness of the original project, the succession of unforeseen changes in the government and the military situation of France, but above all the character of Genet and of Washington, worked to render it abortive. Enough has been said to reveal the fact that this attempt was an important chapter in the history of the Mississippi Valley in its relations to the future of the United States, of France, and of Spain. It is, in fact, a chapter in the long struggle of the people of that Valley to hold the approaches to their great river —a struggle that is not yet ended.

CHAPTER IV

WESTERN STATE-MAKING IN THE REVOLUTIONARY ERA[1]

I

The term "West" in American history is not limited to a single area. At first the Atlantic Coast was the West—the West of Europe; then the lands between tidewater and the Alleghenies became the West. In the second half of the eighteenth century the territory between these mountains and the Mississippi was occupied, and became the West of the Revolutionary era. In consequence of this steady march of the West across the continent, the term represents not only different areas; it stands also for a stage in American development. Whatever region was most recently reclaimed from the wilderness, was most characteristically Western. In other words, the distinctive thing about the West is its relation to free lands; and it is the influence of her free lands that has determined the larger lines of American development.

The country exhibits three phases of growth. First came the period of the application of European men, institutions, and ideas to the tidewater area of America. In this period of colonization, English traits and institutions preponderated, though modified by the new American conditions. But the constant touch of this part of the country with the Old World prevented the

[1] Reprinted by permission from *The American Historical Review*, October, 1895, and January, 1896.

modifying influences of the new environment from having their full effect, and the coast area seemed likely to produce institutions and men that were but modified shoots from the parent tree. Even the physical features of the colonial Americans are described by travelers in colonial days as English: the ruddy complexions, without delicacy of features or play of expression; the lack of nervous energy. The second phase of our growth begins with the spread of this colonial society towards the mountains; the crossing of the Alleghenies, and the settlement upon the Western Waters. Here the wilderness had opportunity to modify men already partly dispossessed of their Old World traits. In adjustment of themselves to completely new conditions, the settlers underwent a process of Americanization, and as each new advance occurred, the process was repeated with modifications. In this reaction between the West and the East, American society took on its peculiar features. We are now in the third phase of our development: the free lands are gone, and with conditions comparable to those of Europe, we have to reshape the ideals and institutions fashioned in the age of wilderness-winning to the new conditions of an occupied country.

Not only is our own development best understood in connection with the occupation of the West; it is the fact of unoccupied territory in America that sets the evolution of American and European institutions in contrast. In the Old World, such institutions were gradually evolved in relation to successive stages of social development, or they were the outcome of a struggle for existence by the older forms against the newer creations of the statesman, or against the institutions of rival peoples. There was in the Old World no virgin soil on which political gardeners might experiment with new varieties. This, America furnished at each successive area of Western advance. Men who had lived under developed institutions were transplanted into the wilderness, with the opportunity and the necessity of adapting their old institutions to their new environment, or of creating new ones capable of meeting the changed conditions.[2]

It is this that makes the study of Western statemaking in the Revolutionary period of peculiar interest. In the colonial era the task of forming governments *in vacuis locis* fell to Europeans; in the Revolution the task was undertaken by Americans on a new frontier. The question at once arises, How would they go about this, and on what principles? Would they strike boldly out regardless of inherited institutions? Would the work be done by the general government; by the separate states that claimed the jurisdiction of these unoccupied lands; or by the settlers themselves? To collect the principal instances of attempts at the formation of states in the West in this era, and briefly to consider the relations of the movement as a whole, is the purpose of this paper. An attempt will be made to interpret the movement from the point of view of the backwoodsmen.

Three types of colonial government are usually mentioned as having flourished on the Atlantic Coast: the charter colonies, outgrowths of the trading-company organization; the proprietary, modelled on the English palatinate; and the provincial colonies, which, having

[2] "The Significance of the Frontier in American History," *Report of the American Historical Association*, 1893, p. 199. [Reprinted in *The Frontier in American History*.]

been established under one of the forms just mentioned, were taken under the government of the crown, and obliged to seek the constitutional law of their organization in the instructions and commissions given to the royal governor. In all these types the transformations due to the American conditions were profound. Colonial political growth was not achieved by imitating English forms, but by reshaping English institutions, bit by bit, as occasion required, to American needs. The product had many of the features of an original creation. But in one type of colonial organizations, which has usually been left out of the classification, the influence of the wilderness conditions was especially plain. The Plymouth compact is the earliest and best-known example of the organization of a colony by a social compact, but it is by no means exceptional.[3] In Rhode Island, Connecticut, New Haven, New Hampshire, and elsewhere, the Puritan settlers, finding themselves without legal rights on vacant lands, signed compacts of government, or plantation covenants, suggested no doubt by their church governments, agreeing to submit to the common will. We shall have to recur to this important type of organization later on in our study.

When the tidewater colonial organization had been

[3] The covenant of the settlers of Exeter, New Hampshire, in 1639, is typical. "Wee, his [Charles I's] loyall subjects brethren of the church of Exeter, situate and lying upon the river of Piscataquacke, with other inhabitants there considering with ourselves the holy will of god and our owne necessity, that wee should not live without wholesome laws & government amongst us, of wch we are altogether destitute doe in the name of Christ & in the sight of god, combine ourselves together to erect and set up amongst us such government as shall be to our best discerning agreeable to the will of god, professing ourselves subject to our sovereign Lord King Charles, according to the liberties of our English colony of the Massachusetts," etc. *N. H. Provincial Papers*, I, 132. Compare Osgood, in *Political Science Quarterly*, March, 1891; Borgeaud, *Rise of Modern Democracy;* J. Adams, *Works*, IV, 110; Jefferson, *Works*, VII, 467; Wells, *Samuel Adams*, I, 429.

perfected and lands taken up, population flowed into
the region beyond the "fall line," and here again vacant
lands continued to influence the form of American institutions. They brought about expansion, which, in itself,
meant a transformation of old institutions; they broke
down social distinctions in the West, and by causing
economic equality, they promoted political equality and
democracy. Offering the freedom of the unexploited
wilderness, they promoted individualism. One of the
most important results of the rush of population into
these vacant lands, in the first half of the eighteenth
century, was the settlement of non-English stocks in
the West. All along the frontier the Palatine Germans
(Pennsylvania Dutch) and the Scotch-Irish Presby-
terians ascended the rivers that flowed into the Atlantic,
and followed the southward trend of the valleys between
the Blue Ridge and the Alleghenies. These pioneers
were of different type from the planters of the South,
or the merchants and seamen of the New England
coast. The Scotch-Irish element was ascendent, and
this contentious, self-reliant, hardy, backwoods stock,
with its rude and vigorous forest life, gave the tone
to Western thought in the Revolutionary era. A log
hut, a little clearing, edged by the primeval forest, with
the palisaded fort near by—this was the type of home
they made. As they pushed the frontier on, they held
their lands at the price of their blood shed in incessant
struggles with the Indians. Descendants of men who
had fought James II, they were the heirs of the political philosophy of Knox and Andrew Melville. Their
preachers, with rifle at the pulpit's edge, preached, not
only the theology of Calvin, but the gospel of the freedom of the individual, and the compact-theory of the

[90]

state. They constituted a new order of Americans. From the social conditions thus created came Patrick Henry, and, at a later time, Andrew Jackson, Calhoun, and Abraham Lincoln. These social conditions gave us the heroes of border warfare, and the men who, in the Revolutionary times, demanded independent statehood for their settlements.

By the middle of the eighteenth century it had become evident that the engrossing of the Eastern lands would induce the rising tide of population to flow across the Alleghenies. As the Old World had produced the tidewater area with its modified English institutions, so the thirteen colonies were now to produce states on the Western Waters, and a political life still more transformed. A multitude of propositions for great land companies, and for new colonial governments in the trans-Allegheny lands, showed a consciousness that the advance was at hand. Fearful of arousing the Indians, and apprehensive that the advance of settlements would withdraw the colonists beyond the reach of British government and trade, the King issued a proclamation in 1763, forbidding the granting of lands or the making of settlements beyond the sources of the rivers that fall into the Atlantic. But neither crown officers nor colonists acted on the theory that settlement was to be permanently excluded. In 1768, at the treaty of Fort Stanwix, the Six Nations ceded to the crown whatever title they had to lands between the Ohio and the Tennessee. At the same time they conveyed to Baynton, Wharton, and Morgan, a firm that traded with the Indians around Pittsburgh and in the Illinois country, a tract comprising about one-fourth of the state of West Virginia, as now constituted. This tract lay between the Little Kanawha and the Monongahela, and was named Indiana. On the basis of this grant a more extensive and ambitious company was formed, which absorbed the Indiana Company and the former Ohio Company and included such men as Franklin in its list of members. After a persistent effort it gained from the Lords Commissioners of Trade and Plantations a report in 1773, recommending the grant of an immense tract, comprising nearly the present state of West Virginia together with that part of Kentucky lying east of the Kentucky River.[4]

All of this area was to be erected into a new colony and to bear the name of Vandalia. It was reported in the American newspapers that the seat of the government was to be at the mouth of the Great Kanawha, and that Mr. Wharton, of Philadelphia, was to be the first governor. Although all of the process of transfer, excepting a few formalities, had been effected, the outbreak of the American Revolution put a stop to the grant. The company soon appealed to Congress, urging that body to assert its right to the crown lands as the property of the whole Union, and to confirm the Vandalia grant. The intrigues of this company had a marked effect on the actions of Congress, and of the Western settlers; and its career is also interesting as illustrating the English policy. At the time when settlement was beginning to cross the Alleghenies, and on the eve of American independence, England had announced her intention to govern the West through great proprietary companies, headed by wealthy or influential men in that country and America.

[4] See map accompanying this paper. The boundaries are described in Franklin, *Works*, X, 348, 349.

The treaty of Fort Stanwix had an additional effect in the impetus it gave to the advance of the frontiersmen by affording them a right to enter these Indian lands. The pioneers had their own ideas of liberty and of government, and were not to have their political destiny shaped without a part in the movement. Already they had reached the mountain wall that separated East and West. Before them lay the Western Waters. From the mountains the backwoodsman, looking to the East, could see, through the forbidding mountain masses, the broken chasms along which flowed the sources of the far-stretching rivers, on whose lower courses the tidewater planters dwelt. Turning away from the rented lands of the old provinces, he saw other rivers cutting their way to the West to join the Mississippi. These river systems constituted four natural areas.

1. The New River, rising in North Carolina near the headsprings of rivers that flowed to the Atlantic, tore a defiant course through the Blue Ridge and the Alleghenies to join the Great Kanawha in West Virginia. Another tributary of the Great Kanawha, the Greenbrier, rising near the sources of the Monongahela, skirted the western edge of the Alleghenies in its southward flow. Here, on the upper waters of the Ohio, was the physiographic basis for a state, a natural unit, rudely cut by the Pennsylvania boundary line, and apportioned between that state and Virginia, in spite of the veto of the Alleghenies.

2. Near to the springs of the New River were the many streams that flowed between the ridges of the Cumberland Mountains and the Alleghenies to join the Tennessee. These affluents of the Tennessee—

Powell's River, the Clinch, the Holston, the French Broad, the Nolichucky, and the Watauga—walled in to east and west by mountains, made another natural unit. Here Virginia's southern line ran right across these river courses, and left the settlements at the head of the Holston in Virginia, while their neighbors lower on the river were under the jurisdiction of North Carolina; and between these settlements and the parent states ran the Allegheny wall. It would be strange if these physiographic facts did not produce their natural result.

3. Passing through Cumberland Gap at Virginia's southwest corner, the pioneer reached another area of Virginia's back lands, the greenswards of Kentucky. This land was bounded on the north by the Ohio, while to the south was the Cumberland, forming a natural boundary, but severed for the most part from the political bounds of the region by the same unreasonable Virginia line that had cut in two the settlements on the Tennessee. These Kentucky fields constituted another natural economic area.

4. Across the Ohio lay the wide Northwest, between the Mississippi and the Great Lakes, its ownership in dispute between Virginia, Massachusetts, and Connecticut, under their charter bounds, and New York, through her protectorate over the Six Nations.

As the pioneer on his mountain height looked eastward and westward, the conviction was forced upon him that he had come to the parting of ways. Not long could he be held by the political reins of the Atlantic Coast; even England had recognized and feared this. But not only did these "Western Waters," as the pioneer called them, reveal the separation of East from West; they insured the unity of the "Western

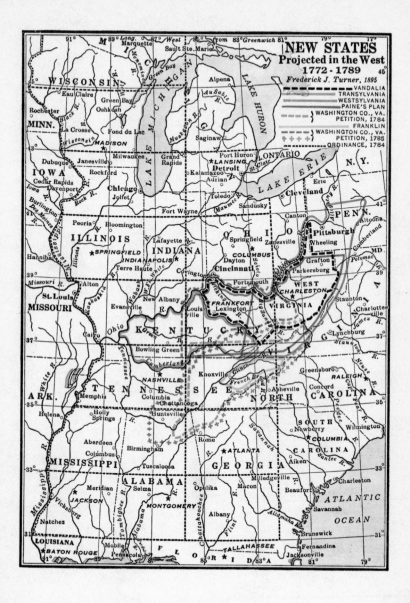

NEW STATES
Projected in the West
1772 - 1789
Frederick J. Turner, 1895

VANDALIA
TRANSYLVANIA
WESTSYLVANIA
PAINE'S PLAN
WASHINGTON CO., VA.
PETITION, 1784
FRANKLIN
WASHINGTON CO., VA.
PETITION, 1785
ORDINANCE, 1784

World"—to use another of his phrases. The waters of the West Virginia region interlocked with the waters of eastern Tennessee; on the borders of the same settlements, Cumberland Gap opened like a door to Kentucky; and all these winding rivers poured their flood into the Mississippi, the indispensable highway of commerce for the Western lands.

Hardly was the treaty of Fort Stanwix made, when Daniel Boone was on his way from his cabin on the Yadkin, "in quest of the country of Kentucke," and James Robertson with his neighbors from North Carolina was settling on the Watauga, in what is now eastern Tennessee. Although the Watauga settlement was within the limits of North Carolina's Western claims, that colony had not given civil organization to the region. Thus the settlers were in the position of the Pilgrim Fathers, or the settlers at Exeter,[5] without formal laws or political institutions. Haywood[6] is authority for the statement that in 1772 the Watauga pioneers formed a written association and articles for their conduct; they appointed five commissioners, a majority of whom was to decide all matters of controversy and to govern and direct for the common good in other respects. Robertson and many of the settlers were from that part of the interior of the Carolinas where the backwoodsmen had found it necessary to "associate" in written agreements for the purpose of "regulating" the horse thieves by summary methods in the absence of efficient courts, or of resisting the fees of colonial officers when they deemed them illegal or extortionate. These Regulators flourished from 1764

[5] Cf. p. 89, n. ante.
[6] Haywood, *Tennessee* (1823), p. 41.

to the time of the settlement on the Watauga.[7] Robertson was also familiar with Husband's "Relation" [8] (1770), which justified these associations; and his friends and neighbors were at the battle of the Alamance in 1771. It is not unreasonable to conclude that the suggestion of the Watauga Association may have been due to the Regulating Associations. But the expedient was a natural one to Scotch-Irishmen, brought up on Presbyterian political philosophy; and it was a common mode of organization at the outbreak of the Revolution.[9] The Watauga settlers petitioned the Provincial Council of North Carolina, in 1776, to extend its government to their community. They had supposed their settlements to lie within the limits of Virginia, and their lands to have been purchased from the Indians by that state, and, therefore, to be open to settlers by preëmption. But, finding their lands south of the line, in unorganized territory belonging to North Carolina, they leased and then purchased them from the Indians. In regard to government their petition [10] declares:

Finding ourselves on the Frontiers, and being apprehensive that for want of a proper legislature, we might become a shelter for such as endeavored to defraud their creditors; considering also the necessity of recording Deeds, Wills, and doing other

---

[7] On the Regulators' associations, see Ramsay, *South Carolina*, I, 210, 211; *Colonial Records of North Carolina*, VII, *passim;* Wheeler, *North Carolina*, II, 301, *et passim;* Moore, *North Carolina*, I.

[8] Putnam, *Middle Tennessee*, p. 19.

[9] For example, Pendleton District, west of Fincastle County, Virginia, informed the Virginia convention that they had "formed themselves into a Society." The system of county associations and the Association of the Congress of 1774 are well-known examples of this Revolutionary expedient. In 1779 settlers at Boonesboro', "for their own and the public good," entered into an association for making rules regarding the raising of a crop of corn. The text is in the Louisville *News Letter*, July 18, 1840 (Draper Colls.).

[10] Ramsey, *Annals of Tennessee*, p. 134. The petition was signed by one hundred inhabitants of "Washington District."

public business; we by consent of the people formed a court for the purposes above mentioned, taking (by desire of our constituents) the Virginia laws for our guide, so near as the situation of affairs would admit; this was intended for ourselves, and was done by the consent of every individual; but wherever we had to deal with people out of our district, we have ruled them to bail to abide by our determinations (which was in fact leaving the matter to reference,) otherwise we dismissed their suit, lest we should in any way intrude on the legislature of the colonies.

Their desire not to be regarded as a "lawless mob," and their petition for annexation to North Carolina, resulted in that state's receiving their representatives in 1776, and in the organization of the settlement as Washington County, in the following year. On the whole, the Association appears to have been a temporary expedient, pending the organization of North Carolina's county government, and comparable to the Western "claim associations" of later times.[11] The same type of government is to be seen in the Cumberland Association. In 1780 James Robertson led an exodus from Watauga to Nashborough at the bend of the Cumberland, and in the spring of that year delegates chosen by the people at the different forts, or stations, assembled and made a compact. Its features resembled those of Watauga; the articles related largely to the mode of regulating disputes in regard to land, and the government was looked upon as temporary.[12] After three years the Cumberland pioneers

[11] See Macy, *Institutional Beginnings of a Western State,* and Shambaugh, *Claim Association of Johnson County, Iowa* (Iowa City, 1894). Bancroft, *Popular Tribunals,* and *Shinn, Mining Camps,* illustrate other phases of the Association.

[12] Putnam and Ramsey give the documentary material for the political history of the Cumberland settlement. See also Roosevelt, *Winning of the West,* II, ch. xi.

were organized as Davidson County of North Carolina. The continuity of the old government and the new is indicated by the fact that the four justices of the new court had all been "judges, or triers" of the former Association.[13] As showing how readily the backwoodsmen seized upon the idea of a social compact in vacant territory, the little settlement of Clarksville,[14] across the Ohio from Louisville, may be instanced. Here, on January 27, 1785, a "convention" was held at which eleven men, calling themselves "a majority of the actual settlers of the town," met and asserted their right, in the absence of congressional government, to make laws not repugnant to the Constitution of the United States, or to the resolves of Congress. They established a tribunal of four magistrates with judicial authority and elected a sheriff to carry out their decisions. The organization continued at least as late as November, 1787. It was the multiplicity of revolutionary associations, and the ease with which they might run into the form taken by the later Vigilance Committees of the Far West, that led even so ardent a follower of revolutionary principles as Patrick Henry to declare in 1786, regarding the defenceless condition of the Western frontiers, "that protection, which is the best and grand object of social compact is withdrawn, and the people, thus consigned to destruction, will naturally form

[13] Roosevelt, II, 366.

[14] Draper Colls., William Clark Papers, I, 103, 105, contain the original minutes of the convention. These collections of the late Dr. Lyman C. Draper, embracing more than four hundred folio volumes of manuscripts on Western history, principally in the Revolutionary period, are the property of the State Historical Society of Wisconsin. These papers are very largely contemporaneous documents, few of which have been published. They constitute a monument to the ability of Dr. Draper as an antiquarian and collector. The present paper is chiefly based upon these documents; and I am indebted to the courtesy of Mr. Reuben G. Thwaites for giving me every facility for using these sources.

associations, disgraceful as they are destructive to government."

Thus the earliest form of government in the region west of the Alleghenies was the Association of the backwoodsmen themselves; but it was soon followed by the attempt of a land company, without governmental sanction, to secure an imperial domain by Indian purchase and to institute a proprietary government. Daniel Boone's Kentucky explorations bore fruit in the formation of the Transylvania Company, January 6, 1775, with Judge Richard Henderson, of North Carolina, at its head. Among the terms of agreement entered into by the nine proprietors, all of them from North Carolina, one had reference to "sitting and voting as a proprietor and giving rules and regulations for the inhabitants." [15] The memories of Clarendon and Monk, and the "Fundamental Constitutions" of John Locke, would seem to have taken possession of the mind of the Carolina jurist, and visions of a new palatinate in the backwoods to have arisen before him. In 1775 this company effected a purchase from the Cherokees of all their lands between the Ohio, Kentucky, and Cumberland rivers, and including Powell's Valley of eastern Tennessee. This domain was Transylvania.[16] Boone and his riflemen had blazed the Wilderness Road to Kentucky, and were holding their grounds against the hostile savages. Here, too, were other bands of settlers, led by Harrod, holding by the tenure of their rifles, and without government. When Henderson arrived, he first opened his land office, and then broached the question

[15] This document and the agreement of the Louisa Company, as well as Henderson's MS. journal, are in Draper Colls., Ky. MSS., I.

[16] The boundaries, with map, are discussed in the *Report of the Bureau of Ethnology*, 1883-4, pp. 148 *et seq*. See Draper Colls., Ky. MSS., I, (A). The boundaries are approximately shown in the map accompanying this paper.

of political organization. If ever the Carolina proprietary had been his model, it suffered a forest-change.
He writes in his Journal: "The plann was plain and
simple—twas nothing novel in its essence. A thousand
years ago it was in use, and found by every years's
experience to be unexceptionable. We were in four distinct settlements. Members or delegates [should be
elected] from every place by free choice of Individuals,
they first having entering [*sic*] into writings solemnly
binding themselves to obey and carry into Execution
such Laws as representatives should from time to time
make, concurred with by a Majority of the Proprietors
present in the Country." This plan met with the frontiersmen's approval; and Henderson appointed May 23,
1775, for the Convention, and "made out writings for
the different towns to sign." Accordingly, delegates
appeared at this open-air convention, six from Boonesboro' and four from each of the other settlements. In
his proprietary address, opening the convention, Henderson declared: "If any doubt remain amongst you
with respect to the force and efficacy of whatever laws
you may now or hereafter make, be pleased to consider
that all power is originally in the people," and that the
laws "derive force and efficacy from our mutual consent." The backwoods legislators passed laws suited to
their needs, which were approved by Henderson, and
they entered into a compact with the proprietors, defining their respective rights, and outlining a legislative
organization, with two chambers, for the colony, when it
should arrive at greater maturity.[17] By retaining the
veto power, the proprietors prevented the possibility of

[17] The Journal of the Proceedings is printed in Collins, *Kentucky*, II, 501.

legislation adverse to their claims; but the proceedings of the convention show how far they had deemed it the part of wisdom to make concessions to the spirit of freedom.[18] The Transylvania Convention never met again. The governors of Virginia and North Carolina denounced the company in proclamations, and felt the greatest indignation over this "infamous Company of Land Pyrates" that had infringed the Earl of Granville's proprietary.[19] But the days of proprietaries, English and American, were numbered. The Revolution had begun, and, in the fall of 1775, the Transylvania proprietors, at a meeting in North Carolina, delegated James Hogg, one of their number, to represent them in the Continental Congress, and to present to that body a memorial desiring Congress to take the infant colony under its protection.[20] The correspondence of this proprietor in January of 1776, from Philadelphia, enables us to see how Congress received the news of this attempt.[21] Mr. Hogg writes that he found the two Adamses friendly, but unwilling to act without the prior consent of Virginia. Jefferson, he said, expressed the wish to see a free government established at the back of Virginia, properly united with them, and desired it to extend westward to the Mississippi, and on each side of the Ohio to their charter line; but he would not consent to congressional action until the proposition had the approval of the Virginia con-

[18] For Powell's Valley, Henderson prepared a form of government, with a separate assembly, for the reason that it was too remote to share in the legislature in Kentucky. It does not seem to have been put into operation. Draper Colls., Ky. MSS., I, (A).

[19] Foote, *Sketches*, p. 49; *North Carolina Colonial Records*, X, 273, 323.

[20] 4 *American Archives*, IV, 553; *N. C. Col. Recs.*, X, 256; Hall, *Sketches of the West*, II, 223.

[21] *N. C. Col. Recs.*, X, 300, 373; 4 *Am. Archives*, IV, 543.

vention. Deane, of Connecticut, held out hopes of a considerable migration[22] from that state, and wrote a long letter[23] advising Transylvania to follow Connecticut ideals of government. He pointed out that Connecticut began with a voluntary compact of government, and governed under it until their charter of 1662. "You would be amazed," wrote Hogg, "to see how much in earnest all these speculative gentlemen are about the plan to be adopted by the Transylvanians. They entreat, they pray that we make it a free government, and beg that no mercenary or ambitious views in the proprietors may prevent it. Quit-rents, they say, is a mark of vassalage, and hope they shall not be established in Transylvania. They even threaten us with their opposition, if we do not act upon liberal principles when we have it so much in our power to make ourselves immortal. Many of them advise a law against negroes."

But Harrod's party in Kentucky petitioned Virginia to take the settlements under her protection, complained against the price of lands fixed by Henderson, denounced the action of the Transylvania Convention, as having been "overawed by the presence of Mr. Henderson," and closed by requesting that if Virginia believed their case more properly belonged to the Continental Congress, she should recommend her delegates to espouse it there.[24] The proprietors, in their reply, scouted as absurd the idea that they had desired to erect a separate government within the limits of another,

[22] On November 12, 1775, Governor Martin, of North Carolina, reported a rumor to Lord Dartmouth that Hogg was negotiating with two thousand Connecticut people to settle in Transylvania. This was not at all impossible. Compare *Am. Hist. Association Rep.*, 1893, p. 333, and *Canadian Archives*, 1890, pp. 103, 156.

[23] *N. C. Col. Recs.*, X, 300; 4 *Am. Archives*, IV, 556.

[24] 4 *Am. Archives*, VI, 1528.

and declared that the measures of the Transylvania Convention were intended as mere temporary by-laws for the good of their little community, and which the necessities of the case justified. This was hardly in keeping with Henderson's address to the Transylvania Convention. "You," he had assured his backwoods listeners, as they stood about him under the mighty elm that made the legislative hall, "You are placing the first corner-stone of an edifice, the height and magnificence of whose superstructure is now in the womb of futurity, and can only become great and glorious in proportion to the excellence of its foundation." But though the proprietors were now ready to yield the glory of commonwealth-builders, for the more substantial benefits of the quitrents, Virginia annulled their title, later compensating them in part with a grant of 200,000 acres.

The settlers, left to their own devices, held a meeting at Harrodsburg in the summer of 1776, and sent George Rogers Clark and a companion as delegates to the Virginia Assembly. Clark had desired the people to choose agents with general powers to negotiate with the governor of Virginia, and if abandoned by that state, to employ the lands of the country as a fund to obtain settlers, and establish an independent state; but he was overruled;[25] and in 1777 Virginia organized this "respectable Body of Prime Riflemen," as, in their petition, they denominated themselves, into a county with the boundaries of the present Kentucky.

In the meantime, the region of the Vandalia Company and western Pennsylvania had become the scene of a new state project. Pennsylvania and Virginia had a

[25] Butler, *Kentucky* (2d edition), p. 38.

boundary dispute involving the possession of the head-
waters of the Ohio, and particularly the region between
the Youghiogheny and the Ohio. In this tract, at the
opening of the Revolution, settlers from these rival
states disputed the ownership of the same pieces of
land, rival local organizations covered the same territory, and the partisans of the Old Dominion and the
adherents of the Quaker state called each other a
"horde of banditti" with reciprocal vehemence. The
anarchical conditions kept the settlers in continual excite-
ment and prevented their union against the Indians, and
even threatened interstate war in the midst of the
struggle against England. The inhabitants of this country, "Miserably distressed & harrassed and rendered
a scene of the most consummate Anarchy & Confusion,"
circulated a memorial to Congress shortly after the
Declaration of Independence, asking organization as a
new state.[26] Between the claims of the Indiana and
Vandalia companies, and the contentions of Virginia
and Pennsylvania, they were all at sea respecting their
property rights, and they felt themselves in a more
deplorable condition than "whilst living on the poor,
barren, rented lands in their respective provinces
below." They recounted their incessant struggles
against the Indians. "Tho' neither politicians nor
orators," said they, "we are at least a rational and
Social People, inured to Hardships & Fatigues, & by
experience taught to dispise Dangers and Difficulties."
They protested that having emigrated from almost
every province of America, "brought up under and
accustomed to various different, & in many respects

[26] Mr. Frederick D. Stone, of the Pennsylvania Historical Society, discovered this memorial. It is printed in Crumrine's *History of Washington
County, Pennsylvania,* p. 187.

discordant & even contradictory systems of laws and
government," and "having imbibed the highest and
most extensive ideas of liberty," they will "with Difficulty Submit to the being annexed to or Subjugated by
(Terms Synonomous to them) any one of those Provinces, much less the being partitioned or parcelled out
among them"; nor will they submit "to be enslaved by
any set of Proprietary or other Claimants, or arbitrarily
deprived and robbed of those Lands and that Country
to which by the Laws of Nature & of Nations they are
entitled as first Occupants, and for the possession of
which they have resigned their All & exposed themselves
and families to Inconveniences, Dangers, & Difficulties,
which Language itself wants Words to express &
describe." With especial vehemence these frontiersmen
deny that they will endure the loss of their rights
"whilst the Rest of their Countrymen, softened by Ease,
enervated by Affluence and Luxurious Plenty & unac-
customed to Fatigues, Hardships, Difficulties or
Dangers, are bravely contending for and exerting themselves on Behalf of a Constitutional, national, rational
& social Liberty." By population and territory they
believed that they were justified in demanding independent statehood. West of the Alleghenies, on the
tributaries of the Ohio above the Scioto, they reported
25,000 families. The seat of government, whether
under Virginia or Pennsylvania, was four or five hundred miles distant, and "separated by a vast, extensive
and almost impassible Tract of Mountains, by Nature
itself formed and pointed out as a Boundary between
this Country & those below it." They therefore
appealed to the Continental Congress as "the Guard-
ians, Trustees, Curators, Conservators, & Defenders

of all that is dear or valuable to Americans," to constitute them a distinct and independent province and
government, by the name of Westsylvania, "a sister
colony and fourteenth province of the American confederacy." The bounds of the prospective state included
most of Pennsylvania beyond the Alleghenies, West
Virginia, and eastern Kentucky.[27] Although Westsylvania did not receive the sanction of Congress, the
project for a state in that region was too well founded
to die out, as the history of the state of West Virginia
proves. During the heat of the Revolution the movement had a moment of lull, but the backwoodsmen kept
in mind the actions of Congress in this period; and as
the two movements are mutually interpretative, we must
turn briefly to recall the actions of Congress in the years
succeeding.[28]

In the fall of 1777, Maryland tried vainly to induce
Congress to assert the power to limit the states which
claimed to the Mississippi, and to lay out the land
beyond the boundary thus fixed into separate and independent states. The little landless states, Maryland,
Rhode Island, New Jersey, and Delaware, made
repeated efforts in the next two years to secure to Con-

[27] See the map. The boundary ran as follows: "Beginning at the Eastern
Bank of the Ohio, opposite the mouth of the Scioto, & running thence in a
direct line to the Owasioto Pass [Cumberland Gap], thence to the top of the
Alleghany Mountains thence with the Top of the said Mountains to the north-
ern limit of the purchase made from the Indians in 1768, at the Treaty of Fort
Stanwix, thence with the said limits to the Alleghany or Ohio River, and
thence down the said River as purchased from the said Indians at the said
Treaty of Fort Stanwix to the Beginning." For the Fort Stanwix line, see
N. Y. Col. Docs., VIII, 136, 137, with map.

[28] Only such a view of congressional action is here given as suffices to
show the relation of this action to the plans of the Westerners. See, for
convenient summaries: Hinsdale, Old Northwest, chs. xii-xiv; Barrett, Evolu-
tion of the Ordinance of 1787; Adams, Maryland's Influence on the Land
Cessions; Stone, Ordinance of 1787. Documentary material is in Journals of
Congress, and Secret Journals of Congress, Domestic, pp. 372, 377, 428, 433;
Secret Journals, Foreign Affairs, III, 161 (1821); Hening, X, 549; Gilpin,
Madison Papers, I, 122; Thomson Papers, in N. Y. Hist. Soc. Colls., 1878,

gress the possession of the back lands, though
Maryland alone continued a consistent opposition to
allowing the jurisdiction of the region involved to
remain with the claimant states. It may have been that
New Jersey's interest was quickened by the strength
which the Indiana Company had in that state, through
the efforts of Col. George Morgan, of Princeton,
the active agent and promoter of the company, and
through the number of New Jersey men interested in
these land speculations. On September 14, 1779,
memorials from the Vandalia and Indiana companies
were presented to Congress,[29] protesting against Virginia's claim to lands beyond the Alleghenies, and
asking an investigation of their claims. About a year
later,[30] Congress recommended to the states a liberal
cession of their Western lands to the Union; and, on
October 10, 1780, resolved that the unappropriated
lands that might be thus ceded should be "disposed of
for the common benefit of the United States, and be
settled and formed into distinct republican States,
which shall become members of the federal union, and
have the same rights of sovereignty, freedom, and
independence as the other states; that each state which
shall be formed shall contain a suitable extent of territory, not less than 100 nor more than 150 miles square,
or as near thereto as circumstances will admit." These
resolutions came at a time when the Westerners were
petitioning Congress for such action,[31] and in their turn
they were circulated throughout the frontier and stimulated action. Shortly after their passage George

[29] *Journals of Congress,* of that date. Cf. Franklin, *Works,* X, 346 (1888).
[30] September 6, 1780.
[31] Besides the Transylvania and Westsylvania petitions, already mentioned,
see the Kentucky petition of May 15, 1780, in Roosevelt, *Winning of the West,*
II, 398, and the projects of western Pennsylvania, to be noted later.

Morgan wrote to a Kentucky friend,[32] that all the country west of the Alleghenies would probably be put under the direction of the United States, and Virginia limited to the waters which fall into the Atlantic. In this case, he thought, several new states would be established, "independent, though united with our present Confederacy of Thirteen," and he promised to send to his correspondent a "pamphlet now in the press on this subject." Within a few weeks[33] Paine's *Public Good* appeared with an elaborate attack on the trans-Allegheny claims of Virginia, and with its proposition that Congress should create a new state to include the Vandalia area, and an additional slice of the Kentucky territory.[34] Paine was accused of receiving compensation from the Indiana Company for this pamphlet,[35] and it may have been the one which Morgan expected to distribute as campaign literature in the West.

In 1780 Pennsylvania and Virginia agreed on a proposition for running a temporary boundary line, and for settling land titles on either side of the boundary by the test of priority of occupation. But the running of the line was much delayed, so that not until 1784 was the southwest corner of Pennsylvania definitively fixed by the two states. In the interval the Virginia men who found themselves likely to come under Pennsylvania's jurisdiction were active in proposing a new

[32] Draper Colls., Clark MSS., L, 76.
[33] The letter was written December 1; Paine's *Public Good* was published December 30, 1780.
[34] See the map. The state's boundaries were to be the Alleghenies, the Ohio as far north as the Pennsylvania line, thence down the Ohio to its falls, thence due south to the latitude of North Carolina's line, and thence east to the mountains again. Conway, *Writings of T. Paine*, II, 62, 63.
[35] Draper Colls., Clark MSS., XI, 10, cites *Virginia Gazette*, April 6, 1782, and *Maryland Journal*, April 2, 1782, to the effect that the company gave Paine a deed for 12,000 acres. Conway, *Life of Paine*, argues against the charge.

state. Questions of taxation, land fees, and the dislike
of accepting the test of priority for their claims were
some of the reasons for discontent.[36] As early as May,
1780, new state meetings were projected in the region,[37]
and, in the fall of the same year, some of the Virginia
partisans drew up a memorial to Congress, urging that
body to encourage the settling of "the Western World,"
by the formation of a new state with such limits as
should seem best to Congress. They complained of
their distance from the parent states on the east; and
of the almost impassable mountain barrier in that direction; while in the opposite direction flowed the Western
Waters, offering an outlet for the produce of their
fertile lands, could they but have a trade established
on those waters. "When we consider our remote situation," say they, "we cannot but reflect that such a
distance renders our Interest incompatible; for when
any part of a State lies so remote from its Capital that
their produce cannot reach the market, the Connection
ceases, & from thence proceeds a different Interest &
consequently a Coolness." Taxation on equal terms
with their Eastern fellow citizens was also a grievance,
for, with no staple commodity that they could send to
the capital, or any other seaport, they could not secure
the specie for paying the tax. "But," say they, with an
idealism common to the West, "were we a separate
state, a Trade on the Western Waters undoubtedly
would be opened for our relief." They advanced the
doctrine, inconsistent with the Articles of Confederation
(and possibly derived from their construction of the
resolutions of Congress of September and October),

[36] Others are mentioned in *Cal. Va. State Papers*, III, 630, 631, 135.
[37] *Hist. of Washington County, Penna.*, p. 232.

that "our Union declares when any state grows too
large or unwieldy, the same may be divided into one or
more States; that the people have a right to emigrate
from one state to another and form new states in different Countries, whenever they can thereby promote
their own Ease & Safety." In addition, they remind
Congress of the King's Proclamation of 1763, and the
Vandalia grant, and ask Congress carefully to investigate all the charters, and "candidly determine all such
Matters and Things as so nearly concern any of the
subjects of America & which tend to sap & undermine
the Liberty of the People." [38] Nor was it only the
friends of Virginia that were considering independent
statehood. The Congressional resolutions mentioned
were regarded in western Pennsylvania as applying to
that state, as well as to the states whose claims ran to
the Mississippi. In Westmoreland County apprehen-
sions were aroused, lest, if Pennsylvania should cede its
unappropriated area, this county would be retained by
the parent state; for, though west of the Alleghenies,
it was more thickly populated than other trans-Allegheny counties of Pennsylvania. "If the unappropriated
parts of the country are relinquished," wrote Thomas
Scott,[39] who went from that district to Congress in
1789, and who was familiar with the views of the settlers, "we must go with it, or Else we shall remain a
people dependent on pennsylvania, Remote in situation,
different in Interests, few in number, and forever prevented of future groath." The agitation continued
through 1781 and 1782, sometimes taking the form of

---

[38] Draper Colls., Shepherd Papers, I, 177, 179, B. Johnston to Colonel
Shepherd, enclosing a draft of the memorial. The letter was begun in
October and sent in November, 1780.
[39] Scott to President Reed, of Pennsylvania, January 24, 1781. 1 *Penna.
Archives*, VIII, 713.

propositions to cross the Ohio and establish a new state near the Muskingum.[40] The Virginia settlers refused to pay taxes, and drove off the Pennsylvania assessors. Besides their uncertainty to whom their taxes were rightfully due, and whether by a new state movement they might not evade them altogether, they found it a peculiar hardship to pay their taxes in specie.[41] To repress these agitations, Pennsylvania enacted a law in 1782, reciting that the unlocated lands were pledged as a fund for extinguishing her obligations to the former colonial proprietors, and declaring any attempt to establish a separate state within her borders high treason, punishable by death.[42] Early the next year, the authorities sent the Rev. James Finley, a prominent Scotch-Irish Presbyterian, who had preached among the Westerners, to investigate matters and allay the disturbance.[43] He found a particularly important field for his efforts, among the clergy of his own denomination; for here, as in other localities, these preachers were promoting the idea of independence and the compact-organization of the state. One of the arguments which Finley had to meet was the way in which the Puritan colonies had been established.

[40] *Washington-Irvine Correspondence*, pp. 231, 233, 109, 244, 266; 1 *Penna. Archives*, IX, 233, 519, 572, 637, 662; McMaster, III, 98. Kentucky settlers projected a movement across the Ohio in 1780 and petitioned Congress for permission. Archives of Continental Congress, XLVIII, 245, 247.

[41] Compare the grievances of the same region in the Whiskey Rebellion. The lack of specie has always been a frontier complaint. In 1783 Virginia allowed her Western settlers to pay one-half their taxes in frontier commodities; the state of Franklin made out a schedule of the specie value of commodities acceptable for taxes and salaries, including linen, beaver skins, raccoon skins, bacon, beeswax, and good rye whiskey.

[42] *Laws of Pennsylvania*, II, 60 (edition of 1810).

[43] 1 *Penna. Archives*, IX, 729; X, 163, 40, 41. He recapitulates the arguments with which he met the demands for statehood.

II

Although in western Pennsylvania the agitation subsided for a time, in the West Virginia region the ferment went on. To understand the situation, it is necessary to recall the proceedings in Congress. On November 3, 1781, a committee recommended the acceptance of New York's cession, covering a considerable portion of Virginia's claim; and also recommended that Congress should refuse to give to Virginia the guaranty of her remaining territory, which she had demanded as the price of ceding her lands beyond the Ohio. It further recommended that, when Congress should come into possession of the tract, the claim of the Indiana Company be confirmed, and the Vandalia proprietors reimbursed in lands for their actual expenditures; but it denied the latter grant as a whole, as incompatible with the interests, government, and policy of the United States. The report was a distinct blow to Virginia, and it marks the high-water point of efforts at congressional control of regions, like West Virginia, just west of the Alleghenies. Through the reasoning of the report ran the theory that the crown lands—that is, all the lands beyond these mountains—had passed by devolution to the whole United States. In accepting New York's cession, Congress clothed herself with the additional title of that state. The report was not acted on until later, but the rumor of it (sometimes exaggerated into the statement that Congress had definitely taken the crown lands) spread through the West, and increased the projects for states and the appeals to Congress. In the summer of 1782 heated debates occurred in Congress over its power respecting the organization of the trans-Allegheny lands. Some argued for the right of Congress to take possession of this country, and to take the petitioning Western settlers by the hand, and admit them as new states. It was intimated that Virginia contemplated the formation of the Western country into distinct subordinate governments, and the sending out of lieutenant-governors to rule them—a repetition of the colonial policy of Great Britain, and likely to bring about another revolution. Virginia was threatened by one speaker with forcible division into two or more distinct and independent states.[44] In the fall of 1782 Congress accepted New York's cession, and there matters rested until the next autumn.[45]

With so critical a situation in Congress, it is not surprising that Virginia settlers beyond the mountains began to sell their lands for low prices, and to take up new claims, expecting to be supported by Congress. Within a few days after they gave the news of this movement, the same newspapers printed a petition[46] to the Virginia Assembly, asking for a new state beyond the mountains. The settlers pointed with pride to their loyalty to the Revolutionary cause even while they were

[44] Thomson Papers, *N. Y. Hist. Colls.*, 1878, pp. 145-150.

[45] Madison's "Observations relating to the Influence of Vermont and the Territorial Claims on the Politics of Congress," May 1, 1782 (Gilpin, I, 122), gives a good idea of the situation from a Virginia point of view, and shows the part played by the land companies and by the revolutionary state of Vermont, where the similar problem of recognizing a state, formed within the limits of other states and against their will, was involved. The *Philadelphia Independent Gazette,* of July 13 and 20, has two numbers of a series entitled: "A Philosophical Discussion on the Rights of Vermont, Kentucky, etc., to aspire to their Separate Stations of Independency among Sovereign States on Revolutionary Principles, by a Revolutionist." These numbers (all I have access to) were chiefly vituperative, and the underlying thought is expressed in the title. The Vermont example was made use of in connection with Western projects. Ramsey, *Tennessee*, p. 312.

[46] Draper Colls., Newspaper Extracts III, *Maryland Journal*, December 9 and December 20, 1783.

suffering hardships in their internal government; and they declared at some length their respect for the federal government. Said the memorialists: "We are, indeed, erected into separate States upon the declaration of our independency: but the very existence of those states separately considered, was necessarily depending upon the success of our federal Union." "Every wise man looks through the Constitution of his own State to that of the confederation, as he walks through the particular apartments of his own house to view the situation of the whole building." An increase of states in the federal Union would, in their opinion, conduce to the strength and dignity of that Union, for, said these frontier members of the Old Dominion, "it is as possible that one state should aim at undue influence over others as that an individual should aspire after the aggrandizement of himself," and this danger an increase of states would lessen. Replying to objections drawn from their social conditions, they say: "Some of our fellow-citizens may think we are not yet able to conduct our affairs and consult our interests; but if our society is rude, much wisdom is not necessary to supply our wants, and a fool can sometimes put on his clothes better than a wise man can do it for him. We are not against hearing council; but we attend more to our feelings than to the argumentation of others." They add that the whole authority of the state rests ultimately upon the opinions and judgments of men who are generally as void of experience as themselves. Nor in their opinion is there occasion to fear the results of a separation of the two parts of the state of Virginia: "Our nearest seaports will be among you, your readiest resources for effectual

succour in case of any invasion will be to us: the fruits
of our industry and temperance will be enjoyed by you,
and the simplicity of our manners will furnish you with
profitable lessons. In recompense for these services you
will furnish our rustic inhabitants with examples of
civility and politeness and supply us with conveniences
which are without the reach of our labour." They ask,
therefore, that Virginia should cede all the territory
west of the Allegheny Mountains and allow the settlers
to form a new government under the auspices of the
American Congress. Early the next year Jefferson[47]
wrote to Madison that it was for the interest of Virginia to cede the Kentucky region immediately, because
the people beyond the meridian of the mouth of the
Great Kanawha would "separate themselves, because
they will be joined by all our settlements beyond the
Alleghany if they are the first movers. Whereas if we
draw the line, those at Kentucky having their end will
not interest themselves for the people of Indiana, Green-
briar &c. who will of course be left to our management,
and I can with certainty almost say that Congress would
approve of the meridian of the mouth of the Kanhaway
and consider it as the ultimate point to be desired from
Virginia. . . . Should we not be the first movers, and the
Indianians & Kentuckians take themselves off and
claim to the Alleghany I am afraid Congress would
secretly wish them well." By the Indianians, of course
Jefferson means the inhabitants of the region of the old
Indiana Company, and it seems likely that the petition
just considered came from these settlers. The reasons
which Jefferson gives for retaining to the meridian of
the mouth of the Great Kanawha included the follow-

[47] Jefferson, *Writings*, III, 401.

ing: These lands (before long to be thickly settled) would form a barrier for Virginia; and the hundred and eighty miles of barren, mountainous lands beyond would make a fine separation between her and the next state. The lead mines were there; and the improvement of the river would afford "the shortest water communication by 500 miles of any which can ever be got between the western waters & Atlantic, & of course promises us almost a monopoly of the western & Indian trade." Evidently the attacks of the land companies, the discontent of the settlers, and the attitude of Congress were having their effects. Virginia was beginning to perceive that she must cede something unconditionally, lest she lose all her Western settlements. Her leaders were coming to see, moreover, the importance of uniting the West and the East by internal improvements—a movement that led the way to the Constitutional Convention. Not long after Jefferson's letter Washington[48] wrote to Governor Harrison, regarding the desirability of connecting the West to Virginia by ties of interest. If Virginia improved the Potomac-and-Ohio route, to draw Western trade to herself, Pennsylvania was in no position to make objections, though part of the road would pass through her territory; for, said Washington, "there are in the State of Pennsylvania at least a hundred thousand souls west of Laurel Hill who are groaning under the inconveniences of a long land transportation," and Pennsylvania "must submit to the loss of so much of its trade, or hazard not only the loss of the trade but the loss of the settlements also . . . toward which there is not wanting a disposition at this moment in that part of it beyond

[48] Washington, *Writings*, X, 407.

the mountains." In the same year Washington was urging that Congress should legislate for the government of the territory northwest of the Ohio. "The spirit of immigration is great," he wrote to Richard Henry Lee, "the people have got impatient; and though you cannot stop the road, it is yet in your power to mark the way; a little while and you will not be able to do either." The truth of this opinion is shown by the attempts of squatters on the western side of the Ohio to form a constitution for a new state in 1785, on the doctrine that it was a right of mankind to pass into vacant territory and there form their constitution.[49] But the federal troops drove off the intruders, in spite of this doctrine of squatter sovereignty, "agreeable to every constitution formed in America."

Propositions for "marking the way" were already under consideration in Congress. The policy had finally prevailed of asking cessions instead of asserting authority, and in October of 1783 Virginia had authorized a cession of her lands across the Ohio. The Vandalia Company made another struggle to secure its claim, and exhibited its New Jersey strength by inducing that state to appoint Colonel George Morgan its agent, in order to bring the Vandalia claim before Congress as a claim of the state of New Jersey, and thus induce Congress to take jurisdiction between the two states of Virginia and New Jersey, under the Articles of Confederation. But that body refused to take the matter up; accepted Virginia's cession; and passed the Ordinance of 1784.[50] It is not within the scope of this paper to discuss the evolution of the territorial government

[49] *St. Clair Papers,* II, 3-5; McMaster, III, 106, 107.
[50] April 23. Donaldson, *Public Domain,* pp. 147-149; Barrett, *Evolution of Ordinance of 1787,* pp. 17-27.

for the ceded lands by Congress. The petition and proposed constitution[51] outlined by the army officers at Newburgh, in 1783; the steps leading to Jefferson's ordinance; Monroe's, and later, reports;[52] and the outcome of all this congressional action in the Ordinance of 1787—we must pass by. But some of the features of the Ordinance of 1784 had a direct effect upon the backwoodsmen, whose attitude is under consideration, and so must be noted. This statute provided that the territory ceded or to be ceded by individual states should, whenever it should have been purchased of the Indians and offered for sale by the United States, be formed into additional states, bounded in the following manner as nearly as the cessions should admit: northwardly and southwardly by parallels of latitude, so that each state should comprise from north to south two degrees of latitude, beginning to count from the completion of 45° N. lat. Eastwardly and westwardly, the boundaries were to be the Mississippi, on the one side, and the meridian of the lowest point of the Falls of the Ohio, on the other; and for the next tier of states, the same meridian was to form the boundary on the west, while to the east the boundary would be the meridian of the mouth of the Great Kanawha. The territory eastward of this last meridian, between the Ohio, Lake Erie, and Pennsylvania, was to be one state in addition. Whatever territory lay beyond the completion of 45°, between the meridians mentioned, was to be a part of the state adjoining it on the south; and where the Ohio cut the parallel 39°, its course to the north of that line was to be substituted for that portion of the parallel.

[51] Pickering, *Life of Pickering*, I, 546-549, Appendix iii.
[52] Stone, *Ordinance of 1787;* Barrett, 33 *et seq.*

Two things deserve particular notice in this arrangement: the rigid application of the rectangular system, with small regard for physiographic propriety;[53] and the number of small states provided for. Jefferson's belief in the West is clearly indicated by this readiness to concede so large a share of power in Congress to the region. The agricultural West might be regarded as a natural political ally of Virginia. It is less easy to see why New England accepted the proposition. Earlier in the year, a Rhode Island congressman wrote: "It is proposed to divide the country into fourteen new states in the following manner. There are to be three tiers of states: one on the Atlantic, one on the Mississippi, and a middle tier. The middle tier is to be the smallest and is to form a balance betwixt the two more powerful ones." [54]

Having thus outlined the course of new-state activity in one of the regions of the Western Waters, and having traced the connection between it and the Congressional legislation, we may next survey the attempts of similar nature in the Tennessee and the Kentucky regions. Here we shall have to be very brief, partly because of the limits of the paper, partly because the essential grievances and methods have been stated in connection with the first region. Moreover, the writers who have related the history of Kentucky and Tennessee have made the attempts in these settlements more familiar. One center of disturbance on the Tennessee waters, however, has been neglected. It will be remembered that Washington County, Virginia, the region on the Holston about Abington, was economically and

[53] See later, p. 125.
[54] Staples, *Rhode Island in the Continental Congress*, p. 479; Barrett, p. 19.

socially a part of the North Carolina region, on the same waters, although separated by the Virginia line; and that the mountains cut this tract off from both the parent states. Moreover, the Virginia counties of Montgomery and Greenbrier, on the tributaries of the Great Kanawha, lay in close connection with Washington County. When the rumor came to these settlements that Congress had resolved against Virginia's claim to their region, they were thrown into commotion, and Arthur Campbell, the fiery Scotch-Irishman who was county lieutenant and justice of Washington County in Virginia, and Colonel William Christian, another noted Indian fighter, brother-in-law of Patrick Henry, agreed upon a plan for holding a convention of delegates from the two counties of North Carolina on the Tennessee waters, and from these three Virginia counties. The delegates were to be chosen by the freemen either in their respective companies of militia, or at the court-houses,[55] on court day, and to meet at Abington. "In the general Confusion and Disturbance we ought to take care of ourselves," wrote Christian.[56] The outcome of the proposition is unknown; but it indicates the delicacy of the Western situation, and the readiness of the frontiersmen to rely on their own assemblies. There is evidence that Arthur Campbell continued in correspondence with congressional leaders. In the summer of 1783, Jefferson reported that Patrick Henry was ready to restrict Virginia to reasonable boundaries, but that instead of ceding the parts lopped off, he was for

[55] Christian preferred the use of militia companies, because "so few meet in common at the annual elections." This is a significant fact. See J. F. Jameson, "Virginia Voting in the Colonial Period," *Nation*, April 27, 1893.
[56] Draper Colls., King's Mountain MSS., IX; *Cal. Va. State Papers*, III, 414, 572; Gilpin, I, 116; Jefferson to Madison, March 24, 1782, *Writings*, III, 53.

laying them off into small republics.[57] Henry had his particularistic tendencies tried in the next few years, when as governor he had to support the unity of the Old Dominion against attempts to withdraw her Western area.

In June, 1784, North Carolina, following the example of Virginia in the cession of her claims beyond the Ohio, ceded to the United States the region now embraced in Tennessee, providing at the same time that the sovereignty should remain in North Carolina until the cession was accepted by Congress. The Ordinance of 1784 had passed on the 23d of the previous April. According to the boundaries provided therein, the settlements of eastern Tennessee would have fallen within one state, and those on the Cumberland in the one just to the west of that. The settlers on the Tennessee complained that after the cession North Carolina lost all interest in them, and stopped the goods she had promised to the Indians in payment for lands. Thereupon the frontiers were attacked by the savages. In this critical situation, abandoned by North Carolina, without proper provision for courts, or for calling the militia to the field, unprovided for by Congress, it is not surprising that the citizens hastened their independent statehood.[58] Committees composed of two representatives from each militia company in the counties of North Carolina on the Tennessee met and recommended the election of deputies to meet in convention at Jonesboro'. The Cumberland men were not represented, for the mountains intervened between them and the Tennessee settlements, and their connections were

[57] Jefferson, *Writings*, III, 334.
[58] Ramsey, *Annals of Tennessee*, gives the documentary material on this state of Franklin.

[121]

more with Kentucky than with this region. The Jonesboro' convention met on the 23d of August and came to the conclusion that it was for their interest to form a separate state. They believed that the increased immigration which would result from their independence would produce an improvement in agriculture, manufactures, and literature. "The seat of government being among ourselves," said they, "would evidently tend, not only to keep a circulating medium in gold and silver among us, but draw it from many individuals living in other states, who claim large quantities of lands that would lie in the bounds of the new state." By implication this would leave the vacant lands within the state to the state itself, rather than to the United States, and it was one of the points with which Governor Martin, of North Carolina, reproached them in the manifesto which he issued against their attempt. At the same time, Martin held out hopes that if they returned to the jurisdiction of the parent state, a future amicable separation might be effected, accompanied by a division of the vacant lands between the two states.[59] Another reason advanced for independence was the fact that the more populous Eastern settlements would render the Western men subservient to them and would legislate against their interests. Finally, they urged that Congress by their resolutions had invited them to assume statehood, and that North Carolina's cession had opened the door. It was their hope that the whole valley of the upper Tennessee might be embraced in the new state; for they resolved to admit any contiguous part of Virginia that might make application to join their association, "after

[59] Governor Sevier of the new state denied that the question of disposing of the public lands had been settled; but the state afterwards opened land offices. Ramsey, *Tennessee*, p. 364. Cf. Henry, *Patrick Henry*, III, 293.

they are legally permitted, either by the state of Virginia, *or other power having cognizance thereof.*" [60]
The italicized words indicate how widespread was the belief in congressional jurisdiction over the West.[61] Although North Carolina repealed her cession and provided judicial and military organization for the region, under the name of Washington District, the movement had progressed too far to be thus arrested. Sevier was chosen governor, and later conventions took the constitution of North Carolina as the model of their government, and adopted the name of Franklin for the state. The Assembly of Franklin petitioned Congress to ignore the repeal of North Carolina's cession and to accept the infant commonwealth. In the summer of 1785 a Washington County, Virginia, man wrote that the "new society or State called Franklin has already put off its infant habit and seems to step forward with a florid, healthy constitution; it wants only the paternal guardianship of Congress for a short period, to entitle it to be admitted with *éclat,* as a member of the Federal Government. Here the genuine Republican! here the real Whig will find a safe asylum a comfortable retreat among these modern *Franks,* the hardy mountain men." But the mountain men were not yet to receive the paternal guardianship of Congress. North Carolina made liberal concessions in postponing taxes and promising forgiveness. The settlers divided into the partisans of North Carolina and of Franklin; rival governments

[60] The italics are mine.
[61] The italicized clause leads Roosevelt (*Winning of the West,* III, 157, 158) to say that "the mountaineers ignored the doctrine of State Sovereignty." These frontiersmen believed in the congressional jurisdiction over the former crown lands; but the italicized words do not warrant the assertion that they ignored the doctrine of state sovereignty. There was much reason for doubting the right of individual states to trans-Allegheny territory.

held courts, summoned militia, passed laws, and collected taxes over the same area. In the midst of this domestic turmoil, Governor Sevier was forced again and again to lead his riflemen against the Indians whom the land hunger of the Franklin men had aroused.

In the meantime, the leaders of Washington County, Virginia, were agitating for union with Franklin. Arthur Campbell lent all of his influence as magistrate and militia officer against continuing with Virginia, and even denounced her taxation on the days when he held court. Rev. Charles Cummings, the backwoods preacher, appealed to his people to stand by their natural rights, and he presided at meetings for separation.[62] Early[63] in January of 1785 a petition from the leaders was read in Congress praying that they might form part of an independent state, bounded by the Alleghenies on the east; the meridian of the Falls of the Ohio on the west; a line from the junction of the Greenbrier and the Great Kanawha to and along the 37th parallel, on the north; and the 34th parallel on the south. In a word, they desired to erect the upper courses of the Tennessee and the territory about Cumberland Gap into a separate state, a greater Franklin. "We are the first occupants and Aborigines of this Country," said these Indian fighters, "freemen claiming natural rights and privileges of American Citizens." They desired that the disposition of the vacant lands be in the hands of the legislature, with the reservation that the proceeds should be paid to the order of Congress. One may be permitted to doubt whether the terms on which they would sell the lands to themselves would leave much

[62] *Cal. Va. State Papers,* IV, 34 *et passim.*
[63] January 13. See the petition in *Cal. Va. State Papers,* IV, 4. This differs in some verbal respects from the copy in the Department of State.

for the congressional coffers. Again, in the spring of
1785, another petition went to Congress from the
deputies of the same county. They proposed modifications in the rigid rectangles that Jefferson had laid down
for the Western states in the Ordinance of 1784. The
eastern meridian line, they complained, passed across a
great number of the most inaccessible and craggy mountains in America, and severed communities naturally
one. The western meridian divided the Kentucky settlers. They proposed two states with natural boundary
lines; the Kentucky settlements bounded by the Great
Kanawha were to make one, and the upper waters of
the Tennessee, including the Muscle Shoals of that
river, another. The Cumberland settlers would have
been left as the nucleus for another of the states provided for by the Ordinance of 1784. As thus modified,
the settlers declared the Ordinance the basis for a liberal
and beneficial compact. With this petition they forwarded an association which they had drawn up, resolv-
ing, among other things, that the lands "cultivated by
individuals belong strictly to them, and not to the government, otherwise every citizen would be a tenant and
not a landlord, a vassal and not a freeman; and every
government would be a usurpation, not an instrumental
device for public good." "For cogent is the reason-
ings," they exclaimed, "when we can with great truth
say: our own blood was spilt in acquiring land for our
settlement, our fortunes expended in making these settlements effectual; for ourselves we fought, for ourselves we conquered, and for ourselves alone have we
a right to hold." [64] But Patrick Henry, then governor

---

[64] They are here using the language of Jefferson's "Proposed Instructions
to the Virginia Delegates," 1774. Ford's Jefferson's *Writings*, I, 437.

of Virginia, was ready to resist the loss of this "barrier and nursery of soldiers," and he regarded the Franklin project as "a matter that may ruin the Western Country which must principally support the glory of America in future Times." [65] The irate Arthur Campbell reproached this orator of the Revolution with incurring the infamy of a Bernard or a Hutchinson; but his attempts were all in vain. [66] The state of Franklin dared not receive the Virginians against the will of so powerful a state, and Virginia, following the example of Pennsylvania, passed an act in the fall of 1785, making the erection of an independent government within her limits, except by an act of her Assembly, high treason, and empowering the governor to call out the militia to repress any combination for such purpose. [67] The state of Franklin, which had steadily lost authority among the settlers, practically expired in 1788. In the fall of the next year, Sevier took his seat in the North Carolina Senate, and the year after that he went to Congress from the Western district of North Carolina. By the lapse of Franklin, one of her settlements, Sevier County, was left stranded on Indian territory not acquired by North Carolina. They organized themselves by the familiar expedient of a social compact, [68] and continued their association until erected into a county of the Territory of the United States South of the River Ohio, in 1794.

When North Carolina ceded the Tennessee country to Congress in 1790, Patrick Henry, who was inter-

[65] Henry, *Patrick Henry*, III, 374.
[66] The evidence respecting Campbell's plans is in *Cal. Va. State Papers*, IV, *passim*. The petitions and association are in Archives of the Continental Congress, No. 48, pp. 281, 287, 297. Cf. Ramsey, *Tennessee*, p. 320.
[67] Hening's *Statutes*, XII, 41.
[68] Ramsey, *Tennessee*, p. 437, prints these interesting Articles of Association.

ested in the Yazoo land company at the time, declared
to a Western correspondent: "I still think great things
may be done in the Tennessee Country and below. For
surely the People of Franklin will never submit to be
given away with the Lands like slaves without holding
a Convention of their own as the Kentucky people have
done under our Laws. But if we had not assented to it,
they would have had a Right to hold one to consult
together for their own Good." He calls the act of
cession "a most abominable Instance of Tyranny," and
says that they ought to do as Vermont has done. "For
being cut off from Government without holding any
convention of the people there to consent to it all the
Rights of Sovereignty over the District and Lands
therein belong to the people there." This doctrine, he
believed, "neither Congress nor any other persons who
understand the principles of the Revolution can contro-
vert or deny." [69]

While the Indian fighters on the upper waters of the
Ohio, and on the tributaries of the Tennessee, had been
striving for independent statehood, the Kentucky riflemen, in their turn, had been seeking the same object.
The lands for which they had risked their lives in conflict with the savages, were being seized by speculative
purchasers from Virginia, who took advantage of the
imperfect titles of the pioneers. One of the most
important features of the economic history of the West
in the eighteenth century, is the way in which preparations for a later aristocracy were being made, by the
amassing of vast estates of wilderness through grant or
purchase. For the time being, these estates did not
materially affect social conditions, for they were but

[69] Draper Colls., King's Mountain MSS., XI.

wilderness; but they served as nuclei for the movement of assimilation of the frontier to the Southern type when the slave population began its westward march. The pioneer had an intuitive sense of this danger. "We have distressing news from Kentucke," wrote a Westerner,[70] in the summer of 1780, "which is entirely owing to a set of Nabobs in Virginia taking all the lands there by Office Warrants and Pre-emption Rights. Hundreds of Families are ruined by it. In short, it threatens a loss of that Country. Should the English go there and offer them Protection from the Indians, the greatest Part will join. . . . Let the *great Men,* say they, whom the Land belongs to, come and defend it, for we will not lift a Gun in Defense of it." It is easy to understand, therefore, why, in the spring of the same year, a petition[71] came to the Continental Congress, praying that body to organize the counties of Kentucky and Illinois into a separate state. Among their grievances was the granting of the waste lands in great tracts, "without Reservation for Cultivating and Settling the same, whereby Setling the Contry is Discouraged and the inhabitants are greatly exposed to the Saviges by whom our wives and Childring are daly Cruily murdered." They objected to being taxed while enrolled and serving in garrisons. Between them and the appellate courts of justice, from six hundred to a thousand miles intervened, and the law miscarried. Although they had taken the oath of allegiance to the United States, Virginia had demanded that they swear allegiance to her, and they knew not to whom they belonged.

[70] Draper Colls., Clark MSS., XLVI, 59.
[71] Printed in Roosevelt, *Winning of the West,* II, 398.

In the next year[72] other attempts at separation were made; and in 1782, as has already been noted, a petition of the Kentucky men aroused a heated debate in Congress.[73] The congressional report of 1781, adverse to Virginia's claims,[74] was circulated in Kentucky by the friends of congressional control; and one of the agitators was tried and fined as "a divulger of false news." Loyalty to Virginia was diminished by the fact that the inhabitants represented many states, and that correspondence was active between them and persons at the seat of Congress.[75] One of the interesting side lights on the period is the fact that at this time James Monroe[76] contemplated removal to Kentucky, and that he solicited confidential communication with George Rogers Clark, the famous Kentucky leader. Monroe favored a new state, on the ground that it would increase the weight of Virginia politics in the Union.

At last, on December 27, 1784, these sporadic attempts at independence culminated in a convention called by a meeting of leading citizens in the previous November. This convention was composed of a delegate from every captain's company. It declared the grievances,[77] already familiar in other Western petitions, of unequal taxes; inefficient administration of

72 *Cal. Va. State Papers,* III, 385; Putnam, *Middle Tennessee,* p. 631; Draper Colls., Shane MSS., XI, 39-44; Draper Colls., Trip, 1860, II, 35; Draper Colls., Clark MSS., XXX, 19.
73 Thomson Papers, *N. Y. Hist. Colls.,* 1878, p. 145. Compare the undated petition in Archives of Continental Congress, Vol. XLI, 102.
74 See page 112, *ante.*
75 Walker Daniel (attorney for Virginia) to Fleming, April 14, 1783; Draper Colls., Clark MSS., XLVI, 78, 79; LII, 91; *Va. Cal. State Papers,* III, 555, 584-588.
76 Monroe to Clark, October 19, 1783, Draper Colls., Clark MSS., LII, 92.
77 Draper Colls., Newspaper Extracts, 1785, p. 1, *Pennsylvania Packet,* May 9, 1785; cf. *Kentucke Gazette,* October 18, 1788.

justice; lack of provisions for calling out the militia; the drainage of specie to the Eastern part of Virginia; and the general neglect due to their remoteness from the seat of government. Among the sources of discontent was the lack of a law for improving the breed of horses—a matter on which the Transylvania legislators had been prompt to act! The convention made provision for a new convention to meet the following May and to take definite action. The subsequent history of Kentucky's struggle for statehood is a subject for treatment by itself, and too extensive for the limits of this paper. It was complicated by the question of the closing of the Mississippi, and by the fear that Congress would consent thus to see the highway of Western trade barricaded. With it were involved the intrigues of Wilkinson and his friends with Spain, the efforts of England to sound the separatist tendencies of the West, and the dilatory caution of Virginia, as well as the fact that in this period the change was effected from the government under the Articles of Confederation to that under the federal Constitution. That in the many blunders and misunderstandings which grew out of this situation, Kentucky adhered to legal methods, indicates much self-restraint on the part of the settlers. But had matters not taken a favorable turn at the time most critical, Kentucky was in a fair way to have crowned this movement for independence by placing itself in the position of a state out of the Union.[78] While Wilkinson was playing his game for a Spanish alliance, or at least for Spanish bribes, even such honest Westerners as

[78] The best general account of these movements is in Roosevelt, III; but the documentary material in Gayarré's *Louisiana*, Green's *Spanish Conspiracy*, and *Report on Canadian Archives*, 1890, as well as in the Draper Collections, is important.

Sevier and Robertson entered into correspondence with
Spanish agents in the critical period of 1788; and
George Rogers Clark offered to expatriate himself and
accept the flag of Spain in return for a liberal land grant
for a trans-Mississippi colony. Colonel George Morgan, hopeless of securing from Congress his desire for
Indiana Company lands, sought the Spanish power, and
was promised an immense domain opposite the mouth
of the Ohio, for a colony to be called New Madrid. In
this period also was formed the Yazoo company, whose
agent, Dr. O'Fallon (Clark's brother-in-law), proposed
to the Spaniards that his colony should become subjects
of Spain, if unmolested by that power.[79] The appre-
hensions of Patrick Henry and Grayson regarding the
relinquishment of the Mississippi by Congress under the
proposed federal Constitution, all but turned Virginia
against that instrument in the ratification convention.[80]
The Kentucky radicals desired to establish a state
regardless of Virginia's consent, and without securing
the permission of the federal government, and thus to
be in a position to ratify or reject the new federal Constitution; to make terms with Spain; or to stand alone
and await events. "Our Political era is at hand!"
exultantly wrote Judge Wallace,[81] of the Kentucky convention, to Arthur Campbell in 1788.

All along the border the party favorable to new
states had been balked. The hopes awakened by the
Ordinance of 1784, of congressional organization of
the whole West, had so far borne no fruit in the settled
regions, although the unoccupied Northwest had been

[79] Compare Isaac Sherman's proposed Connecticut colony beyond the
Mississippi; *Can. Archives*, 1890. See Haskins' "Yazoo Land Companies,"
American Historical Association Papers, V, 395.
[80] Elliot's *Debates*, III; Stone, *Ordinance of 1787*.
[81] Draper Colls., King's Mountain MSS., IX.

splendidly provided for in 1787. Checked or rebuffed
by the parent states, neglected by Congress, their very
industrial life threatened by the closure of the Mississippi, it was not surprising that they gave to the separatist movement a more aggressive form. The
Kentuckians had reason to think that the whole frontier
sympathized with them. The Western counties of
Pennsylvania were excited;[82] the French on the Illinois
had grown impatient of the lack of government and the
insecurity of their land titles; the surviving Franklin
partisans were ready to join in a Western uprising; the
people of Cumberland sent their agents to ask to be
incorporated in the state of Kentucky;[83] and Arthur
Campbell was in correspondence with leading advocates of Kentucky separation, and was proposing a
general coalescence of the Western country.[84] Added
to all of these evidences of unrest was the attitude of
England and Spain, both of whom were sounding the
West regarding its readiness to cast off the connection
with the Union.[85] Such facts show how impossible it
would have been to have governed the West by any
system of provincial administration.

If these forces of disunion had prevailed, the indications point rather to a Mississippi Valley federation,
a union of the Western Waters, than to a lapse into
independent communities indifferent to each other's
fate. The readiness of the settlers to appeal to each

[82] Draper Colls., Clark MSS., XI, 153, citing *Maryland Journal*, July 3,
1787.
[83] McDowell to A. Campbell, September 23, 1787, Draper Colls., King's
Mountain MSS., IX; Speed, *Danville Political Club*, p. 136; Putnam, p. 280.
[84] C. Wallace to A. Campbell, Sept. 19, 1788, Draper Colls., King's Mountain MSS., IX.
[85] Interesting material on the situation in the West in 1789 is in *Report
on Canadian Archives*, 1890. See Gayarré, *Louisiana, Spanish Domination*, pp.
206, 228; Green, *Spanish Conspiracy;* Roosevelt, *Winning of the West*, III.

other for aid, the negotiations for mutual political connection at various times in this period, the physiographic unity of the Mississippi Valley, and the dangerous neighborhood of England and Spain, all lead to the same conclusion.[86]

The results of this study may be summarized in conclusion. We have found that the writers on the organization of the West have made the Ordinance of 1787, and the vacant country beyond the Ohio, the object of their inquiry and that they have thus been led to slight the occupied area involved—that is, the lands between the Alleghenies and the Ohio. It follows that the part played by the frontiersmen themselves has been neglected. The documents surviving in their rude chirography and frontier spelling, the archives of Congress, and the newspapers of the time, have enabled us to show that, so far from being passive spectators of the congressional plans for their political future, the frontiersmen were agitated by every new proposal of that body. They tried to shape their own civil destiny.

We have noted, too, the importance of the physiographic explanation of the movement. The new-state activity extended all along the frontier; but in three areas, natural economic unities, separate states were proposed. The eastern tributaries of the upper Ohio made the area of Vandalia, Westsylvania, part of Paine's projected state, and the many unnamed states projected in the period from 1780 to 1784. The persistence of the physiographic influence in this unit is seen in the Whiskey Rebellion in Western Pennsylvania, and in the continuous struggle of West Virginia against

[86] Roosevelt, *Winning of the West*, III, 127, 128, 94, 95, holds the contrary view.

control by the Eastern section of that state, until at last her object was gained in the Civil War, and an independent state on the lines of Vandalia, though not of Westsylvania, was formed. The second economic unit, around the upper course of the Tennessee, was the area of the Watauga Association, the state of Franklin, and the proposed greater Franklin of Arthur Campbell. Virginia retained her portion of this tract, and assimilated the descendants of these leaders to the great-planter type; but the Tennessee region was organized as the Territory of the United States South of the River Ohio, in 1790, and six years later it became a state. The union of the Cumberland pasture-lands with the mountain tracts of East Tennessee was physiographically unnatural. In the debates at Nashville, preceding the Civil War, the proposition for organizing a Union state of Franklin out of the mountain lands received much attention,[87] and it was this area that furnished most of the Tennessee soldiers for the Union army in that war, and which today holds to the Republican party, while the rest of the state has usually given its votes to the Democratic party. In the Kentucky unit, too, after a decade of struggle, independent statehood was acquired. All of these movements were natural expressions of physiographic influences. They were all led by sons of Virginia, and the same era that saw the decline of her tobacco-planting aristocracy seemed likely to witness the restriction of Virginia's vast domain to limits narrower than those imposed in the Civil War. But she was able to resist the full effects of these influences.

Another result revealed by this general view is the variety of the new governmental plans, and the fact

[87] Phelan, *Tennessee*, p. 104.

that there appeared in this area of vacant lands, as in
the colonial area long before, plans of proprietary companies, and social compacts, or associations. The Ordi-
nances of Congress, moreover, provided for a type of
government comparable to that of the royal colonies;
the idea of close control by the general government was
common to both; but the type was revolutionized by the
American conditions. The weakness of the proprietary
plans, also, shows the influence of the wilderness training in liberty. The theory of the associations was a
natural outcome of the combined influences of Puritan
political philosophy, in its Scotch-Irish form, the revolutionary spirit, and the forest freedom. All through
these compacts runs the doctrine that the people in an
unoccupied land have the right to determine their own
political institutions. In announcing the doctrine of
"squatter sovereignty," therefore, Cass and Douglas
merely gave utterance to a time-honored Western idea.[88]

This idea was, nevertheless, merely an extension of
the principles and methods of the Revolution to the
West. In interpreting the history of colonial settlement
so as to meet the needs of the revolutionary arguments,
John Adams had held that the original colonists carried
with them only natural rights, and having settled a new
country according to the law of nature, were not bound
to submit to English law unless they chose it. Jefferson
had compared the original colonial migrations to the
migrations of their Saxon ancestors to England; and he
had asserted that the colonists "possessed a right which
nature has given to all men, of . . . going in quest of new

---

[88] A committee of the Wisconsin legislature declared in 1843 that it was
a doctrine well understood in this country, that all "political communities
have the right of governing themselves in their own way within their lawful
boundaries."

10

habitations and of there establishing new societies under
such laws and regulations as to them shall seem most
likely to promote public happiness. . . . Settlements having been thus effected in the wilds of America, the emigrants thought proper to adopt that system of laws
under which they had hitherto lived in the mother country." Such were the theories urged by the revolutionary leaders respecting the political rights of settlers in
vacant regions, at the very time when the frontiersmen
were occupying the lands beyond the mountains. These
doctrines formed convenient bases for the formation of
associations, for the assertion of the ownership of their
lands by the settlers in defiance of the parent state, for
their complaints against the actions of these states, and
for their demands for independence. The revolutionary states found themselves obliged to repudiate some
of their own doctrines in dealing with their Western
communities. In the Franklin convention the Declaration of Independence was read to show that reasons for
separation from England urged in that document
applied equally well to the relation of the Western
counties to the counties of the coast.

It is a noteworthy fact, however, that so many of
these associations accepted the laws and constitution of
an older state. The frontier did not proceed on the
principle of *tabula rasa;* it modified older forms, and
infused into them the spirit of democracy.[89]

Examining the grievances of the Westerners, one is
impressed with the similarity of the reasons for wishing
independent statehood, in all the petitions from all the
regions. They were chiefly the following: disputed
boundaries; uncertain land titles; inefficient organization

[89] Compare the Exeter covenant, where the "liberties of our English Colony
of the Massachusetts" were asserted.

of justice and military defense, due to the remoteness
of the capital; the difficulty of paying taxes in specie;
the dislike of paying taxes at all when the pioneers
were serving in Indian warfare, and were paying
money into the state treasury for their lands; general
incompatibility of interests between the frontiersmen
and the planters, and the aggravation of this fact by
the control which the East retained in the legislatures.[90]
Perhaps no factor in the explanation of the new-state
activity is of more importance than the Westerners'
desire to organize states that should own the vacant
lands within their bounds. This would enable them to
determine the price of the public lands, and this would
enable them to reduce taxes while assuming government. But it was just this that Congress could not be
expected to permit. The policy of Calhoun to win
Western support at a later period by yielding to the
states the public lands within their limits, was based on
a thorough understanding of Western traits.

Through all these petitions and memorials runs the
sentiment that Congress might, or ought to, assume
jurisdiction over the West. The frontiersmen exerted
a constant pressure on Congress to exalt its powers.
The crown had asserted its control over the lands beyond the sources of the rivers flowing into the Atlantic,
by the Proclamation of 1763, when it forbade settlement and the patenting of land therein. On the eve of
the Revolution, it had all but completed a grant to the
Vandalia Company, providing for a colonial government in the limits of Virginia's trans-Allegheny claim.
This company tried to persuade Congress to assert the
possession and jurisdiction of the lands beyond the

[90] Compare Jefferson, *Notes on Virginia*, 127 (1853); *Debates in Virginia
Constitutional Convention*, 1829-1830; Brevard, *Digest of S. C. Laws* (1814),
pp. xiv ff.; *N. C. Colonial Records*, VII, pp. xix ff.

mountains, as the property of the whole Union by devolution from the crown when independence was declared. To the Westerners the theory of congressional control was attractive. It seemed to exact nothing and to promise much. They looked for organization into independent states of the Union; they looked for deliverance from the rule of the coast counties in the legislatures, the rule of a section radically unlike the West; they looked for lighter taxation and for all the advantages of self-government; they hoped to own the lands within their borders. It is not strange that with these ideals they appealed to the central government for organization into states. But, in any case, there were strong national tendencies in the West. These communities were made up of settlers from many states, and this mixture of peoples diminished the loyalty to the claimant states, and increased the tendency to appeal to national authority. It was chiefly, however, because the national power could promote the interests of the West that that section was so ready to turn to it. It was ready to abandon this attitude when its interest was threatened, as the Mississippi question clearly shows. But for the most part it has been for the interest of the national government to legislate in the interest of the West, and so the West has been, not only in the era of the Revolution, but ever since, a great nationalizing force in our history.

In fine, we see in these agitations along the Alleghenies the early political efforts of the rude, boisterous West, checked as yet by the tidewater area, but already giving promise of the day when, in the person of Andrew Jackson, its forces of democracy and nationalism should rule the republic.

CHAPTER V

THE POLICY OF FRANCE TOWARD THE MISSISSIPPI VALLEY IN THE PERIOD OF WASHINGTON AND ADAMS [1]

The interest of France in the Mississippi Valley extended over nearly two centuries. It falls into three main periods: (1) the unsuccessful attempt to outrival England as mistress of this region in the struggles of the colonial era; (2) the alliance with the United States in order to disrupt the British empire in our War for Independence; (3) the efforts to render the United States subservient to France and to rebuild French power in the interior of North America, ending with the cession of Louisiana. There is a striking continuity in the efforts of France to unite the fortunes of the region beyond the Allegheny Mountains with those of the province of Louisiana and to control the Mississippi Valley. This she desired to do, as a bar to the advance of England; as a means of supplying the French West Indies; as a lever by which to compel the United States to serve the interests of France; and as a means of promoting French ascendency over Spanish America. France recognized that the effective boundary of Louisiana must be the Allegheny Mountains, not the Mississippi River.

[1] Reprinted by permission from *The American Historical Review*, January, 1905. This paper makes free use of two earlier articles by the present writer, published in the *Atlantic Monthly* for May and June, 1904, under the title, "The Diplomatic Contest for the Mississippi Valley." The principal purpose of this paper is to furnish the necessary citations for some of the assertions made in these articles and to consider more fully the French side of these diplomatic intrigues.

It is desired here to present some of the evidences of this policy, to exhibit the various forms which it took at different periods, and to explain the causes that affected the desire of France to control this important region. As will appear, the problem was a part of the larger problem of successorship to the power of Spain in the New World, but the specific forms that French policy assumed were more immediately dependent upon the Louisiana question.

The suggestion made by France in the peace proposals of 1761, that a barrier country, or Indian reservation, should be formed between Louisiana and the Allegheny Mountains, exhibits an early form of her desire to prevent the encroachments of English-speaking people into the valley,[2] and the use to be made of the Indians as a means of holding this region open to the purposes of France and Spain, closely allied in the family compact of that year. The refusal of England and the final defeat of the allies led to the readjustment of 1763, by which France yielded her American possessions east of the Mississippi to England. She ceded New Orleans with the province of Louisiana to Spain.[3] The cession of Florida to England by Spain left the Gulf of Mexico divided between these last-named powers. Doubtless France yielded the province without keen reluctance, for it had been an unprofitable possession; but the intimate connection between Spain and France seemed to make the transfer something less than an absolute relinquishment.

[2] Winsor, *The Mississippi Basin*, p. 416.
[3] See the important paper, based on Spanish documents, by Dr. William R. Shepherd, in *Political Science Quarterly*, September, 1904 (XIX, 439-458), "The Cession of Louisiana to Spain."

The English policy with regard to the interior must certainly have been acceptable to her recent enemies, for, by the proclamation of 1763, the King reserved the lands beyond the Alleghenies to the Indians, and declared that until the crown was ready to extinguish the Indian title, lands should not be patented within that area, nor settlers enter it. Although the Indian line was changed by purchases, and the colony of Vandalia was all but organized at the opening of the Revolution,[4] yet, when France had to determine her attitude toward the United States at the outbreak of that war, the trans-Allegheny region was still, in the eyes of the English law, almost entirely Indian country.

It is impossible here to review the connection of France with the colonies during the Revolution; but some of the essential features of the policy of Vergennes must be stated in order to understand later events, and to perceive the continuity of French policy.

There was published in Paris, in 1802, a *Mémoire historique et politique sur la Louisiane, par M. de Vergennes*.[5] This document was found, according to the statement of its editor, among the minister's papers after his death, with his coat of arms at the head of the memoir. It is not known whether this memoir is to be found in the French archives, and, without further proof of its authenticity, doubts may be raised concerning it. Nevertheless, apparently both French and American

[4] G. H. Alden, *New Governments West of the Alleghanies*, Bulletin of the University of Wisconsin, Economics, Political Science and History Series, II, 19 ff., 38 ff.; V. Coffin, *The Province of Quebec and the Early American Revolution*, ibid., I, 398-431.

[5] There are copies in the library of Harvard University, in the Library of Congress, and in the Wisconsin State Historical Library. John Quincy Adams notes in his diary (IV, 126) in 1818 that de Neuville, the French minister to the United States, "returned the Memoir of Count de Vergennes upon Louisiana, which he had some time since borrowed of me."

[141]

bibliographers have accepted its genuineness.[6] The memoir was written prior to the alliance of 1778, and it includes, not only a survey of the resources and history of Louisiana, but also an examination of the proper policy for France toward the United States, in the event of the independence of the latter power. Apprehending that the new republic would prove harmful to the interests of France and Spain in America, Vergennes (assuming that he was, indeed, its author) advised the King to insist, in the treaty which France expected to dictate to England at the conclusion of hostilities, that the territory beyond the Alleghenies and east of the Mississippi should revert to herself. He contended that this territory was properly a part of Louisiana, and not rightfully to be claimed by the American colonies under their charters. To carry out this idea, he proposed the plan of a treaty to be imposed upon England at the termination of the war. This provided for the cession to France by England of the trans-Allegheny territory and for such a partition of Canada as would insure Louisiana from attack by way of the Great Lakes. The

[6] In his *Voyage à la Louisiane* (Paris, 1802), pp. 4-5, Baudry des Lozières, influenced, possibly, by the apprehension of a competing account of Louisiana, expresses doubts of the authenticity of this memoir, in the following passage:

"Mais instruit que la Louisiane allait nous être rendue, je me ressouvins de mes notes, et je travaillais à en tirer quelque parti pour la chose publique, quand parut un ouvrage intitulé: *Mémoires de M. de Vergennes, ministre des affaires étrangères.* Je le lus d'abord rapidement; je le parcourus de nouveau, et je m'en voulais à moi-même de ne pas le trouver digne de son auteur. Enfin, après l'avoir bien examiné, je me décidai à croire que le nom de l'auteur était supposé. Si M. de Vergennes a quelque part à ces mémoires, ce n'est que pour très-peu, et le reste est d'une obscurité telle qu'il est impossible d'avoir, d'après cette lecture, une idée nette de la Louisiane.

"Cependant je dois dire que celui qui a été sur les lieux, supplée aisément à ce qui manque à ces mémoires, et que ce qu'on y voit n'est obscur que faute d'avoir été rédigé par une personne qui connaisse l'objet qu'on traite. Néanmoins cet ouvrage n'est pas sans mérite pour l'homme d'état; et quel que soit celui qui se cache sous le nom imposant de M. de Vergennes, il ne rend pas moins des services par plusieurs de ses vues qui sont très-sages. Persuadé que ces mémoires ne pouvaient faire de tort à mon projet, je continuai mon travail, et ce que je vais dire n'est que le développement des notes que j'avais déjà prises dans mes voyages."

proposed boundaries were outlined in the document.[7]
The territory thus to be acquired was to be joined with
Louisiana, which, he proposed, should be retroceded to
France. Thus a revived French colonial empire would
be created on both banks of the Mississippi, reaching to
the Great Lakes and dominating the Gulf of Mexico.
He warned the King that when the people of the United
States once obtained their independence, they would not
rest content with having defended their own hearth-
fires, but would desire to expand over Louisiana, Florida, and Mexico, in order to master all the approaches
to the sea. On the other hand, if France possessed the
Mississippi Valley, the Great Lakes, and the entrance
to the St. Lawrence, and if she allied herself with the
Indians of the interior, she could restrain the ambitions
of the Americans. Such were the proposals of this interesting memoir.

It is obvious that, if the work was that of Vergennes,
M. Doniol has omitted an essential document for under-

---

[7] The substance of this project is as follows (*Mémoire*, pp. 108-114):

ARTICLE I. England shall restore to France all the conquests which she
made in North America during the last war. ARTICLE II. France shall
reserve Louisburg and other specified areas about the mouth of the St. Lawrence and to the north. ARTICLE III. The English are forbidden to fortify
within ten leagues near the eastern coast of Nova Scotia, etc. "ART. IV.
Que la France rentrera aussi en possession de toute la partie occidentale du
Canada, à la réserve du pays concédé à l'ouest des montagnes Apalaches;
c'est-à-dire, le pays des Iroquois, les terres et rivières au sud de l'Ohio et
de son cours, depuis ses sources jusqu'à la Rivière-Neuve inclusivement; dans
lequel pays les Anglais ne pourront non plus conserver, ni avoir d'autres
fortifications, que le fort d'Osvego, sur la rivière Chouagen, ni sur l'Ohio,
que celui qu'ils ont bâti à la place du fort du Quesne. ART. V. La France
conservera pour bornes au nord du pays des Iroquois et de la Nouvelle-Yorck,
la rivière à la Plance et le lac du Saint-Sacrement, et à l'ouest le lac Ontario
et le lac Crié [Erie], avec la propriété de toutes les terres et rivières au nord
de l'Ohio, ainsi que la propriété du pays au sud de cette rivière; c'est-à-dire,
des terres et rivières au-dessous, et depuis la Rivière-Neuve exclusivement
jusqu'à l'embouchure de l'Ohio dans le Mississipi. ART. VI. Que pour
prévenir les discussions que pouraient occasionner entre les sujets de sa
majesté Très-Chrétienne et ceux de sa majesté Britannique, la trop grande
proximité de leurs établissements, dans cette patrie, les Français ne pourront
en aucun temps et sous aucuns prétextes, construire ni bâtir aucuns forts
sur la Belle-Rivière, entre ses sources et l'embouchure de la Rivière-Neuve,

standing the connection of France with the American Revolution.[8] The subsequent actions of Vergennes are entirely consistent with the view that he was the author of this memoir. It is true that, by the treaty of alliance of 1778, France renounced the possession of territories in North America that had belonged to England, but the student of French diplomatic relations with the United States during the Revolution will remember that the French ministers to the United States supported the Spanish contention that American rights did not extend beyond the Alleghenies, and tried to get from Congress a renunciation of the claim to that region. Vergennes instructed his representatives, also, that France did not intend to raise the United States to a position where she would be independent of French support. The proposal shown by Rayneval, the secretary of Vergennes, to Jay in 1782 presented the ideas of France. Roughly speaking, this provided that the land south of the Ohio, between the Alleghenies and the Mississippi, should be

[8] Doniol, *Histoire de la Participation de la France à l'Établissement des États-Unis d'Amérique.*

qui se dégorge à cent quatre-vingts lieues au-dessous du fort du Quesne, n'y établir les terres qui se trouvent entre le lac Crié [Erie] et la rive septentrionale de l'Ohio, depuis la rivière Casconchiagou jusqu'à l'embouchure de la rivière Souhiato; c'est-à-dire, que toute cette étendue de pays restera inculte, inhabitée et en désert. ART. VII. Qu'afin néanmoins que la France puisse mettre ses sujets et ses possessions à l'abri et à couvert des incursions des sauvages, cette couronne conservera, de son côté, le fort de Catarakoui, ou Frontenac sur le lac Ontario et le fort de Niagara, au nord du lac Crié, comme aussi le droit de se fortifier dans les autres limites, lors et ainsi qu'elle le trouvera à propos. ART. VIII. Il sera libre à toutes les nations et peuples sauvages, sous quelques dominations qu'ils soient, de changer à leur volonté de domicile, et de se retirer et de s'établir suivant leurs goûts et leurs caprices sur les domaines de l'Angleterre ou de la France, sans qu'aucune de ces deux puissances puisse jamais y porter obstacles ou s'en formaliser. *Nota.* Cet article est fondé sur l'amour de la liberté, inné chez tous les sauvages, et l'on ne peut, sans injustice, leur ôter le droit primitif de propriété sur les terres où la providence les a fait naitre et placés." ARTICLE IX. Freedom of the Indians to trade with either power, but prohibition of the passage of traders of either country into the territory assigned to the other. ARTICLES X, XI, and XII provide arrangements regarding fugitives from justice among the Indians.

free Indian country divided by the Cumberland River into two spheres of influence, the northern to fall under the protection of the United States, and the southern under that of Spain.[9] The argument for this proposal submitted by Rayneval, and approved by Vergennes,[10] was based upon the recognition of the independence of the Indian tribes east of the Mississippi. England was held to have admitted this by her proposals in regard to limits in 1755, and by her proclamation of 1763. By the latter document the colonies were held to be debarred from claiming to the Mississippi, and it was argued that neither Spain nor the United States had the least right of sovereignty over the savages in question.

The system of France becomes clearer when it is remembered that, under pressure from that court, in 1781, Congress had rescinded its ultimatum with regard to a Mississippi boundary, and had instructed its representatives to be guided by the advice of France as to the terms of peace. What this advice would be is shown in the *Mémoire*[11] and in the proposition of Rayneval. By this proposal of an independent Indian country, Vergennes would avoid breaking the terms of the treaty of 1778, in regard to acquisition of English territory, and at the same time he expected effectually to withdraw

[9] Wharton (ed.), *Revolutionary Diplomatic Correspondence of the United States*, VI, 25 ff.; *Secret Journals of Congress*, IV, 74-78; Winsor, *Narrative and Critical History of America*, VII, 118, 148.

[10] Circourt, *Histoire de l'Action Commune de la France et de l'Amérique pour l'Indépendance des États-Unis*, III, 290.

[11] Besides the projects of the *Mémoire* itself, note this significant passage (p. 103):

"Quelque soit l'issue de la guerre des Anglais et des Américains, la fin de cette révolution ne peut finir sans que les puissances belligérantes de l'Europe ne se mêlent de la querelle, ou ne servent de médiateurs. Dans ces deux cas, un congrès général peut changer les dispositions du traité de Versailles; et, en supposant que les Provinces-Unies de l'Amérique soient séparées de leur métropole, la France est en mesure pour réclamer ses anciennes possessions."

the region from the Americans. Although Oswald, the English representative in the American negotiations, did not possess full information as to this device of France, nor as to her readiness to make concessions to England north of the Ohio, his construction of her policy in his letter to Shelburne, September 11, 1782, was not unfounded. He writes:

"M. de Vergennes has sent an agent [Rayneval] over to London on some particular negotiation, it is thought in favour of Spain. That Court wishes to have the whole of the country from West Florida of a certain width quite up to Canada, so as to have both banks of the Mississippi clear, and would wish to have such a cession from England, before a cession to the Colonies takes place." [12]

So far, then, the actions of Vergennes accord with the ideas set forth in the memoir. A further striking evidence of the consistency of his policy with this document is the fact that he also tried to acquire Louisiana from Spain. Godoy, the Prince of Peace, declares that Vergennes, counting upon the close union of the two cabinets connected by the family compact, employed every means of persuasion "to induce Spain, already so rich in possessions beyond the sea, to give to France her ancient colony." Charles III and the Count of Florida Blanca were not averse to consenting to this demand, but under the condition of reimbursement of the expenses which Spain had made for preserving and improving Louisiana. "The lack of money," says Godoy, "was the only difficulty which suspended the course of

[12] Fitzmaurice, *Life of Shelburne*, III, 258. For Rayneval's interview with Shelburne, and his suggestion that England would find in the negotiations of 1754, relating to the Ohio, the boundaries that England then saw fit to assign the colonies, see Circourt, III, 46, and Doniol, V, 133.

the negotiation." [13]   It is clear, therefore, that the essential elements in the policy outlined by the memoir were followed by Vergennes in his diplomacy. The anxiety of Vergennes to protect the interests of Spain in the country between the Alleghenies and the Mississippi, when interpreted by the memoir and by his efforts to procure Louisiana from Spain, proves to be in reality an anxiety to promote the interests of France. Expecting to be put in possession of Louisiana, France herself was vitally interested in the disposal of the lands between the Mississippi and the Alleghenies. Vergennes believed that in assenting to a Mississippi boundary for the United States, England had given a territory which she did not possess, and which, in fact, belonged in part to Spain and in part to the Indians. [14] The matter is important inasmuch as it reveals the emphasis which France at this period laid upon the connection of the trans-Allegheny country with Louisiana.   It puts in a strong light her desire to become an American power, to place boundaries to the expansion of the United States, and to hold that country in a position of subordination to her policy.   The system of Vergennes in the American Revolution cannot be rightly understood so long as the historians of the negotiations fail to comprehend his expectation that France would replace Spain in Louisiana. [15]

[13] J. B. D'Esménard, *Mémoires du Prince de la Paix, Don Manuel Godoy* (Brussels, 1836), III, 113.

[14] Doniol, V, 362-365.   Compare treaty of alliance, 1778, Articles VI and XI.

[15] There are some grounds for suspecting France of desiring to evade the pledges regarding conquest in the Revolution.   The question of the Canada invasion and the occupation of Detroit is one.   See D'Estaing's proclamation to the French, and Lafayette's to the Indians, Kingsford's *Canada*, VI, 342, VII, 13; Washington's fears are in Sparks's *Washington*, VI, 106; cf. *Secret Journals of Congress*, II, 125; Lafayette to Vergennes, July 18, 1779, *Stevens's Facsimiles*, Vol. XVII, No. 1609, from Archives des Affaires Étrangères, États-Unis, IX, No. 42, fol. 154: "Shall we free our oppressed

POLICY OF FRANCE

The close of this war which France had waged against England left her without the financial resources to achieve the possession of Louisiana, and her interest turned to domestic affairs. Anticipating the possibility of the dissolution of the Union, England and Spain took measures to keep in touch with the Western communities. Spain, having acquired Florida from England as a result of the war, gained the control of the navigation of the Mississippi and opened and closed the door to Western prosperity at her pleasure. She established her ascendency over the Southwestern Indians by treaties of alliance and protection, and used them to check the American advance. Hoping to add the Kentucky, Franklin, and Cumberland settlements

---

brethren, recover the fur trade, our intercourse with the Indians, and all the profits of our former establishments without their expenses and losses? Shall we throw into the balance of the new world a fourteenth state, which would be always attached to us, and which by its situation would give us a superiority in the troubles that may at some future day set America at variance? Opinions are very much divided on this point; I know yours, Monsieur le Comte, and my own inclination is not unknown to you. I do not therefore dwell on it in any sense, and regard this idea only as a means of deceiving and embarrassing the enemy." But Vergennes's policy seems to have been to leave Canada to England (Doniol, III, 566).

Colonel La Balme's attempt to take Detroit in the fall of 1780 with a force of Illinois and Indiana Frenchmen who proclaimed that they would not recognize any authority but that of the king of France, and who were aroused against the American rule by La Balme, is certainly suspicious. La Balme was in 1777 inspector of horse in Armand's legion. He was relieved from service under Congress in 1778. On June 27, 1780, from Fort Pitt, he gave a report to Luzerne, the French minister, of his proposed Western visit, figuring in his talks to the Indians as a French chief, who had come to learn the real inclinations of the children of the king of France (*Report on Canadian Archives, 1888*, p. 865). On his arrival in Vincennes and the Illinois settlements, he encouraged the Frenchmen to resist American authority; they were "buoyed up with the flattering hopes of being again subject to the King of France," according to reports by Americans resident in the French villages. Indeed, he was reported to have told the Indians that, in the spring, there would be French troops in the Illinois country. His expedition against Detroit miscarried, and he was killed and his papers sent to Canada. Had Detroit been taken by Frenchmen of the Illinois country, who professed independence of the United States, complications to the advantage of France might have been raised in the discussion of the terms of peace. See *Michigan Pioneer Colls.*, IX, 641; Canadian Archives, Series B, Vol. 122, p. 569; Vol. 123, p. 3; Vol. 182, p. 489; *Report on Canadian Archives, 1887*, p. 228; *1888*, pp. 865, 882; George Rogers Clark MSS., Vol. 50, pp. 51, 66, 71; *Calendar Virginia State Papers*, I, 380.

to the Spanish empire, she intrigued with their leaders to bring about secession.[16] England, also retaining her posts on the Great Lakes, held the Northwestern Indians under her influence and was able to infuse some degree of unanimity into their councils and into their dealings with the Americans. Her influence, and the material aid furnished to the Indians, enabled them to resist the American advance across the Ohio. While Spain intrigued with the West, England also sounded the leaders of that region, and in the fall of 1789 instructed Lord Dorchester, the governor of Canada, that it was desirable that the Western settlements should be kept distinct from the United States and in connection with Great Britain.[17] The Lords of Trade, in a report of 1790, declared that it would be for England's interest "to prevent Vermont and Kentuck and all the other Settlements now forming in the Interior parts of the great Continent of North America, from becoming dependent on the Government of the United States, or on that of any other Foreign Country, and to preserve them on the contrary in a State of

[16] For material on this subject the reader should consult Gayarré, *History of Louisiana*, III; Winsor, *Westward Movement;* Roosevelt, *Winning of the West,* III; T. M. Green, *Spanish Conspiracy.* McGillivray, the half-breed chief of the Creeks, informed White, the Indian agent of the United States in 1787, that if Congress would form a new state south of the Altamaha (presumably composed of the Indians), he would agree to take the oath of allegiance to it and to cede the Oconee lands to Georgia. *American State Papers, Foreign Relations,* I, 20-22. Compare *American Historical Review,* VIII, 283, for evidence that the state of Franklin considered the proposition of admitting the Cherokees to representation in her legislature. For the Spanish attitude regarding the independence of the Indians, see *American State Papers, Foreign Relations,* I, 278-280; *Indian Affairs,* I, 17-19. Instructions were given to the governor of Louisiana by Spain, May 24, 1793, that the Americans should be kept from the Mississippi and the mouth of the Ohio, and that the Cumberland settlers should be restrained to the north of the Cumberland River. George Rogers Clark MSS., XL, 63. By her Indian treaties of 1792, Spain professed to have extended her limits on the east bank of the Mississippi forty leagues in one direction and sixty leagues in the other. George Rogers Clark MSS., A.
[17] Canadian Archives, Series Q, Vol. 42, p. 153.

Independence, and to induce them to form Treaties
of Commerce and Friendship with Great Britain."[18]

France, at the same period, was not free from interest in Western affairs. Her archives have not been
sufficiently explored to make clear how far she adhered
to the desire to regain Louisiana. De Moustier, the
French minister to the United States, was instructed
in 1787 by Montmorin, minister of foreign affairs, that
principles were in favor of Spain in the matter of the
navigation of the Mississippi, and that it would pain
the King if the United States should embroil themselves
with that power over the question; but he was not to
offer the good offices of the King, lest all parties should
be compromised. This minister was further instructed
that it was for the interest of France that the United
States should remain in their actual condition rather
than form a new constitution, because, if they secured
the unity of which they were capable, they would soon
acquire a force and power which they would probably
be very ready to abuse.[19]

Various memoirs were transmitted to the government at the close of the Confederation, describing the
advantages which France would gain by recovering
Louisiana,[20] and De Moustier sent a dispatch to his
court reciting the advantages which would come to
France by the retrocession of Louisiana. By this
France would obtain, he argued, a continental colony
which would guarantee the West Indies, the most beau-

[18] *American Historical Review*, VIII, 84.
[19] *American Historical Review*, VIII, 713. Cf. page 143, *ante*.
[20] See the intercepted memorial written about 1787, Chatham MSS., 345,
and in *Report on Canadian Archives, 1890*, pp. 108-119. Dorchester informed
his government that De Moustier forwarded it to his court. It is possible that
this was the work of Pierre Lyonnet; see *Report of American Historical
Association*, 1896, I, 946.

tiful entrepôt of North America, for her commerce, and an almost complete monopoly of the products of the states situated on the Mississippi—and, in fine, the solution of the problem of French influence upon the United States—by furnishing a means of holding the government by the party which was the most sensible of its interest and its prejudices.[21]

It was in these closing years of the Confederation, also, that various French travelers visited the United States and reported the conditions of the lands beyond the Alleghenies. Of these the most important were Brissot and Clavière, the former afterward the real master of the foreign policy of France during the ascendency of the Brissotins or Girondists, the latter the minister of finance in the period of the dominance of that party.[22] Brissot's opinion was that the Westerners would resent the attempt of Spain to shut them off from the sea, and that "if ever the Americans shall march toward New Orleans, it will infallibly fall into their hands."

When, in the spring of 1790, war seemed imminent between England and Spain over the Nootka Sound affair,[23] there was every prospect that a descent would be made by the former power upon New Orleans. Indeed, Pitt listened to the plan of Miranda, the Vene-

[21] See the letter of Fauchet, February 4, 1795, in *Report of American Historical Association, 1903,* II. Jefferson had evidently received hints of De Moustier's project, for he wrote to our representative, Mr. Short, August 10, 1790, warning him to be on his guard even in communications to France. "It is believed here, that the Count de Moustier, during his residence with us, conceived the project of again engaging France in a colony upon our continent, and that he directed his views to some of the country on the Mississippi, and obtained and communicated a good deal of matter on the subject to his court." *The Writings of Thomas Jefferson* (ed. Ford), V, 220.

[22] Brissot de Warville, *Nouveau Voyage dans les États-Unis* (Paris, 1791); Brissot et Clavière, *De la France et des États-Unis* (London, 1787); Brissot and Clavière, *Commerce of America with Europe* (New York, 1795).

[23] *American Historical Review,* VII, 706 ff.; *Atlantic Monthly,* XCIII, 680.

zuelan revolutionist, for an attack upon Spain's American possessions with a view of giving freedom to those colonies, and thereby opening their commerce to England and insuring to her a predominance in their political relations. Jefferson, seeing the danger to the United States, menaced by the possibility of England's acquiring Louisiana and Florida and thus completely surrounding us in the rear and flanks while her fleet threatened our seaboard, turned to France for assistance and instructed our representative there to attempt to secure the good offices of that nation to induce Spain to yield to us the island of New Orleans; or, since that idea might seem extreme, to urge her, at first, to recommend to Spain the cession of "a port near the mouth of the river with a circumadjacent territory sufficient for its support, well defined and extra-territorial to Spain, leaving the idea to future growth." He instructed our minister to Spain to ask for New Orleans and Florida and to argue that thus we could protect for Spain what lay beyond the Mississippi.[24] His policy was, in brief, to make advances to France and Spain, but at the same time to offer neutrality to England, if she would carry out the treaty of 1783 and attempt no conquests adjoining us.

But France had other plans. After considerable discussion she finally proposed to Spain a new national pact in place of the family compact, and sent Bourgoing in 1790 to negotiate. He suggested to Spain as a consecration of their proposed new alliance the restitution of Louisiana to France.[25] But Spain was not ready to agree to such terms; she distrusted the revolutionary

[24] *The Writings of Thomas Jefferson* (ed. Ford), V, 220, 229.
[25] Sorel, *L'Europe et la Révolution Française*, II, 94.

advances and came to terms with England. France, perceiving the family compact no longer applicable to the new conditions, adjusted her policy to the prospect of a complete rupture with Spain. This had a most important bearing upon the New World; for France, with the fires of the Revolution destroying the old order of things, saw the opportunity to rebuild her colonial empire at the expense of Spain.

In 1792 Talleyrand and other French agents negotiated with England informally to withdraw her from the formidable list of enemies that were uniting against France. If England joined them, the French islands would be exposed to her attack. The instructions to these agents, drawn by Dumouriez, argued that the New World was large enough for partition. Has not the time come, it was asked, to form a great combination, between France and Great Britain (including, if necessary, the United States), by which the commerce of the Spanish possessions should be opened to these three powers? [26] But England was in no mood to accept the alliance of antimonarchical France, and turned a cold shoulder to these advances. France, in isolation, took up the revolutionary projects which Miranda had in 1790 unfolded to Pitt, and turned to the United States for assistance.

The need was great, for the French islands were likely to fall a prey to England in case of war, and French commerce would be exposed to the fleets of the same power. The time was also favorable, for, before the close of 1792, Washington, realizing the dangers to which the United States was exposed, with England

[26] *Ibid.*, pp. 384 ff., III, 17-21. Compare Robinet, *Danton Émigré*, p. 243; G. Pallain, *Le Ministère de Talleyrand sous le Directoire*, pp. xii, xlii.

and Spain both holding unfriendly relations with the Indians on the flanks of the United States, broached to Jefferson the question of a closer connection with France. Jefferson caught eagerly at the proposal, for, as he said, a French alliance was his "polar star." [27] Fortunately, however, Washington's policy turned eventually to a strict neutrality and complete freedom from foreign entanglements.

The result was Genet's mission to the United States.[28] Here only the essential elements of French policy in respect to the mission can be given. In the inception of the plan, Brissot proposed to send Miranda [29] to San Domingo, where the French garrisons, together with local troops, would serve as the nucleus for inaugurating a revolution among the Spanish colonies. Other forces were to be raised in the United States.[30] Lebrun, minister of foreign relations, sent word to Washington, in November of 1792, that France would revolutionize Spanish America, and that forty-five ships of the line would leave in the spring for that purpose, under command of Miranda. According to the further statement of Colonel Smith (the son-in-law of Vice-President Adams), who was the bearer of this news, they intended to begin the attack at the mouth of the Mississippi, and to sweep along the Gulf of Mexico southwardly, and

[27] *The Writings of Thomas Jefferson* (ed. Ford), I, 212.
[28] See Chapter 3. The documentary material, edited by the present writer, is in the *Report of American Historical Association, 1896*, I, 930-1107; *1897*, pp. 569-679; and *1903*, II, 201-286; and in the *American Historical Review*, II, 474, and III, 490. See also the additional material cited in the introduction to the documents in the *Reports* above mentioned.
[29] See Antepara, *South American Emancipation Documents* (London, 1810); Marquis de Rojas, *El General Miranda*; A. Rojas, *Miranda dans la Révolution Française*; Tejera, *Life of Miranda*; p. 59, *ante*; *American Historical Review*, III, 674, ff., VI, 508; *Edinburgh Review*, XIII, 288; *Athenæum*, April 19, 1902; Sorel, *L'Europe et la Révolution Française*, III, 175 *et passim*.
[30] See A. Rojas and Antepara for the early ideas of a general movement against Spanish America on the lines of Miranda's proposals in 1790 to Pitt.

would have no objection to our incorporating the two
Floridas.[31] Under the influence of this information,
Jefferson drafted new instructions for our commissioners to Spain, wherein he countermanded the proposal
to guarantee Louisiana to Spain on condition of the
cession of the Floridas. The former proposal, made
in 1790, would have interfered with the freedom of
the United States to act according to the new circumstances.

France, however, hesitated to plunge into this vast
enterprise of Spanish-American revolution until she had
overcome Holland and made herself the mistress of the
Dutch marine. Then, in the opinion of Dumouriez, it
would be possible to crush England and execute
Miranda's project. This general, therefore, left to participate in the operations in the Netherlands and to
suffer the loss of prestige which his disastrous defeat
brought about. It is doubtful whether the Gironde
leaders had reached an exact conclusion regarding the
disposal of Louisiana and the Floridas when Genet[32]
was sent to the United States.[33] The memoirs found in

[31] *The Writings of Thomas Jefferson* (ed. Ford), I, 216-217. Compare
American State Papers, Foreign Relations, I, 144; A. Rojas, p. 9; Antepara,
p. 172.

[32] Genet was born in 1763. He was the son of the head of the bureau of
translation in the foreign office. He studied international law at Giessen, was
attached to embassies at Berlin and Vienna, and was made chief of the
bureau of translation at the death of his father, in 1781. He went to London
in 1783 as secretary of a special embassy. In 1787 he became secretary of
legation, and afterward chargé d'affaires at St. Petersburg. His revolutionary
enthusiasm was so violent, however, that the Empress Catherine dubbed him
"un démagogue enragé," and in the summer of 1792 he was obliged to leave
the country. On his arrival at Paris, he was selected for the ministry
to Holland, but it was finally determined to send him to the United
States, possibly because of his relations to the King through his sister,
Madame Campan, who was lady in waiting to the Queen. The Girondists
had seriously considered the banishment of the King to the United States,
and it was thought that Genet might accompany the family. See *Washington,
Jefferson, and "Citizen" Genet, 1793,* a pamphlet privately printed in 1899
by the late George C. Genet, son of the minister; see also p. 62, *ante.*

[33] *Report of American Historical Association, 1896,* I, 946, note, 949, 952,
953.

the archives show that the alternatives were considered of giving them to the United States, of establishing them as independent republics, and of making them a French possession; but there can be little doubt as to what the action of France would have been in case of successful occupation of New Orleans.

Genet's instructions of December, 1792, and January, 1793,[34] written when the prospect of a war on the part of France against both Spain and England was imminent,[35] required him to endeavor to secure a treaty with the United States, which should guarantee the sovereignty of the people and punish the powers which had an exclusive commercial and colonial system, by declaring that the vessels of these powers should not be received in the ports of the contracting nations. This compact, in the opinion of the ministers, "would conduce rapidly to the freeing of Spanish America, to opening the navigation of the Mississippi to the inhabitants of Kentucky, to delivering our ancient brothers of Louisiana from the tyrannical yoke of Spain, and perhaps to reuniting the fair star of Canada to the American constellation." It will be observed that Canada alone was indicated as a possible acquisition by the United States. Genet was further authorized, in case of timidity on the part of the American government, to take all measures which comported with his position to arouse in Louisiana and in the other provinces of America adjacent to the United States the principles of liberty and independence. It was pointed out that Kentucky would probably second his efforts without compromising

[34] *Report of American Historical Association, 1896,* I, 957-967; 1903, II, 201-211.
[35] War was declared against England February 1, 1793, and against Spain, March 9, 1793.

Congress, and he was authorized to send agents there and to Louisiana.

From these instructions it is clear that the conquest of Louisiana was a fundamental purpose in Genet's mission, and that he was even to proceed by an intrigue with the frontiersmen in case the American government should not connive at his designs. Under the guise of neutrality, the United States was expected to furnish in fact an effective basis for French operations. Moreover, he was instructed to make use of the Indians, "the ancient friends of the French nation," against the enemies of France. By combining the large French population of Canada and of Louisiana, where the seeds of revolution were already sown, with the frontiersmen and the Indians in the interior, there was reason to hope for a successful outcome of the enterprise.

On his arrival in Charleston, early in April, 1793, Genet found an efficient lieutenant in Mangourit, the French consul at that city.[36] The frontiersmen of Georgia and the Carolinas had suffered from the hostility of the Cherokees and the Creeks on their frontiers, and were eager to destroy the influence by which Spain supported them in their resistance to American advance. Mangourit was therefore able to enlist the services of

[36] See F. Masson, *Le Département des Affaires Étrangères pendant la Révolution*, pp. 323-325. Mangourit's career illustrates the fact that the representatives of France in America were influential persons. In 1789 he edited for a few months *Le Héraut de la Nation*, and was the orator of his section in the National Assembly. He came to Charleston March 2, 1792, as consul. Returning after the downfall of Genet, he was sent on a mission to consider the situation of France in regard to the Two Sicilies and Spain. He was nominated as one of the members of the new commission of foreign relations in 1794, but refused the position, and was subsequently appointed first secretary of legation in Spain. Instructions were made out for him to succeed Adet in the United States in 1796, but, probably owing to the representations of Monroe against this appointment, it was not made. He afterward held various positions in the foreign service of France, among other missions being one to incite the Greeks to insurrection. Mangourit's correspondence during Genet's mission is published in the *Report of American Historical Association, 1897*, 569-679.

important leaders. One of them, Samuel Hammond,[37] of Georgia, was assigned the task of making treaties with the Creek Indians[38] and of rallying the Georgia frontiersmen for an attack upon East Florida. William Tate,[39] another frontier leader, was to negotiate with the Cherokees and the Choctaws, and to collect the frontiersmen of the Carolinas for a descent upon New Orleans by way of the Tennessee and the Mississippi. The draft of the Indian treaties[40] provided for an alliance between France and these nations, and guaranteed to the Indians the free and peaceable possession of their lands. Genet afterward, while denying that he had authorized the collection of forces against Spain on territory of the United States, admitted that he had granted commissions to men who desired to go among "the independent Indian tribes, ancient . . . allies of France," to retaliate on the Spaniards and English.[41] The connivance of Governor Moultrie, of South Carolina, seems to have been secured. Thus Genet and his lieutenants had initiated plans for the filibustering enterprise before he had broken definitely with Washington. The Southern part of the plot was seriously interfered

[37] He had been a colonel of cavalry in the Revolution and surveyor-general at Savannah, and was afterward a member of Congress.

[38] *Report of American Historical Association, 1897,* pp. 591 ff.

[39] If we may believe Mangourit, Tate had "all the virtues of the adventurers who conquered the two Indies, without their vices and ignorance; extremely severe to himself, drinking nothing but water; . . . a firm disciplinarian and having in his brain the coolness and the heat necessary to execute a great enterprise with small means. He conceives in the minute, decides on the instant; he carves in the right joint." *Ibid.,* p. 646. Tate afterward led a band of free lances in the service of France, whither he went after the failure of Genet's plans. One of his expeditions was the descent upon Ireland (the Fishguard Bay incident) in 1797. See E. Desbrière, *Projets et Tentatives de Débarquement aux Iles Britanniques* (Paris, 1900), p. 238; and M. E. James, *The Fishguard Invasion by the French in 1797.* See the index to *Report of American Historical Association, 1897,* under "Tate." In the Archives Nationales, A. F., iii, 186b, are interesting letters from Tate to [Elijah] Clarke, proposing a descent upon the Bermudas in 1796.

[40] *Report of American Historical Association, 1897,* pp. 591 ff.

[41] *American State Papers, Foreign Relations,* I, 311.

with, later, by an investigation by the legislature of South Carolina, and by the discovery that the Girondists, and Genet in particular, were "friends of the blacks."

On his arrival at Philadelphia, Genet found much popular discontent with Washington's proclamation of neutrality issued on April 27, and he came to the conclusion that he would be able to reverse the executive policy by procuring a majority in Congress favorable to his plans. The "appeal to the people" which he proposed was rather an attempt to secure a majority friendly to France in Congress, for he believed that in that body rested the sovereignty. Determining to accept the propositions of George Rogers Clark, of Kentucky, for a frontier attack upon New Orleans by way of the Mississippi, he appointed him "Major General of the Independent and Revolutionary Legion of the Mississippi." In July, 1793, Genet made known his plans to Jefferson.[42] Expecting war with Spain and understanding Genet's proposition to be that of giving freedom to Louisiana and the Floridas, Jefferson made only a formal protest against the implied violation of our neutrality; and he intimated that a little spontaneous uprising in New Orleans might prove to the advantage of the American plans.

Genet's project involved not only the organization of the frontiersmen and the "independent" Indians of the Southwest against the Floridas, while George Rogers Clark rallied the Kentuckians against New Orleans, but he proposed to block the mouth of the Mississippi by a French naval force at the same time. It was for this reason that, on July 12, 1793, he so recklessly sent the

[42] *Report of American Historical Association, 1896,* I, 948; *The Writings of Thomas Jefferson* (ed. Ford), I, 235.

"Little Democrat" to sea, against the protest of the administration.[43] At the same time, he made preparations for the use of a fleet against Canada.[44] It is unnecessary here to relate the misfortunes that befell Genet's projects. His plan of securing an advance on the indebtedness due to France by the United States failed. Lacking financial resources, the operations in the interior were delayed, and the use of parts of the fleet was prevented by mutinous crews. Washington prepared to use the military forces of the United States to prevent a violation of our neutrality, and Genet himself lost his following, even among the more radical of the democratic leaders. France, under the Reign of Terror, fully occupied on her own borders and torn by internal party dissension, was unable to carry out her American plans, and Genet was superseded and disavowed.

The new embassy to the United States consisted of Fauchet,[45] as minister plenipotentiary, La Forest,[46] consul general, Petry, consul for Pennsylvania, and Le Blanc, secretary of legation. By the terms of the

[43] *Report of American Historical Association, 1896,* I, 990.

[44] For Genet's activity in respect to Canada, see the *Report on Canadian Archives, 1891,* Note D, pp. 57-84. There is considerable material throughout the reports of 1891 and 1894. The connection of Vermonters with this intrigue called out a mass of material; but it is not the purpose of the present paper to discuss the Canadian side of the French activity.

[45] Jean-Antoine-Joseph Fauchet was born in 1761 and died in 1834. He was chief of the bureau of administration of war (1791), secretary of the mayor of Paris (1792), and, in the same year, secretary of the executive power. After his mission to the United States (1794-1795), he became a partisan of Napoleon, and was prefect of the Var and of the Gironde, successively. In 1810 he was made a baron. *Report of American Historical Association, 1903,* II, 288.

[46] Antoine-René-Charles-Mathurin de la Forest, son of the Marquis de Paulmy, was born in 1756. He became an attaché in the French legation to the United States in 1778, and was made vice-consul at Savannah in 1783. In 1785 he was charged with the management of the affairs of the *consulat général* in the United States. He replaced Barbé-Marbois in this place March 2, 1792. Recalled November 17, 1792, with the other agents who had served the crown, he desired to remain in America, but finally returned in order to avoid complications between France and the United States. Returning as con-

instructions[47] given November 25, 1793, no measure which interested the republic could be undertaken without the agreement of a majority of the commissioners. By this it was desired to avoid the indiscretions into which Genet had fallen. The commission, in accordance with these instructions, disavowed the conduct of Genet. By the proclamation of March 6, 1794, Fauchet, not without regret, revoked the commissions of the filibusters and forbade the violation of the neutrality of the United States. But, in spite of the fact that under the Jacobin administration France was ready to disavow the proceedings of the Girondists in respect to the violation of American neutrality, she by no means abandoned her interests in the Mississippi Valley. By their instructions the new commissioners were required to inform the officers of the American government that negotiations with Spain regarding the navigation of the Mississippi would be incompatible with the ties which bound the United States to France. In the earlier part of his mission, Fauchet devoted himself to a policy of "wise delay and useful temporizing," conceiving that the interest of the republic was to obtain from the United States a prolonged inertia. He therefore contented himself with observing the development of our domestic policy, and particularly the events on our frontiers during the period of Indian wars and the Whiskey Rebellion. Of all of this, as well as of the

[47] *Report of American Historical Association*, 1903, II, 288-294.

sul general with Fauchet, he fell under the suspicion of that minister, and was recalled. On his return to France, he received from Talleyrand the appointment of chief of the *Direction des Fondes,* where he served until 1799. He was connected with the negotiations of the treaty of 1800 with the United States, and also served in the negotiations of the treaty of Lunéville. In 1801 he was minister plenipotentiary at Munich, and was a councilor of state for foreign relations under the Empire. See Masson, *Le Département des Affaires Étrangères pendant la Révolution,* pp. 320, 321, 407-408, 455-464.

English policy in the Northwest, he gave detailed accounts to his government. He was active in sending provision fleets to France, and in protests against English violations of our neutral commerce. At this period other interests were entirely subordinated to the important consideration of the provisioning of France by the United States. The insurrection in the French West Indies gave him concern; but, on the other hand, he pointed out that the revolution of the blacks had established an eternal seed of repulsion between the West Indies and slaveholding America, so that there was less danger of American acquisition of these islands. It was not until the news of Jay's treaty reached him that he turned to the subject of Louisiana. As soon as he was fairly well informed of the purport of this treaty (in February, 1795), he proposed a radical programme for meeting the situation.[48] He reminded his government that he had energetically protested against our failure to enforce the rights of neutral commerce against England; but now Jay's treaty threatened even more unfavorable conditions by its concessions to Great Britain in the matter of neutral rights, and the alliance of 1778 had become worse than useless. Yet, as Fauchet pointed out, France had no means of intimidating the United States. The ocean separated the two powers, and the French West Indies, far from threatening the United States, were actually in danger of starvation in time of war if American trade was cut off. He quoted Jefferson's remark, "France enjoys their sovereignty and we their profit." A war to compel the Union to follow French policy would deprive the republic of the indispensable trade of America. Some other means

[48] *Ibid.*, Fauchet's dispatch of February 4, 1795.

must be found, and the solution of the problem, in Fauchet's opinion, was the acquisition of a continental colony in America: "Louisiana opens her arms to us." This province would furnish France the best entrepôt in North America, raw material, and a market for her manufactures, a monopoly of the products of the American states on the Mississippi, and a means of pressure upon the United States. He predicted that, unless a revolution occurred in Spanish policy, the force of events would unite Louisiana to the United States, and in the course of time would bring about a new confederation between this province and the Western states, which would not remain within the United States fifty years. In this new union the superior institutions and power of the American element would give to it the sovereignty. But if France or any power less feeble than Spain possessed Louisiana, it would establish there the sovereignty over all the countries on the Mississippi. If a nation with adequate resources, said he, understood how to manage the control of the river, it could hold in dependence the Western states of America, and might at pleasure advance or retard the rate of their growth. What, then, he asks, might not France do with so many warm friends among the Western settlers? The leaven of insurrection had been recently manifested in the Whiskey Rebellion; it would depend upon France to decide the question of dismemberment. In this way, by pressure on our borders, she could bend the United States to her will, or in the possession of the Mississippi Valley find a means of freeing herself and her islands from their economic dependence upon the United States. Such was the line of thought presented by Fauchet to the French authorities; he preferred diplomatic negotiation to war or the filibustering system of Genet.

How far this dispatch of Fauchet may have affected the policy of France in the negotiations at Basel is not certain, but these negotiations, by which Spain came to terms with France, were exceedingly important for the Mississippi Valley. Barthélemy was instructed [49] May 10, 1795, to demand from Spain certain cessions as the price of peace. The Spanish portion of San Domingo, the Basque province of Guipuscoa, and Louisiana were desired, but upon Louisiana he was ordered to insist— "the rest would be easy." "C'est sur la Louisiane qu'il faut insister et le citoyen Barthélemy aura soin de diriger tous ces efforts vers ce but." In support of her demand, France argued that it would be a great gain to Spain to place a strong power between her American possessions and those of the United States, particularly since England had by Jay's treaty guaranteed to the United States the freedom of navigation of the Mississippi, and it was to be feared that these new allies would seize Louisiana.

At this juncture Godoy, the Duke of Alcudia, was in control of the foreign policy of Spain. Alarmed by conditions in Europe, and chagrined at England's arrangements with the United States at a moment when Spain trembled for the fate of Louisiana,[50] he made peace with France at Basel (July, 1795); but he refused to yield Louisiana, preferring to abandon the Spanish portion of San Domingo. This only rendered

[49] Sorel, in *Revue Historique*, XIII, 46. See also XII, 295, XIII, 274; and D'Esménard, *Mémoires du Prince de la Paix*.

[50] In a letter of December 29, 1794, Short informed the Secretary of State of Godoy's mortification at Jay's treaty and of his bitterness against England. Godoy intimated that the points for a treaty between the United States and Spain might easily be arranged. Nevertheless, he continued to procrastinate. See Morrissy, "William Short's Career" (Cornell, thesis, MS., 1900, p. 530).

France the more determined to secure the continental colony needed to support her West Indian possessions; and in the negotiations, later, over the terms of alliance she pressed hard for the additional cession.

It is this situation which explains the treaty that Godoy made with the United States not long after. He was most reluctant to give up Louisiana, but France demanded it as a condition of her alliance. Threatened thus with isolation, and confronted by the prospect of a war with England, he was disposed to conciliate the United States, lest she join England and take Louisiana by force. When, therefore, Pinckney's threat to leave for London was made, Godoy interpreted it as an indication that Jay's treaty had made contingent provision for a joint attack by England and the United States against Louisiana. He had previously tried in vain to persuade Pinckney to engage the United States in an alliance with France and Spain. In alarm he hastily came to the American terms, and in the treaty of San Lorenzo (October 27, 1795)[51] he conceded the navigation of the Mississippi and our boundary on that river, and agreed to give up the Spanish posts north of New Orleans within the disputed territory. Thus relieved of the danger of an American invasion, Godoy was in a better position to resist the efforts of France to force him to cede Louisiana.

By the close of the year 1795, therefore, Washington's administration had by Jay's treaty secured possession of the Northwest, and by Pinckney's treaty had received the promise of the evacuation of the disputed posts on the east of the Mississippi by Spain. The flanks of the Mississippi Valley were apparently insured to

[51] D'Esménard, *Mémoires du Prince de la Paix,* II, ch. xxx (part i).

the United States. But the former diplomatic conditions were reversed after Jay's treaty and the treaty of Basel. France and Spain were no longer enemies. Spain had broken with England; and the United States, swinging away from the French alliance, was embracing the friendship of England. To Spain and France, there seemed to be a menace, in these new relationships, against the Spanish-American colonies. It became a cardinal point in French policy, therefore, to press to a conclusion the negotiations for Louisiana, to suspend diplomatic relations with the United States, and to attempt to alarm her into a reversal of her friendly attitude toward England. But it was not the policy of France to force the United States into war. Adet,[52] who arrived as the successor of Fauchet in June, 1795, later informed his government that a rupture with the United States would be a disadvantage for France:

"You know that our colonies would be without provisionment and perhaps actually conquered, that all hope of commerce with America would be cut off thereafter, while England would receive 30,000 sailors of the United States, and Louisiana and the Floridas would shortly fall under the power of our new enemies and of Great Britain; that New Mexico would soon see their banners waving, and who knows where the habit of pillage and the ambition of conquest may conduct them in a country so badly defended as the Spanish possessions and where already germs of discord exist and the ferment of discontent?"[53]

[52] Pierre-Auguste Adet was born in Paris in 1763. He was the author of some important chemical works, was the secretary of the first commission sent to San Domingo; then *chef de l'administration des colonies,* and afterward connected with the ministry of marine. He served for a time in Geneva, whence he was transferred to the United States. Adet's instructions and correspondence are in the *Report of American Historical Association, 1903,* II.
[53] Adet's dispatch of February 3, 1797, *ibid.*

The treaty of Basel had provided for peace between France and Spain, but it did not include the terms of an alliance. France now tried to reap the fruits of her success by dictating the conditions of the treaty. In the spring of 1796, the Directors sent General Perignon to Madrid to arrange terms of a formal alliance.[54] He was instructed to warn Spain that French influence in America was nearing its end. War with the United States promised France no satisfactory results, and to punish the Americans by restrictions on their commerce would deprive France of a resource which the European wars rendered necessary to her. These, however, were merely temporary difficulties. "Who," asked the Directors, "can answer that England and the United States together will not divide up the northern part of the New World? What prevents them?" The instructions went on to give a forceful presentation of the rapidity with which settlers were pouring into Kentucky and Tennessee, and of the danger to Louisiana from filibustering expeditions. The concession of the navigation of the Mississippi, in the opinion of France, prepared the ruin and invasion of Louisiana whenever the United States, in concert with Great Britain, should "give the reins to those fierce inhabitants of the West." The English-speaking people would then overrun Mexico and all North America, and the commerce of the islands of the Gulf would be dependent upon this Anglo-American power. Only France, in alliance with Spain, argued the Directors, can oppose a counterpoise, by the use of her old influence among the Indians: "We alone can trace with strong and respected hand the bounds of the

[54] See the instructions in *Report of American Historical Association, 1897*, pp. 667-671; *Atlantic Monthly*, XCIII, 810.

power of the United States and the limits of their territory." All that France demanded was Louisiana, a
province that, so far from serving the purpose of its
original cession as a barrier against England, was now
a dangerous possession to Spain, ever ready to join with
her neighbors. It had remained in a condition of infancy
while the United States had acquired irresistible
strength on its borders. This country was now daily
preparing the subjects of Spain for insurrection by
intrigues and by the spectacle of its prosperity. "On
the other hand," continued the Directors, "if this possession were once in our hands, it would be beyond
insult by Great Britain, to whom we can oppose not
only the western settlements of the United States, who
are as friendly to us as they could possibly be, but also
the inhabitants of Louisiana, who have given clear evidence of their indestructible attachment to their former
mother-country. It gives us the means to balance the
marked predilection of the federal government for our
enemy, and to retain it in the line of duty by the fear
of dismemberment which we can bring about." "We
shall affright England by the sudden development of an
actual power in the New World, and shall be in a position to oppose a perfect harmony to her attacks and her
intrigues." They therefore urged Spain to act at once,
in order that the political and military campaigns might
begin in America that very year.

But Godoy resolutely refused to give up Louisiana,
and Perignon was obliged to content himself with a
treaty of alliance without this important concession.
France thereupon recalled him, and sent a successor
with the particular purpose of persuading Spain to yield
Louisiana by the offer to join her in the conquest of

Portugal; but the Prince of Peace remained immovable; nor did he consent even when, in 1797, after Napoleon's victories in Italy had given the papal legations to France, she offered them to the royal house of Spain as an equivalent for Louisiana. Had religious scruples not prevented, however, Spain would probably have accepted this proposition.[55]

While France negotiated with Spain, she prepared the ground in America. In the winter of 1795, Colonel Fulton, one of George Rogers Clark's officers in the Genet expedition, was sent to intrigue with the Southwestern Indians[56] and to consult with Clark.

By the close of 1796 Fulton, having returned, furnished the Directors information as to the best season for occupying Louisiana, and assured them that Clark's old soldiers were loyal to France, and asked only arms, ammunition, and uniforms, and "their country will find itself in the vast regions which the Republic will pos-

[55] See Sorel's study of the relations of France and Spain, 1792-1797, in *Revue Historique*, XIII, 46, 274; and *Mémoires du Prince de la Paix*, III, 116; Barras, *Memoirs* (New York, 1895), II, 359.
[56] See *American State Papers, Indian Affairs*, I, 463; *Report of American Historical Association, 1896*, I, 1063, and index under "Fulton." Samuel Fulton was one of the interesting American adventurers of the type of Tate. He was a North Carolinian who removed to the Creek country about 1791. Refusing to swear allegiance to the king of Spain, he was forced to leave in 1793. The spring of 1794 found him acting as an assistant to George Rogers Clark in the service of France, with the position of major of cavalry. After the failure of the expedition he went to Paris to collect the claims of Clark and himself against the French government. Here he was commissioned as colonel in the cavalry, but he writes, "I begin to be D—d tired of Paris." In the summer of 1795 he was back in the United States and was sent by the minister, Adet, to report on the situation of the followers of Elijah Clarke, who had fled to Amelia Island after the failure of the Genet project in which they had a part. Adet regretted that the peace of Basel compelled him to withdraw French support from this promising movement against the Spanish possessions (*Report of American Historical Association, 1897*, p. 663). Fulton then went to Kentucky some time prior to November 2, 1795, to inform George Rogers Clark that the French government ratified the proceedings of Genet and himself (*ibid., 1896*, I, 1095). Colonel Charles M. Thruston wrote to his son Charles at Louisville, under date of Frederick Co., Va., February 17, 1796: "We have a report here that Col. Fulton has returned from France with a commission for Gen! Clark of Major General in the French service, with an appointment of three hundred dollars a month for him and commissions for all his officers. If this be true it must have reached you before this; and if

sess." [57] Toward the end of 1796, France sent a new commission to George Rogers Clark, as brigadier general, on the theory, as Delacroix, the minister of foreign relations, declared, that it was to the interest of France to foster a favorable disposition among the Westerners. "In case we shall be put in possession of Louisiana," he wrote, "the affection of those regions will serve us in our political plans toward the United States." [58]

Information regarding the Southwestern tribes was also procured from Milfort, a French adventurer who, after passing twenty years among the Creeks as an agent of Spain, went to offer his services to France.[59] He had married a sister of McGillivray, and claimed to be the principal war-chief of the Creeks. In 1795 Milfort had left the Indians and had presented his plans for organizing the Indians of the Southwest under the French, and, according to his statement, Fauchet

[57] Fulton to Delacroix, October 24, 1796. Affaires Étrangères, La. et Fla., Vol. 7, fol. 44.

[58] *Ibid.*, États-Unis, Vol. 47, fo. 305.

[59] His *Mémoire ou Coup d'Œil Rapide sur mes Différens Voyages et mon Séjour dans la Nation Crêck* is one of the sources for our knowledge of these Indians; but he was a hopeless liar, one of his most interesting concoctions being a statement to the French government that he had defeated ten thousand regulars under George Rogers Clark near Detroit by a force of six thousand Northern Indians under his command (De Villiers du Terrage, *Les Dernières Années de la Louisiane Française*, p. 364). For his career, see, in addition to his *Mémoire,* the *State Papers and Correspondence bearing upon the Purchase of the Territory of Louisiana,* p. 20; *American State Papers, Indian Affairs,* I, 395; Pickett, *Alabama* (1851 ed.), I, 115 ff.; *Report of American Historical Association, 1896,* I, 1053.

it be so, I beg you, present my congratulations to the General, and my best respects. For his country has been ungrateful enough to let his valuable services pass by unregarded and neglected" (Draper MSS., Trip, 1868, IV, 223). Chisholm, who was connected with Blount's conspiracy, informs us (in Declaration of November 29, 1797, State Dept. MSS., Bureau of Indexes and Archives, Dispatches, England, Vol. 5, No. 57) that, in the winter of 1795, he met, between the towns of the Creek and the Cherokee nations, a person named Fulton, who said he was a colonel of horse in the French service. "He told me," says Chisholm, "that he had come from France in order to get the Indians consent for the establishment of a Republic in the Floridas, as they the French were to take it, or to get it (I don't recollect which) from the Spaniards; as I was friendly to the United States I advised him to leave the country as soon as possible which I believe he did as I have not heard of him since; the said Fulton is a tall handsome man upwards of six feet high, well

approved them. He was put off in Paris by the fact
that France was negotiating with Spain, but the Directory took him up, and on March 26, 1796, gave him
the title of general of brigade. In 1798 he presented a
memoir to the Directory offering them a large portion
of Creek territory by which they might destroy the
Americans and facilitate the acquisition of Louisiana.
The matter was favorably received by Talleyrand.

Not only did France again draw together the threads
of intrigue with the "independent" Indians and the
frontiersmen, but also in the summer of 1796 she
determined to send Mangourit to America to replace
Adet.[60] Monroe reported rumors that France was to
make an attempt upon Canada, "which is to be united
with Louisiana and the Floridas to the south, taking in
such parts of our western people as are willing to unite."
Monroe's protest against Mangourit's appointment was
effective; but the significance of the selection of this
energetic companion of Genet in the early attempt upon
Louisiana and Florida is obvious.

In the meantime, Adet, the French minister to the
United States, exerted every effort to prevent Congress
from voting the appropriations to carry out Jay's

[60] *Ibid., 1903,* II, gives the draft of his instructions. See also *American
State Papers, Foreign Relations,* I, 742.

mounted and handsomely equipped in every particular, appeared to be about
twenty-five years of age." Fulton arrived in Philadelphia in the middle of
March, after his long and disagreeable journey *(Report of American Historical
Association, 1896,* I, 1098), and returned again to France, bearing Adet's
dispatches, about April 19, 1796 (Affaires Étrangères, E.-U. Corresp., Vol. 45,
fol. 378). In a letter of George Rogers Clark to Fulton, dated March 2, 1797,
he refers to a letter from Fulton of "last December" enclosing copies of pat-
ents of general of brigade accorded to Clark by the Directory (Baron Marc
de Villiers du Terrage, *Les Dernières Années de la Louisiane Française,* p. 362).
On May 26, 1797, Delacroix, minister of foreign relations, refers to the granting of a commission to George Rogers Clark as general of brigade without
activity, and says: "It is not indifferent to our interests to preserve among
these people and the men who have their confidence, all the dispositions which
are favorable to us." Affaires Étrangères, États-Unis, Vol. 47, fol. 305.

treaty. In fact, as it turned out, the vote was a close one, but Adet, foreseeing defeat, and acting in accordance with the desire of his government, in March, 1796, commissioned General Victor Collot,[61] formerly governor of Guadeloupe, to travel in the West, and to make a military survey of the defenses and lines of communication west of the Alleghenies, along the Ohio and the Mississippi. Collot was gone about ten months, and as he passed down the rivers he pointed out to men whom he trusted the advantages of accepting French jurisdiction. He made detailed and accurate plans of the river-courses and the Spanish posts, which may still be seen in the atlas that accompanies his *Journey in North America,* published long afterward. As the military expert on whose judgment the French government had to rely, his conclusions have a peculiar interest, and may be given in his own words: "All the positions on the left bank of the river [Mississippi], in whatever point of view they may be considered, or in whatever mode they may be occupied, without the alliance of the Western states are far from covering Louisiana: they are, on the contrary, highly injurious to this colony; and the money and men which might be employed for this purpose would be ineffectual." In other words, a Louisiana bounded by the Mississippi could not be protected against the neighboring settlements of the United States. He emphasizes the same idea, in another con-

[61] For Adet's policy in this period and his relations with Collot, see *Report of American Historical Association, 1903,* II. Collot's report is in print in part: Collot, *Voyage dans l'Amérique Septentrionale* . . . *avec un Atlas de 36 Cartes* (2 vols.; Paris, 1826); and in English: *Journey in North America* (Paris, 1826), also with the atlas. The *Portfolio,* Jan. 28, 1804, p. 30, published a prospectus of the work. See also Gibbs, *Memoirs* (1846), p. 350 *et passim;* Smith, *St. Clair Papers,* II, 395; Jefferson, *Works* (1854), IX, 200; Gayarré, *Louisiana,* III, 383; Cruzat, in *New Orleans Picayune,* March 18, 1901; *Michigan Pioneer Collections,* XXV, 171; *Report on Canadian Archives, 1891;* Pickering Papers indexed in *Massachusetts Historical Society Collections,* Sixth Series, VIII, 44 *et passim.*

nection, as follows: "When two nations possess, one the coasts and the other the plains, the former must inevitably embark or submit. From thence I conclude that the Western states of the North American republic must unite themselves with Louisiana and form in the future one single compact nation; else that colony to whatever power it shall belong will be conquered or devoured."

As the logical accompaniment of this conclusion that Louisiana must embrace the Western states, Collot drew up a plan for the defense of the passes of the Alleghenies, which were to constitute the frontier of this interior dependency of France to protect it against the United States. The Louisiana that Collot contemplated, therefore, stretched from the Alleghenies to the Rockies.[62] The importance of his report is made clearer by the facts that the minister, Adet, and the consul general who remained after he left, continually refer to Collot's work as the basis for their views on Louisiana, and that Livingston reported in 1802 that it had been expected that Napoleon would make Collot second in command in the province of Louisiana, and that Adet was to be prefect.[63]

[62] In view of these designs, there is significance in the "Farewell Address," which Washington issued while Collot was making his investigations. Washington informed the West that "it must, of necessity, owe the secure enjoyment of indispensable outlets for its own productions, to the weight, influence, and the future maritime strength of the Atlantic side of the Union, directed by an indissoluble community of interest as one nation. Any other tenure by which the *West* can hold this essential advantage, whether derived from its own separate strength, or from an apostate and unnatural connexion with any foreign Power, must be intrinsically precarious." He added that the treaties with Spain and England had given the Western people all that they could desire in respect to foreign relations, and asked: "Will it not be their wisdom to rely for the preservation of these advantages on the union by which they were procured? Will they not henceforth be deaf to those advisers, if such there are, who would sever them from their brethren and connect them with aliens?" *American State Papers, Foreign Relations*, I, 34-38.

[63] *State Papers and Correspondence bearing upon the Purchase of the Territory of Louisiana* (Washington, 1903), p. 29.

As he descended the Mississippi, Collot learned of a plot for an attack under the English flag upon the Spanish dependencies, and on his return, early in 1797, he notified the Spanish minister to the United States, who promptly informed the secretary of state. In the investigation that followed, it was ascertained that the British minister had been privy to the plans, and United States Senator Blount, of Tennessee, lost his seat as a result of the revelations which involved him. The incident revealed how widespread were the forces of intrigue for the Mississippi Valley, and it gave grounds for the refusal of the Spanish authorities to carry out the agreement to yield their posts on the right bank of the river while New Orleans was threatened by an attack down the Mississippi.

The documentary material for the Blount episode has already been published in the *American Historical Review*. Here its lines can be hardly more than indicated.[64] On October 24, 1795, the English government had charged Lieutenant Governor Simcoe, of Canada, to cultivate such intercourse with the leading men of the Western settlements of the United States as would enable England to utilize the services of the frontiersmen against the Spanish settlements, if war broke out between England and Spain, and to report what assistance might be afforded by the Southern and Western Indians in such an event. Information was also desired with regard to the communications between Lake Michigan and the Mississippi, with the evident idea of using Canadian forces in the operations. These "most private and

---

[64] See *Atlantic Monthly*, XCIII, 813. The documents are in Vol. X of the *Review*, pp. 574-606.

secret" instructions [65] cast light upon England's policy at this time; and the explicit injunctions of caution, lest the government should be compromised with Spain and the United States while matters were preparing, help us to understand that whatever was to be done must be managed secretly. War was declared by Spain against England in the fall of 1796, and rumors of the approaching acquisition of Louisiana by France alarmed the land-speculators like Blount, as well as the former Tory settlers about Natchez. The gist of the plan with which Blount's name is connected was that a combined body of frontiersmen and Indians, working in concert with the English fleet and an expedition from Canada, should seize Louisiana and the Floridas for England. Liston, the minister, was acquainted with the essential features of the plan, canvassed the practicability of Canadian assistance with the authorities of that province, and finally communicated the matter to his government. In the meantime, it had become known, and England disavowed responsibility.[66]

From the point of view of the larger diplomatic problem, the most tangible result of the affair was the retention by Spain of Natchez and the other posts east of the Mississippi, under the sincere apprehension that if they were evacuated, in accordance with the treaty of 1795, a clear road would be opened for the British into Louisiana. Not until the spring of 1798 did Spain,

[65] British War Office (Colonial) Secret Entry Book and *Report on Canadian Archives, 1891,* "Upper Canada," p. 59.

[66] On the whole matter see the following: Collot, *Journey in North America,* II, 11, 64, 65, 229; Aff. Ét., États-Unis, Vol. 47, folios 124, 126, 130, 137; *American State Papers, Foreign Relations,* II, 66 ff.; *Annals of Fifth Congress, 1797-1799,* pp. 498, 2245 ff., 3131 ff.; King's *Correspondence of King,* II, 195-199, 208, 209, 216-218, 236, 253-256, 258. The disclosures to King made by Chisholm are in the Department of State, Bureau of Indexes and Archives, Despatches, England, Vols. 4 and 5, and also in the King MSS. in the New York Historical Society, folio A, pp. 378, 385, 386, 391. See also the British

under the anti-French policy of Godoy, actually evacu-
ate these forts.[67]

After the rupture of diplomatic relations with France,
the Federalists proceeded in the early summer of 1797
to enact laws for raising an army and providing a fleet,
and for the necessary loans and taxes in preparation for
war with the republic. But, less radical than some of his
advisers, and ready to make another effort to adjust our
affairs with France, President Adams sent a commission
to reopen negotiations, in spite of his chagrin that the
previous minister, C. C. Pinckney, had been summarily
refused and ordered out of France.

When this commission sailed, Talleyrand had just
become the master of the foreign policy of his country.
He had returned from his sojourn in the United States,
convinced that Americans were hopelessly attached to
England,[68] and that France must have Louisiana. In a
memoir to the Institute, April 4, 1797, he had pointed
out that Louisiana would serve the commercial needs of
France, would prove a granary for a great West Indian
colonial power, and would be a useful outlet for the
discontented revolutionists, who could find room for

[67] See Henry Adams's account of Godoy's relation to this action and of his
loss of power under French influence (*History of the United States*, I, 350-351).
[68] See his letter to Lord Lansdowne, 1795, in *Revue d'Histoire Diplomatique*,
III, 64-77, and his *Memoir concerning the Commercial Relations of the United
States with England, etc.* (London, 1806). The French original I have not seen
(*Recueil des Mémoires de l'Institut*, 1st Series, II, 1799). Cf. Talleyrand's
Memoirs (New York, 1891), I, 188.

Public Record Office, America, XVIII (containing Liston's correspondence on
the subject); *Report on Canadian Archives, 1891*, "Upper Canada," 71, 77, and
"Lower Canada," 149 *et passim; Michigan Pioneer Collections*, XXIV, 666,
XXV, 27; *Massachusetts Historical Collections*, Sixth Series, VIII, 44 *et passim*
(Pickering Papers); Upham's *Pickering*; Gibbs, *Memoirs of the Administra-
tions of Washington and Adams*, I, 474 *et passim*; Roosevelt, *Winning of the
West*, I, p. xi (citing the Blount MSS., sent him by the Honorable W. D.
Stephens, of Los Angeles, California), IV, 212 and index, *s.v.* Blount; M. J.
Wright, *Life and Services of William Blount*; Riley, "Spanish Policy in Mis-
sissippi after the Treaty of San Lorenzo," in *Report of American Historical
Association, 1897*, p. 177; Hinsdale, "Southern Boundary of the United States,"

[176]

their energies in building up the New World.[69] It was his policy to play with the American representatives, refusing to deal with them except informally through agents, and, while detaining them, to negotiate with Spain for Louisiana. These so-called X. Y. Z. negotiations extended till the spring of 1798, when Marshall and Pinckney, outraged by demands for bribes and hopeless of results, left Paris. Gerry, deluded by Talleyrand, remained to keep the peace, and while the adroit diplomat deceived Gerry, he instructed Guillemardet, his minister at Madrid, to make Spain realize that that government had been blind to its interests in putting the United States into possession of the Mississippi forts; they meant, he declared, to rule alone in America, and to influence Europe. No other means existed for putting an end to their ambition than that of "shutting them up within the limits which Nature seems to have traced for them." There can be little

[69] There were many French travelers who visited the United States and described the Mississippi Valley between 1790 and 1803. See *Report of American Historical Association, 1903,* II (introduction). In 1798 Dupont de Nemours and some other French philosophers, a delegation from the National Institute, had applied through Sir Joseph Banks for passports from the English government, the Directory having given them passports to go to the United States with a view to improve and extend the sciences. Mr. King, the American minister, wrote that he understood that the object of the mission was to form an establishment high up the Mississippi, out of the limits of the United States, and within the boundaries of Spain. President Adams agreed with Mr. King that no encouragement should be given to this mission. Adams, *Works,* VIII, 596. The possible connection with the political designs of France is obvious. Compare Michaux's Journal (Thwaites, *Early Western Travels,* III, 53, 89, 90).

ibid., 1893, p. 331; Gayarré, *History of Louisiana,* III; Marbois, *History of Louisiana* (1830), pp. 163-165; Winsor, *Westward Movement,* pp. 561-573.

General George Rogers Clark, of Kentucky, wrote on March 2, 1797, to his old companion in the Genet expedition, Colonel Fulton, then in the service of the Directory of France: "We have here English agents from Canada to enrol volunteers destined to march against Louisiana. Some days ago I received propositions from the governor of Canada to march at the head of two thousand men against the Spanish establishments of New Mexico." The plan, he explains, was to occupy St. Louis, then to divide the army; one party would descend the Mississippi and the other march upon Santa Fe. Terrage, *Les Dernières Années de la Louisiane Française,* pp. 362-363.

doubt that Talleyrand intended the Alleghenies by this expression. France, he argued, if placed in possession of Louisiana and Florida, would be a "wall of brass forever impenetrable to the combined efforts of England and America." [70] In a memoir of July 10, 1798, Talleyrand reported to the Directory the yielding spirit of Spain and her increasing favor toward the plan of having French troops, rather than Spanish, meet the expected invasion of Louisiana by England and the United States. In the course of a discussion of the policy to be adopted toward Portugal, the minister proposed an exchange of some of the provinces of that country for Louisiana. [71] Thus Talleyrand increased his aggressive policy toward the Spanish peninsula and Spain's North American dependencies immediately after the retirement of Godoy and contemporaneously with the policy of deceiving the United States into inactivity. Spain and her provinces bid fair to become appanages of France.

The situation led Pitt to consider again the proposition[72] to revolutionize Spanish America, with the coöperation of the United States. Again Miranda raised the veil of the future and summoned England and the United States to give freedom to the colonies

[70] H. Adams, *History of the United States*, I, 355 ff.
[71] Pallain, *Le Ministère de Talleyrand sous le Directoire*, p. 312.
[72] *Atlantic Monthly*, XCIII, 815. The dispatches of the American minister to England, Rufus King, during the early months of 1798 show that Grenville and Pitt seriously contemplated freeing the Spanish-American colonies by joint operations on the part of England and the United States, in case Spain fell completely under French control. King embraced the project eagerly. Hamilton's connection with the matter, as effective head of the American army, is an interesting feature. The episode has its importance for the present discussion, in showing how closely Spanish-American matters were involved in the Louisiana question; how certain it was that the United States would be involved in the European alliances so long as the fate of the Mississippi Valley was uncertain; and how Jefferson's project of combining with England, in case France occupied New Orleans, was prefigured in this Federalist negotiation. See King, *Correspondence*, II, 278, 283, 305, 367, 392, 453, 454, 511, 519, 650, 654, 657. The works of Adams and Hamilton should also be consulted.

of Spain, complete the passage of the Isthmus of
Panama by a waterway, and enter into the commerce of
the New World. But John Adams proved stubborn in
his refusal. Pitt finally determined to await events and
see whether Spain could resist incorporation in the
French power.

So it was that Napoleon found Louisiana ripe for the
picking in 1800. His plan of taking possession was on
the same lines as were the plans of those who guided
the Louisiana policy of France before him. In his
instructions to the captain general[73] in 1802, he referred
to the fact that as the mistress of both banks of the
Mississippi at its mouth, France held the key to its
navigation—a matter of the highest importance to the
Western states. "Whatever may be the events which
this new part of the continent has to expect, the arrival
of the French forces should be marked there by the
expression of sentiments of great benevolence for these
new neighbors." These were not reassuring words! But
the rest was more alarming: "A little local experience
will soon enable you to discern the sentiments of the
western provinces of the Federal Government. It will
be well to maintain sources of intelligence in that country, whose numerous, warlike, and sober population
may present you a redoubtable enemy. The inhabitants
of Kentucky especially should fix the attention of the
captain-general. . . . He must also fortify himself
against them by alliance with the Indian nations scattered to the east of the river."

It is reasonably clear that Napoleon's policy
resembled that of Vergennes. He would intrigue with
the Westerners, use the control of the navigation to

[73] H. Adams, *History of the United States*, II, 8, 9.

influence them, make of the Indians a barrier, and
gradually widen the borders of his province until the
Gulf of Mexico should be a French lake, and perhaps
the Alleghenies the boundary of the United States.
Lord Hawkesbury, the English minister of foreign affairs, saw the danger and warned Rufus King in 1801
that "the acquisition might enable France to extend her
influence and perhaps her dominion up the Mississippi
and through the Great Lakes, even to Canada. This
would be realizing the plan, to prevent the accomplishment of which the Seven Years' War took place."

But Lord Hawkesbury saw it no more clearly than
did Thomas Jefferson, who had turned his attention to
the West ever since he encouraged George Rogers Clark
to go forth from Virginia and conquer the Illinois country in the Revolution. He had learned the truth that
the possession of New Orleans by any European power
meant that the United States would essentially be a
part of Europe. "The day that France takes possession
of New Orleans," he wrote,[74] "fixes the sentence which
is to restrain her forever within her low-water mark.
It seals the union of two nations, who, in conjunction,
can maintain exclusive possession of the ocean. From
that moment, we must marry ourselves to the British
fleet and nation. We must turn all our attention to a
maritime force, for which our resources place us on
very high ground; and having formed and connected
together a power which may render reinforcement of
her settlements here impossible to France, make the
first cannon which shall be fired in Europe the signal
for the tearing up any settlement she may have made,
and for holding the two continents of America in

[74] Jefferson's *Works* (ed. H. A. Washington, 1853-1854), IV, 432.

sequestration for the common purposes of the United British and American nations." [75]

It is evident that the policy of Vergennes found supporters in the subsequent French governments. Even under the Bourbons, De Moustier, the minister to the United States, urged the reacquisition of Louisiana. In the beginning of the French Revolution, the French government first proposed to unite with England in dividing Spanish America, and then the Girondists sent Genet to conquer Louisiana and the Floridas by the aid of the trans-Allegheny settlers. His successor urged the recovery of the province by diplomacy, and France made strenuous efforts, at Basel in 1795 and in the negotiations over alliance with Spain under the Directory in 1796, to procure its restitution. Her military expert advised an Allegheny frontier for Louisiana, and, as the prospect of war between France and the United States grew imminent, in 1796 the republic renewed the commissions of George Rogers Clark and other Americans and expected aid from the frontiersmen. From that time until Napoleon's power reduced Spain to essential vassalage and forced the cession of Louisiana, hardly a year elapsed in which France did not make an effort to secure that province and the Floridas. She proposed to use the ascendency which she would

[75] When the French minister, Adet, was striving to secure the election of Jefferson to the presidency in 1796, he reported to his government this estimate of Jefferson's character: "I do not know whether, as I am told, we will always find in him a man entirely devoted to our interests. Mr. Jefferson likes us because he detests England; he seeks to unite with us because he suspects us less than Great Britain, but he would change his sentiments toward us to-morrow, perhaps, if to-morrow Great Britain ceased to inspire him with fear. Jefferson, although a friend of liberty and the sciences, although an admirer of the efforts which we have made to break our chains and dissipate the cloud of ignorance which weighs upon mankind, Jefferson, I say, is an American, and, by that title, it is impossible for him to be sincerely our friend. An American is the born enemy of European peoples." (Adet's dispatch of 1796, *Report of American Historical Association, 1903*, II.)

POLICY OF FRANCE

possess over the river and the gulf to force the United States to become her servile ally, or to lose the West by reason of French pressure upon the frontiersmen. The language of Talleyrand indicates his belief that the Alleghenies were the natural boundary for the United States. Napoleon's Louisiana policy was, therefore, simply the continuation of a long series of consistent attempts by the French government.

Through the whole period, France relied upon the friendship of the frontiersmen and upon negotiations with the "independent Indian tribes" of the Southwest to further her plans for dominating the trans-Allegheny region.

The real question at issue was whether the control of the entire Mississippi Valley and the Gulf of Mexico should fall to France, England, or the United States. In view of Spain's decline, the fate of Spanish America hinged upon the decision. The contest abundantly illustrates the fact that a river is not a barrier, and consequently not a permanent boundary. No one who has studied the evidence of long-continued menace to the connection of the West with the rest of the United States made by the Alleghenies[76] prior to the railroads, can doubt that the danger was a real one, and that a European power might have arisen along the Mississippi Valley and the Gulf of Mexico, dominating the interior by its naval force, and checking, if not preventing, the destiny of the United States as the arbiter of North America and the protector of an American system for the New World.

[76] This danger was increased, owing to the indifference, and, at times, the antagonism, of the Northeastern commercial section to the trans-Allegheny lands.

CHAPTER VI

GEOGRAPHICAL INFLUENCES IN AMERICAN
POLITICAL HISTORY [1]

The frontier[2] and the section[3] are two of the most
fundamental factors in American history. The frontier
is a moving section, or rather a form of society,
determined by the reactions between the wilderness and
the edge of expanding settlement; the section is the
outcome of the deeper-seated geographical conditions
interacting with the stock which settled the region. Sections are more important than states in shaping the
underlying forces of American history.

The economic, political, and social life of the United
States, even its literature, psychology, and its religious
organizations, must be described by sections; there is a
geography of public opinion. In spite of similarity of
traits and institutions throughout the nation, it is also a
congeries of sections. Political leaders usually gain a
national position by first convincing their own section,
expressing, as well as leading, its ideals and wishes, and
then combining it with other sections, under political
adjustments.

Political sectionalism exhibits itself most obviously:

[1] Abstract of an address before the joint meeting of the American Geographical Society and the Association of American Geographers, in New York,
on April 4, 1914. Reprinted by permission from the *Bulletin of the American
Geographical Society,* Vol. XLVI, No. 8, 1914.

[2] F. J. Turner, "Significance of the Frontier in American History," *Report
of American Historical Association, 1893,* p. 199. Reprinted in *The Frontier in
American History.*

[3] See chapter II. See also the author's articles on "Frontier" and "Sectionalism" in Hart and McLaughlin (editors), *Cyclopedia of American Government* (1914).

1. In a group of states contending with other groups, or with the nation, as in the case of North against South, West against East, or the Northeastern group of Federal states against the rest of the nation. Such a grouping by states, however, conceals interior divisions and needs further analysis.

2. A sectionalism by congressional districts, not confined within state lines, is exhibited by mapping votes in Congress, attributing to the district the views of its representative in the House. Such maps of votes show that party voting is often subordinated to sectional voting; the sections reflect the influence of physical geography as well as of other factors. This method of exhibiting geographical influence is limited by the frequency of the cases where the congressman does not fairly represent the mass of his constituents, as well as by the size of the congressional districts, and by the practice of "gerrymandering" the districts in order to gain a party advantage.

3. By mapping presidential and state elections, using towns or counties as the unit, a closer approximation to the geography of political areas is possible. Such maps show more clearly the geographical influence, and in greater detail. They disclose the fact that there are both interstate and intrastate party areas persisting in some cases for many decades or even generations and having clear relations to natural geographic factors. But the county itself is too large an area to tell the whole story. It often lies athwart diverse geographical areas, and has diverse economic and social groups within it.

4. The final refinement of such mapping would be by election precincts, which would be a much more satis-

factory mode of exhibiting the relations of voting to soils, resources, position, population, etc. But at present this has been insufficiently carried out.

Limitations of the method must be noted. The existence of a minority is concealed, though the vote may be close. Great political changes may occur, where a mere plurality is the test, without materially altering the appearance of maps based on county units, inasmuch as the size of the plurality is not recorded; the city in one corner of a state or a county may outweigh all the varied sections of the rest of the state; even the bulk of a party vote may theoretically lie in the areas not depicted as the areas of this party. Moreover, parties are held together by combining various issues in order to hold dissenting elements, and by stating issues ambiguously; platform and candidate are also sometimes inconsistent. Thus the issue for which a geographical interpretation is sought may be confused, if the question is one of political opinion rather than of party habit.

The method, therefore, has its special value in revealing the party inertia of geographical areas rather than in its use for the natural history of political parties, as organizations, though it is also useful in this respect. By mapping votes by percentages, as in the presidential election of 1880, mapped in *Scribner's Statistical Atlas,* many of these objections may be met. Such a system, however, confirms the general correctness of the coarser reconnaissance system of mapping by pluralities, used in illustration of the present paper. Areas of transition and of political instability are brought out more clearly by percentage mapping, but the more durable and pronounced political areas remain substantially the same under both systems. In other respects, also, the limitations noted in theory are not so important in practice as they might seem.

Conceding the limitations of the method, it nevertheless reveals a most significant geographical influence in American political history, which needs further study.[4] The series of maps illustrating the various modes of mapping described above, show that geographical influence exists both in regard to the groups by states and in groups by lesser units. Refinement of the mapping discloses increasingly the importance of the geographical factor. Groups of states, like the New England-New York Federalist group, tend to reappear whenever issues reappear affecting the interests of capital, as in the election of 1828, the Bland-Allison Act of 1878, and the Gold Democrats of the Chicago Convention of 1896. The areas mapped by congressional districts also show marked persistence and relationship to lines of communication and centers of capital.

In the mapping of presidential elections by county pluralities from 1836 to the present, the most obvious distribution is into Northern and Southern political zones, with ragged, intermingling edges. But this fails to

[4] The studies of political geography which were begun in the author's seminary in American history with a paper by Orin G. Libby, now professor in the University of North Dakota, in 1894, on "The Distribution of the Vote on the Ratification of the Federal Constitution," have been continued since by my students and myself. More recently the Carnegie Institution has undertaken the publication of an atlas of American history, in which the method of mapping votes will be used. The writer has not had the advantage of consulting this work as yet, and the present study is in the nature of a reconnaissance paper. For studies of state sectionalism see lists in *Turner Essays in American History*, p. 207; A. W. Small, *General Sociology*, pp. 282-3, note; C. A. Beard, *Economic Interpretation of the Constitution*, p. 5. See also W. E. Dodd, "Fight for the Northwest," *American Historical Review*, Vol. XVI, p. 788, map; Boyd, "Antecedents of the North Carolina Convention of 1835," *South Atlantic Quarterly*, January and April, 1910; J. A. Morgan, "State Aid to Transportation in North Carolina," *N. C. Booklet*, Jan., 1911; F. H. Giddings, "Conduct of Political Majorities," *Political Science Quarterly*, Vol. XVI, p. 116.

reveal fundamental differences between the Eastern and Western wings of the various parties, held together by an unstable party alliance. Composite maps exhibiting state elections about 1800 and 1830, indicate the importance of this difference between Eastern and Western areas at different early periods. It is also clearly shown in recent political history.

The Northern area, which tended to be, first, Federalist, then Whig, and then Republican, is broken by groups of opposition counties, chiefly in interior regions. The strength of the Whig-Republican area is along such lines of communication and industry as the Great Lakes, the Potomac, and the upper Ohio. It is strongest, generally, along the routes of capital, commerce, industrial energy, and density of population, with frequent exception of the great cities, where class voting modifies the rule. Even in the city, however, bipartisan organizations tend to make party lines conceal a real identity with the geographic distribution above noted.

This Whig-Republican Northern zone was deeply influenced by the distribution of the descendants of New England stock (including the later generations of central and western New York), who occupied the shores of the Great Lakes—particularly in western New York, the "triangle" in northwestern Pennsylvania, the Western Reserve in Ohio, and in parts of Michigan—and the prairie regions of southern Wisconsin, northern Illinois, and part of Iowa, Kansas, and Nebraska. Here the persistence of feelings aroused by the issues of the Civil War is also noteworthy.

The Democratic areas in the Northern Zone give distinct evidence of the location of the Southern Upland settlers who came to the forested area, before the New

GEOGRAPHICAL INFLUENCES

York-New England settlers. Here factors of social origin coincided with geographical influences proper. These persistent political groups appear in a series of maps of elections in Ohio, Indiana, and Illinois, between 1828 and 1908. For example, the counties bounded by the lines of the Western Reserve on Lake Erie normally vote in the same way, year after year. In Indiana the political grouping is in persistent vertical tiers of counties. In Illinois a map of party grouping looks like a map of the original forest and prairie areas, with the glacial lobe extending from Lake Michigan clearly visible.[5] In eastern Wisconsin and in the Illinois counties adjacent to St. Louis, the German area emerges— in the former as a group of Democratic counties in a Republican region, whenever special issues call it forth; and in the latter regularly as a group of Whig or Republican counties in a Democratic area.

In the Lower South from 1836 to about 1850 (when the slavery issue blurred the old divisions), the Whig and Democratic areas are strikingly reflective of geological formations. By combining the results of the presidential elections of 1836 to 1848, inclusive, to show how pluralities were distributed in three or all of these four elections, it appears that the Whig area was practically identical with the chief cotton-raising counties, and that the most important Whig counties were in the belt where the negro was nearly or quite the majority of the population. Of the counties within the Black Belt (i.e., where the negroes were an actual majority of the population), the Democrats carried but two in

[5] Compare E. B. Greene, "Sectional Forces in the History of Illinois," *Transactions of Illinois Historical Society*, 1903, p. 75; H. H. Barrows, *Middle Illinois Valley*; A. Shaw, *Local Government in Illinois*; J. P. Goode, *Geography of Illinois*.

Georgia, three in Alabama, and four in Mississippi, in three-fourths of these elections. Outside of the chief cotton counties, the Whigs carried few counties in the same states. The Democratic counties in the same states for this period were almost entirely in the regions of inferior soils.

More particularly, the Whig counties occupied the best cotton soils of eastern and central Georgia (the majorities becoming weaker or vanishing in the Pine Hills strip running through the Cotton Belt). They were located in that part of Alabama known as the Inner Lowlands, bounded on the south by the cuesta (especially by the Chunnemugga Ridge), and on the north by the Pine Hills and the Tuscaloosa strata. The Whig belt, resting on this intermediate strip of calcareous black prairie, swings northwestwardly into the closely divided Whig and Democratic counties at the eastern edge of Mississippi. The alluvial belts along some of the rivers, and the limestone area of the Tennessee in northern Alabama, supplement this central cotton belt, but in northern Alabama the Democratic influence is the stronger. In Mississippi the Whig counties are largely confined to the alluvial zone adjacent to the Mississippi River, and adjacent counties. Tennessee's three natural geographical areas find marked reflections in the political map of these four elections, the Whig areas being the cotton counties of the west (adjacent to the Mississippi), the limestone island of middle Tennessee, and the counties in the fertile valleys of eastern Tennessee. The Democratic counties, with rare exceptions, were the less fertile, rocky soils bounding these Whig areas. The geographical influence becomes clearer the farther this analysis

[189]

is refined in each of these main areas.

These divisions of the Lower South,[6] obliterated in large measure in the era of civil war and reconstruction and in the later Solid South under the influence of the negro problem, still tend to reveal their outlines when tested by mapping minorities and by primary elections in which the negro issue is eliminated. This distribution has also its social aspect, inasmuch as when the area was settled, in the bidding for the best cotton lands the wealthier slaveholder excluded the non-slaveholding white, whom economic considerations, and in part his tendencies as a pioneer farmer, turned to the upcountry and the sand barrens. The Whig aristocracy naturally supported the banking policy of its party, inasmuch as property and the credit needed in their cotton planting were basal in their economy. In Kentucky, conditions existed comparable to those in Tennessee, and a similar analysis is possible for other parts of the South.

In the Southern Appalachian area, similar composite maps for both the Whig and the Republican period, from 1836 to 1908, show that the Whig area was strongest on the lines of communication, and in the bottom lands, while the Democrats were strongest in the upper country. The Republican area shows continuous extension along the Southern Appalachians, becoming a wedge thrust down into the South from Pennsylvania. It is made up only in part of former Whig areas, for it tends to include normally the "white" counties above the thousand-foot contour, as well as the lines of communication.

[6] See also U. B. Phillips, "Southern Whigs," in *Turner Essays in American History*, pp. 209, 214-215.

Many minor geographical aspects might be noted, such as the tendency of the area of the Dismal Swamp canal to go with the Northern parties; the persistent trough of Federalists and Whigs running to the interior of North Carolina diagonally from the coast; the efforts of the Tennessee River to assert its presence again and again by showing Whig and, later, Republican counties along its course.

In recent political struggles between West and East, the relations of Grangers to the prairie, wheat-raising areas, and of the Populists to the later wheat- and silver-producing areas, are significant. The factors of declining prices of crops, mortgaged farms, appreciating gold and declining silver values as the silver mines were exploited, coincide with transportation problems to produce significant reactions between geography and political history; and these factors are significantly emphasized both by the study of the section made up of groups of states and by the closer analysis of counties.[7]

Perhaps the most fundamental generalization is that there are areas influenced or controlled by geological factors wherein capitalistic considerations are strongest, and that such areas tend to be Whig and, later, Republican. These capitalistic basins, and the conduits of communication between them, show increasing tendency to gain at the expense of the intermediate regions less favored by geographical advantages.

Such a generalization is subject to exceptions; there is not absolute geographical control; social or psycho-

[7] See, for example, O. G. Libby, "Study of the Greenback Movement," *Wisconsin Academy Transactions*, Vol. XII, p. 530; C. O. Ruggles, "Economic Basis of the Greenback Movement," *Proceedings of the Mississippi Valley Historical Association*, 1912-1913, p. 143; S. J. Buck, *Granger Movement* (maps); E. E. Robinson, "Recent Manifestations of Sectionalism," *American Journal of Sociology*, Vol. XIX, p. 446.

logical considerations sometimes reverse the result. But there is in each state a normal antagonism between certain sections, on whichever side they take their party stand. As a further consideration it is important to repeat that interstate migration has tended to distribute such groups of settlers as those of New England ancestry, and those of Southern Upland ancestry, in special geological provinces. Party inertia is as fundamental as any one factor in determining the result.

The problem resembles that of a complex geological area and demands the use of the multiple hypothesis. Where there are so many possible factors for use in interpretation, it is possible to select with unconscious prejudice and so reach unscientific conclusions.

But, whatever the difficulties of interpretation, the main thesis, that there is a geography of American politics and that the relation between geography and political history becomes clearer the farther the method of investigation is refined, seems established. The facts demand combined investigation by geographer and historian.

CHAPTER VII

GEOGRAPHIC SECTIONALISM IN AMERICAN HISTORY [1]

Sectionalism in American history has been so commonly conceived of by historians as the struggle between North and South over slavery, that the much more complicated sectionalism, involving all the various geographic provinces of the United States and the regions within them, and exhibiting itself in economic, political, and cultural fields, has been neglected. But, as it is fundamental to an understanding of America, and of particular interest to the human geographer, I venture to present here some analysis of the subject from the point of view of the historian. As the years go on and the United States becomes a settled nation, regional geography is certain to demand at least the same degree of attention here as in Europe. The United States being practically as large as all of Europe, it must be thought of in continental, and not merely in national, terms. Our sections constitute the American analogue of European nations. In their normal relations with each other, economically, politically, and socially, we find startling resemblances to the international processes of European history, except for the appeal to arms. But these phenomena have been concealed by the disproportionate attention to federal legislation, to state legislation, and to political parties, without digging beneath the surface.

[1] Reprinted by permission from *Annals of the Association of American Geographers,* June, 1926.

[193]

As soon as we cease to be dominated by the political map, divided into rectangular states, and by the form of the Constitution in contrast with the actualities, groups of states and geographic provinces, rather than individual states, press upon the historian's attention. John Taylor of Caroline, senator from Virginia in the early days of our government, urged state sovereignty as the best means of preventing Congress from becoming an assembly of geographical envoys from the great sections; but in fact there was hardly a case of the serious assertion of state sovereignty except where sectional coöperation gave it force, and there [were] various examples of its collapse as a threat when the section in which the state lay refused concurrence. Before his death, Calhoun, the political philosopher of state sovereignty, learned this lesson by heart.

Of course the federal system and the state governments are very real things themselves, and cannot be ignored. Even in intersectional relations the constitutional structure is influential, in view of the equal representation of states in the Senate and, in part, in the electoral college and in national party conventions. Inasmuch as this feature of the Constitution operates to give certain groups of states a sectional power beyond that to which population or property and income-tax payments would entitle them, it has particular significance in the adjustment of balance of power in legislation and in party. Thus the eleven states, large in area, which extend from the western boundary of Michigan across to the Pacific on the northwest—a distance further than from Paris to Constantinople—have only about fourteen million people, while New York alone has over eleven million, and New York and Pennsylvania together have about twenty and one-half million. Of the taxes levied on personal incomes by the federal government in 1922, New York and Pennsylvania together paid ten times those paid by this Northwestern zone. And yet New York and Pennsylvania have but four members of the Senate, while these eleven states have twenty-two. In view of bills providing for expenditure of revenue in the United States as a whole, and for tax rates, it is obvious that here is a situation certain to create sectional antagonisms. This is emphasized by the difference in interests and in social ideals between the two regions. Owing to the facts that New England frequently acts in conjunction with New York, and that the six states of New England have twelve senators, most of them from small states, the sectional disparity is measurably alleviated.

The larger outlines of the sectional picture may be rapidly drawn. In the colonial era, in the seventeenth century, physiography and the different colonizing peoples, each with distinctive psychological traits, produced the three well-known sections, New England, the Middle Region, and the South. Toward the close of that century and especially in the middle of the next, publicists began to speak of the desirability of embodying these sections politically. Indeed, the New England Confederation, and later the "Dominion of New England," illustrate this aspect, though they both had but a brief existence. When the Plan of Union was considered in the Albany Congress of 1754, and again when the Constitutional Convention of 1787 discussed the terms of union, three groups of colonies were seriously considered as factors in a new government or as substitutes for a single government. One of John

Jay's ablest papers in the *Federalist* had to do with the dangers that would follow a division into sectional unions, both with regard to foreign interference and in respect to domestic peace. From the first, also, there were subdivisions in these colonial sections, corresponding in considerable measure to the geographic regions of the physiographer, which complicated sectional policy and made the exact boundaries between sections hard to draw. The Middle Region, mixed in its stocks, in its institutions, economic life, religions, just as it was in its geologic provinces, was a bone of contention between the Southern and the Eastern colonies.

Toward the end of the first century of colonial life, this aspect of sectionalism became complicated by the frontier advance. First, by the development of a sectionalism of the coastal area as a whole and of the evolving West. There was, in the first half of the eighteenth century, the occupation of what I have called the Old West. In interior and northern New England, central and western New York and Pennsylvania, and in the Piedmont region of the South, the contact with the wilderness produced a frontier society, and later a more developed Western type of society which made a sharp contrast with the East. This became a migratory sectionalism of West against East; the rule of the majority against minority rights in their vested interests, and property; innovation against conservatism; debtors against creditors. It went on until, not only the frontier *line,* as mapped by Henry Gannett, could no longer be depicted, but until the frontier *phase* of our history drew to its close. From Bacon's Rebellion to the La Follette revolt, there are almost continuous manifestations of the sectional contests of East and West, of the frontier and the older areas.

But, second, for many years the three Eastern sections conceived of the West as merely an emanation from themselves, and regarded it as a battle field in the struggle for power between the original sections, the raw material wherewith political and economic, and even religious, preponderance could be built up. On the other hand, the West, almost from the beginning, wherever it lay at the time, thought of itself as an entity, a substantial and separate section in the Union, and as destined to rule the nation in the future.

Third, this frontier advance was not into uniform space, but into a series of geographic regions which progressively opened to the pioneer. Potentially, they were the equivalents of European nations in area, in variety, and in resources. One by one these provinces were discovered, conquered, settled, and exploited or developed. Into these regional areas were poured the various colonizing stocks. The settlers and the Eastern capitalists transformed the wilderness, but in the very process they were themselves transformed by the conditions with which they dealt. Whether by adjusting to the environment or by the kind of labor and thought involved in modifying it, the process of pioneering created new societies, new sections. New England in central and western New York was not the New England from which the settlers came. The Yankees of the Middle West were not the Yankees of their old homeland. The South Central Southerner was not the same as the tidewater Southerner.

And, fourth, as the frontier advance drew to a close, as these provinces were no longer regions to be crossed, or merely to be exploited, but home-sections of perma-

nent settlers, the final stage was reached. These
sections and regions, like the older ones, became self-
conscious, in politics, in economic life, in literature.
Mural paintings in the newer, as in the older, provinces;
sectional historical pageantry; the marking of trails;
local-color fiction and poetry; the circulation of newspapers; the gathering of sectional societies, in all the
fields of human activity—such indications of self-
conscious sections revealed a new era. The nation is
now in reality rather a federation of sections than a
federation of states. In a sense, therefore, there was
compressed into the relatively brief time of two or three
centuries in America, something very like that process
of nation-building which had occupied ages in Europe.
Before the geographer and the historian, and the allied
social scientist, lies the opportunity to study these reactions between nature and man, with ample documenta-
tion and with much of the process under our very eyes.

Today there are clear evidences that these varied
sections are attempting to express themselves institu-
tionally and administratively, that American geography
is demanding recognition of itself governmentally.

First, I may mention less formal revelations of geographic sectionalism. Votes in Congress reveal a steady
trend toward *blocs* or sectional alliances, made up of
a discontented wing of the dominant party with the
opposite minority party, such as the farmers' *bloc*—a
combination of the West and North Central States,
together with the Democratic South. This, however, is
far from being a new thing, though it has gained a new
name.

Again and again, throughout our political history,
there have been a breakdown of party voting and these

alliances between regional groups regardless of party affiliations. Calhoun's whole political career shows a desire to use a sectional balance of power and to combine the West with the South. Van Buren would have an *entente cordial* between the plain republicans of the Middle Region and the planters of the South led by Virginia. Henry Clay and John Quincy Adams would join the Northern zone of the Ohio Valley and the North Atlantic. Benton wished to hold the West to a position where, as its political power increased with the admission of new states and with the growth of population, it should be "bid for," as he said, by the older sections. All of these statesmen consciously recognized that a struggle was going on between all sections, and that their task as statesmen was to find a formula which should unite a sufficient number of sections to carry out a program by combination of interests.

Presidents had felt obliged to warn their countrymen against the dangers of geographic sectionalism. Read the Farewell Messages of Washington and Jackson, the utterances of Wilson and Harding, for illustrations. In the Whig platform of 1856 appears this plank: "*Resolved,* That the government of the United States was formed by the conjunction in political unity of widespread geographical sections, materially differing not only in climate and products, but in social and domestic institutions; and that any cause that shall permanently array the different sections of the Union in political hostility and organized parties, founded only on geographical distinctions, must inevitably prove fatal to a continuance of the national Union."

But all these historic examples are perhaps less significant of geographic sectionalism than the present-day steps toward sectional integration. I may mention the attempts to procure united action of the interior in behalf of the so-called "frustrated seaway" of the Great Lakes-St. Lawrence deep-water route to the ocean. "Upon the map of economic divides indicated by geography—the Atlantic seaboard, the Gulf territory, and the Pacific slope—there is, as it were," runs the argument, "an economic desert a thousand miles east and west, five hundred miles north and south beyond the radius of logical rail haul to either coast." And now this interior sectional complaint, not without implied threats, has won President Coolidge's assent for the project of the Great Lakes-Gulf of Mexico waterway. For my purpose it is not necessary to pass upon the economic profitability of such sectional demands. To New England it has seemed like destruction of its industrial power. To New York the choice of the St. Lawrence waterway looks like placing the Great Lakes basin at the mercy of England, unless the route runs by way of the Erie Canal. To Chicago, as expressed in one of this section's leading dailies, the refusal of Congress and the government to meet the wishes of that metropolis in such matters as the drainage canal, seems to demand that the entire Mississippi Valley "rise in revolt against a tyranny which now threatens its very existence." "Our Middle Western agents," is what this paper calls the section's congressmen.

New England shows quite as vigorous sectional tendencies. The Boston press has long been accustomed to urge the section to act as a unit, and to point out that state lines are really artificial and no real barriers.

More recently the papers have announced what one of the periodicals dubs "A League of New England States"—a New England States commission of seventy-two members, twelve from each state, with an annual conference.

Of course the unity of the Pacific Coast is exhibited whenever the Oriental question arises, as is the solidity of the South when the race question, in the form of the negro, is raised.

But, going further, there is in progress a movement of legal integration of geographic sections—a possible equipment of new units for federal government in the form of groups of states. Recently the *Yale Law Journal* (May, 1925) published an article by Professor Felix Frankfurter, of the Harvard Law School, which ably sets forth the legal aspects of the application of the Compact Clause of the Constitution as a phase of interstate adjustments. State compacts have included boundary agreements, state-debt agreements, compacts over navigable waters, over drainage and irrigation basins, over criminal jurisdiction, control of floods, fishing, tunnels, etc. More recently there are the Colorado River Compact of 1921, between seven states, regarding the equitable apportionment of the waters of the Colorado River; the New York-New Jersey ports agreement of the same year; the Columbia River Compact of 1925; and the proposed Delaware River compact, between Pennsylvania, New Jersey, and New York, in which the disposal of sewage, hydraulic construction, and a supervising administrative agency are involved.

As the plans for coördinating hydroelectric power plants within different sections are formulated, the realization becomes increasingly keen that the states must be tied into groups for effective action in this field, which may conceivably become an important instrument in reshaping America's legislative and administrative units. Regional solution of problems by use of the Compact Clause of the Constitution, which permits state agreements by consent of Congress, will probably be invoked in the development of what has been called super-power systems and electrical giant power combinations. The problem of interstate arrangement, regarding power, not long ago engaged the correspondence of Governor Smith, of New York, on behalf of her water power, and Governor Pinchot, of Pennsylvania, regarding her coal fields. Secretary Hoover, who was influential in procuring the Colorado Compact, believes that the United States will be divided into several power areas: New England and the Mid-Atlantic states, the area from the Mississippi River to the Alleghenies, the South Atlantic, the lower South Central, and the North Central States—each with separate problems, unsuited to federal legislation, either by the actual conditions or by constitutional limitations.

In these important new power developments, state machinery can provide for local regulation, and there can be general federal oversight; but there is needed a new sectional, regional provision for coördination in groups of states, each presenting distinct problems. For such governmental machinery the way is now preparing through sectional councils, like that of New England, and sectional agreements, such as these under the Compact Clause, with national consent through Congress. A new governmental organization appears to be evolving, not by theory, but by the pressure of solid geographic realities, and by economic interests, peacefully preparing the way for recognition of the geographic section as an integral part of the national machinery. The regional arrangement of the Federal Reserve Bank; the proposed regional consolidation and administration of the railroad systems; the regional analysis of census statistics—all add to the same conclusion.

Does this indicate a dissolution of the Union? Are we to become another Europe? Are sections to evolve into nations? I do not think so. While we are becoming conscious of our sections, Europe is attempting to bind her nations into a league. We have become aware of the reality of the geographic region in our political, as in our economic and cultural, life, and Europe is now becoming aware of the need of bringing within a single political organization the interdependent nations that make up that continent. The *Pax Americana* is not without its influence upon the war-torn continent of the Old World.

Not only is there this world tendency toward integration, with preservation of autonomy, but the United States has found in practice a bond of union which, as yet, Europe does not possess. Rival political parties, national (that is, intersectional) in their scope and following, exist here. As yet, Europe has not acquired international political parties, continental in their scope, as they would have to be to correspond with those of the United States.

In this country there is an interesting geography of party preponderance. Too complicated for statement in brief, in general the situation may be described, geographically, as regional conflicts within such different sections or larger groups of states as the South, or the North Central States. The rough country, the least valuable farm lands, the illiterate counties, tend, by and large, to be Democratic, as do the principal immigrant populations of the greater cities. The favored-soil regions, the least illiterate areas, the most highly capitalized and industrial districts, tend to be anti-Democratic, Federal, Whig, Republican, according to the era. Where there are important exceptions, as along the foothills and ridges of the Carolina mountains, which have been Whig and Republican often, the explanation is usually traceable to historic factors, such as the conflict of the slaveholding Whig coast against the upcountry over legislative apportionment, taxation, internal improvements, and slavery. It was a contest of regions, of economic and social ideals. Physical geography, taken simply, was far from dictating the precise way in which the region acted. The Black Belt in central Georgia and Alabama, and western Mississippi, was strongly Whig, with a small degree of white illiteracy, the abode of wealthy aristocrats. But in the mountain counties of the Carolinas, among the illiterate poor whites, they found political companions in arms. As a rule there were, and are, within each section as classified in the Census Atlas, divergent subdivisions, geographic regions, sometimes running to neighboring sections, or finding allies in similar though isolated regions in other sections. These sections usually show political preponderances (taking the county as the unit) of one or the other party. This is a check upon purely sectional parties, or upon exploitive and ruthless action by the section which controls a major political party. Within each section, moreover, partly due to the regional factor, and partly due to the factors of migration and inherited political faiths, the parties are closely divided. To this, the South since the Civil War is an exception; but the Northern industrial wedge pushed down along the mines, the mills, the hydroelectric powers of the Alleghenies and their foothills, constitutes a menace to Southern solidarity. With these regional varieties, with these close party majorities, there are checks to sectional particularism. Its political power is in a state of unstable equilibrium. It stands in danger of disintegration itself, unless its cause overwhelmingly appeals to its people.

National party, then, has been in America a flexible bond, yielding in extreme cases to sectional insurgency, yielding often, in the construction of bills, to sectional demands and to sectional threats, but always tending to draw sections together toward national adjustments by compromise and bargain. A common language, law, and institutions, absence of sectional concentration of religions and races, absence of historical hatreds, have helped to prevent America from splitting apart and falling into European conditions; but regional geography, quasi-continental parties, and a national, that is, intersectional (our equivalent of international), congressional organization by which sectionalism could express itself in voting instead of by war—these are important factors in the contrast between European and American ways of settling difficulties, and are important explanations of our continued unity.

What is now needed is coöperation between the geographers who have come from geologic training to an interest in the regional aspect of human geography; the statisticians who have aimed to divide the nation into convenient sections for census data; the politicians, economists, and bankers who have tried to map the

Federal Reserve districts; the railroad experts; business
men in general; the historians; the students of literature
and of society—to make a more adequate survey of what
are actually the natural regions in human geography,
as shown by human action. Across the provinces, as
delimited by the geologists and the physiographers,
flowed the migration of men from the seaboard sections,
the later immigrants, the whole flood of social and industrial developments, changing the obvious influences of
physiography—a glacial invasion of humanity, as it
were, modifying but not obliterating the older land-
scape. We need a mapping by human geographers that
shall take account of these factors, in politics, economics, society, literature—in all the social sciences.
Until then, sectional delimitation can only be in the
nature of a reconnoissance, needing refinement.

CHAPTER VIII

SINCE THE FOUNDATION [OF CLARK UNIVERSITY (1889)][1]

Measured by years, the foundation of Clark University is not remote. From 1889 to 1924 is a little over a generation; Dr. Stanley Hall, Clark's first president, still lives and writes robustly and wisely for the present time. Measured by the changes in social conditions in the years between 1889 and the present, all universities are young, and Clark stands among a group of sisters rather than an infant in arms.

Few epochs in history have included such startling changes within a single generation as that between the eighties and the present. It is a hazardous task to attempt to portray the large outlines of a nation's changes and tendencies for the era of the present generation, especially an era of revolutionary changes in the material, political, and social composition of a people. There have been generations of such stationary character that the historian's task in dealing with them is simple if not inspiring. But the very fact that the generation which has passed since Clark University was founded, is one of such complexity and of such extraordinary change that it daunts the historian and almost forbids the attempt, is at the same time a challenge. For unless the American people turn at times from the rushing current of events, to take observations, to look

---

[1] Reprinted by permission from *Publications of the Clark University Library*, February, 1924. Reprinted in *The Historical Outlook*, November, 1924.

to the chart of their course, to measure their progress or decline, and survey its stages, they are not likely to comprehend the direction in which they are going, the meaning of the voyage, or the measures to pursue in the coming years. No one is wise enough, no one is far enough removed from the action, adequately to make this survey. The prepossessions and the prejudices, the survival of old conceptions, the complexity of the problems, are too great. It requires the base line which only coming generations can draw, to measure the full meaning of these recent years and to reckon the things that should have been done and those that should have been undone.

Nevertheless, a generation that does not attempt to consider its recent past is like the merchant who ignores his ledger, the mariner who takes no observations. However imperfect the results, it is necessary that the attitude of mind should be achieved. I have often thought that our New England ancestors who kept diaries as well as ledgers, and who at the year's end made a dead reckoning of their use of the year, their conformity to the will of God, and who planned the coming year, showed not only the Puritan quality, but also revealed the elements of strength which the stock exhibited in its best days.

Let us, then, briefly consider some of the many factors that have appeared in the nation's history in that generation that has passed since this institution of learning and research was born. We are set in a changing world as well as a changing nation. It is manifestly out of the question to attempt, even for so brief a period as has passed since 1889, to comprehend the mighty changes that have come upon this planet. But let us refresh our memories concerning some of the changes which have directly affected our own nation.

When the census of 1890 was taken, our population had reached the middle of the Dakotas, lay like an island around the Black Hills, omitted the sandy lands of northwest Nebraska, swung like a huge lariat around central Colorado and the valleys of the Rio Grande and Pecos in New Mexico, had formed an island in the center of the Indian enclave of Oklahoma, and had advanced in Texas to the western quarter on the meridian of the panhandle. Beyond were the mining camps of the upper Missouri and Columbia waters, and the settled areas of the Pacific Coast. The Mormons of the Great Salt Lake basin constituted another outlying settlement.

Today practically all of the West unoccupied in 1890 has been taken up, except the mountains, the desert, and other lands unsuited to settlement. We have extended our territory to include the Hawaiian crossroads of the Pacific, the Philippines at the edge of Asia, and other strategic islands in the Pacific as well as in the Caribbean Sea, which controls the Isthmian canal. Our population has overflowed into Canada, our capital into Mexico. We have fairly begun the occupation of Alaska, and our aerial navy contemplates the discovery of hoped-for new lands and resources in the regions beyond the Arctic Circle. The era of the Pacific Ocean has begun, with all its problems of new relations with the Oriental world, whose teeming millions also seek new outlets on the shrinking planet.

The population of the Union has grown from sixty-two and one-half millions in 1890 to about one hundred and ten millions today. In 1890 the rural population greatly exceeded the urban; we were still an agricultural commonwealth. Today the urban population exceeds the rural. One-fifth of the population dwell in large cities of over 250,000. New York City proper is larger than all the rest of the state, and its metropolitan district holds eight million souls, or more than all New England—almost as many as all the Mountain States and the Pacific Coast. So great has been the movement from country to city and from east to west that, by the census of 1920, one-third of the counties of the Union had declined in population. By a process of geographical selection the rural areas lost ground. Millions of men changed their state.

Not only did the city gain upon the country, industrialism upon agriculture, but Europe moved into the United States in millions. In the decade of the nineties, over three million, seven hundred thousand immigrants arrived in the United States; over eight millions in the next decade; and over six millions in the following. Between 1887 and 1924 nearly twenty-two million immigrants entered this country—a population which excels that of the states of New England and New York combined, or all the states of the Old Northwest. But there was also a large return movement of Europeans who came here to find wages and food and then went home. If one-third of them returned, this still leaves about fourteen millions, which could more than replace the population which now lives in New England and Ohio combined, or in all the states west of Kansas to the Pacific Ocean, except Texas. The persons of foreign birth and parentage, combined, exceeded the total population of New England, New York, New Jersey, and Delaware in 1920. Since the foundation date of Clark, this immigration has come largely from southern and eastern Europe instead of from northern and western, the source of the old immigration.

If we could imagine this torrent of European immigrants actually expelling the native element in these great regions since this university began at the close of the eighties, we should more keenly comprehend the size of the inundation. To a large extent they swelled the labor population of the North Atlantic industrial centers; congestion aggravated the problem. In New York City proper, with a population of nearly six millions, there are two million foreign-born (or one-third), and over four million (or two-thirds) of "foreign stock." The Jewish Year Book for 1923-1924 estimates that there are one million, six hundred and forty-three thousand Jews in the city, or about twenty-nine per cent of the city proper. In Massachusetts, in 1910, only a third of the population was native white of native parentage, and in that native white was included a large proportion of the descendants of immigrants who had been coming in great numbers ever since the Irish famine—over two generations—and the birth rate of the native stock is lower than that of the alien.

A careful statistician has worked out the estimate that about one-third of the Americans are wholly descended from those who resided here in 1790. If so, the people of the United States are now about one-third of the old native stock, one-third of foreign birth or parentage, and one-third of those who are partly descended from immigrants who arrived in the intermediate period. These proportions are largely due to the mass movements of European peoples into the nation since the middle eighties—the peaceful conquest of the old stock by an international army of workers. The Secretary of Labor reports that, of nearly fourteen million white people of foreign birth, less than half are naturalized citizens. To a disturbing extent they have carried their national self-consciousness with them, interpreted America in terms of Europe, and have tried to impress their Old World conceptions upon the United States. There is a marked tendency among their spokesmen to insist upon the preservation of their racial groups, to resent the ideal of the "melting pot," and to class the older stock as "hyphenated Anglo-Americans." The preëminence of New York City as the center for writers and journals which influence American thought, emphasizes this factor.

Turning from this indication of the extent to which our population has been changed in these years, let us consider some of the changes that invention and science have brought over the nation since the founding of this university. An important group of inventions, made before the eighties, first gained widespread use and general significance in American life after 1889. Many of them related to more effective means of communication, the lessening of the importance of the factor of distance, and the acceleration of business. The perfected typewriter transformed office work, modified literary style, and gave a new outlet for feminism in contact with business through secretarial employment. It would be difficult to estimate the influence of this machine upon the rise of women to activity in the business world, who more often than is realized are the efficient though unknown brains of the office.

By 1890 the telephone had just achieved effective systematization and extension. In 1924 there were between fourteen and fifteen million telephones in the United States—over three-fifths of the world's supply, and about one for every eight persons of the Union. The total expenditures of the Bell System in 1922 were practically the same as the expenditures of the United States government before the World War.

The automobile began to be an occasional sight shortly after Clark was founded. Its manufacture was not reported in the census of 1890, but by 1923 over fourteen millions were registered in the United States, or about as many automobiles as telephones—one for every seven or eight people in the nation. The bicycle had led the way; but the "safety" was just established, the pneumatic tire had just made itself useful in the later eighties, and the gasoline engine for motor vehicles had just been made practical. So rapidly did the automobile supersede these pioneer vehicles that we have almost forgotten the foot-driven bicycle. Our streets are congested with motor cars; street planning and policing have been transformed. Localism has been diminished, rural life deeply changed, and the good-roads movement has worked a revolution in intercourse and recreation. Henry Ford has reached the ranks of the wealthiest men of the world, and Detroit has risen from a city of two hundred thousand in 1890 to nearly a million souls.

The first overhead trolley had just been tried out the year before Clark began. It is unnecessary to say that city life has been profoundly changed by this invention. The automobile has checked, or in places extinguished, its growth in the country; but the city has spread its suburbs and tunnelled under rivers and beneath the great buildings as the trolley, the common people's car, has extended.

Eastman invented the photographic film in 1888, the Kodak became a household instrument, and now, to country as well as to city, the moving picture has brought the weekly news and the scenes of other cities and lands. It has deeply influenced the psychology of youth, for evil as well as for good; but in any case it has added new means for seeing the world and has profoundly modified the simplicity and localism of our life. But the first year of commercial moving-picture-film production was only in 1895.

Even more striking is the rise and spread of the radio. Marconi's first experiments date from 1894, though, as in all these cases of invention, a long period of scientific discoveries prepared the way. Not until 1903 was a complete message sent across the Atlantic. Today men talk through the air between the cities of the United States and those of the Old World. MacMillan in the polar ice of the Arctic hears and sends messages to his friends in New England; the steamships call for aid or chat between themselves and between their ports of departure and arrival. The silence and the loneliness of the ocean have gone; and in remote farmsteads as well as in the great cities, the symphony hall, the preacher's pulpit, the news of ball field, the shouts of the prize ring, the voice of the President of the United States, are brought to the listener's ear. It is estimated that five million radio sets are now in operation. Truly the planet is shrinking.

Emerson wrote in the forties that the world was not yet ready for the flying machine; but by 1903 the Wright brothers conquered the air. Airplanes have crossed the Atlantic, have revolutionized the art of war, transformed the significance of England's island isolation, and rendered it doubtful if the navies of the world and sea power are not obsolete. For we have seen Tennyson's "Vision of the world" come true, and ourselves have

> Heard the heavens fill with shouting, and there rained
> a ghastly dew
> From the nations' airy navies grappling in the central
> blue.

Speed undreamed of, heights inconceivable, have been mastered, and the airplane and the Zeppelin are still in their infancy. To many of us, that huge silver fish, the "Shenandoah," which recently floated over New England, borne aloft by helium, was a new and thrilling sight. As the air was conquered, so was the sea, for the success of the submarine belongs also to these years. The World War revealed its full significance.

It is needless to recount all the achievements of invention in these marvelous years. Electricity has been made to light our homes and our streets, to carry water power from mountain streams and Great Lake cataracts hundreds of miles to furnish energy for factory and household. New industrial centers have arisen, and super-power projects are under way which promise to coördinate and distribute energy through great sections to a degree hitherto hardly conceived. To this generation belongs the development of high-speed tools, the use of carborundum, bauxite, helium, aluminum, the extraction of nitrates from the air to fertilize impoverished soils, the electric furnace and electric welding, the alternating-current motor, and all the wonders of high-power current, even to rivaling the lightning flash.

The wonders that "creative chemistry" has opened in our day cannot be enumerated in detail. They may be suggested by the reminder that the business application of chemical synthesis to the coal tars has made a new era in dyes, medicines, explosives, and even food flavors; that the chemist's researches have found new means of extracting the needed fertilizers for the soil; that biochemistry, physical chemistry, and similar combinations have opened new realms for research into the mysteries of the universe.

The physicists have made more refined examinations of atomic weights, have developed instruments of precision, have measured Betelgueze, revealed the electron, developed the use of the telescope, the microscope, the spectroscope, astrophotography, and kindred devices. Largely in these decades since Clark University began, they have carried explorations into the infinitely little and the infinitely large, until the mind staggers under the revelations of the new universe. We measure and weigh the stars, we see their composition, we find new galaxies in the immensity of space, and, as the scientist resolves the molecule into the atom and the electron and explores radioactivity, we come with awe to a new realization of the mysteries of matter and force, and the vastness of space. Earlier generations learned that the universe was not geocentric. We are becoming aware that our starry system may well be, like the atom, only one of an infinite number of whirling, complex worlds, beyond the reach of telescope and photographic plate. Einstein's doctrine of relativity has brought new conceptions of the relations of space and time, to be tested and applied by future generations. In all this tide of discovery and speculation one realizes both the decreasing size of our planet, the widening scope and power of the mind of man, and the meaning of university science in the training of that mind.

Nor is it alone in the physical universe that these discoveries have been made. The biologists, to whom Mendel's work was hardly known when Clark began, have worked out results in their studies of heredity, mutation, the processes of life, that open new vistas; the bacteriologists, following the lead of Pasteur and Koch, have revolutionized medical science and have gone far to wipe away the scourges of malaria, typhoid, yellow fever, diphtheria, and other germ diseases. Medicine and surgery, building on the research of laboratory and clinic, have made marked advances in the alleviation of suffering and the prolongation of human life. Explorers have sought out the unknown regions of the earth. The North Pole was reached by Peary in 1909, the South Pole by Amundsen two years later, and then the Northwest Passage sought for centuries was found by the same navigator. The engineers, whose marvels have kept pace with these other builders and revealers of a new world, have opened the long-sought Straits of Anian by joining the waters of Atlantic and Pacific, changing thereby the problems of transportation strategy and the commercial rivalries of sections and nations.

The geographers have mapped and minutely studied the regional geography of many parts of the earth, and brought the relations of peoples and places into new relations, so that it is now recognized that this science is entitled to the special study and broad development which this university gives it. For human geography and the older study of the earth go hand in hand and are essential to understanding the course of history, the bases of industrial and social life. On the steppes of Asia have been found fossils that afford new revelations of the course of evolution and of the spread of animal life. The valley of the Amazon is being explored and the riches of Brazil as a future iron supply for the world are being made known. Africa is opened to the rivalry of European peoples, and the congress of partition in 1885 has been followed by the formation of new states, new mandates, and the exploitation of its natural resources. From all quarters of the globe have been brought back to America plant life that may be adapted to the different regions of the Union. Climate has been studied descriptively and historically. The "pulse of Asia" has been felt by study of the desert lands where civilizations flourished and fell, and daring hypotheses have been made of the relations of climate and civilization as related to sun and planets.

But it were too venturesome a task to do more than touch upon some of the suggestions of what science has done since the foundation year. Every scientist would protest that the half has not been told and that some things have not been understandingly told. But at least they will agree, I think, that for the historian it is important to realize how deep and vast have been the changes in our knowledge of the planet; how important has been the work in prolonging life and so increasing the population of the earth, and in disclosing both the opportunities for living on this earth, our narrowing home, as well as the limits and the dangers that beset us from the pressure of population upon the soil and natural resources of the earth; and the colossal developments of industry in this age of domination by the machine. Bergson the philosopher has been reported as declaring that the World War was the outcome of the fact that man's control over nature had increased faster than his spiritual power.

But, with this rapid survey of the world forces of science and invention that played upon the United States in the years we are considering, let us next turn for a few minutes to discuss the results in the United States. Some of them I have already indicated. The opening up of the iron deposits of the Lake Superior basin, about the period when Clark was founded, and the fuller utilization of our coal supplies centering around Pittsburgh, brought about the growth of that cyclonic manufacturing power which resulted in quadrupling the iron and steel production of the United States between 1890 and 1920. By the latter date the Union produced over two-thirds of the pig iron of the world—double that of England, Germany, and France combined. Even before the World War the production of the United States was about equal to that of all those great industrial nations. In steel production in 1920, this country produced twice the tonnage of the powers that I have named, and was two-thirds of that of the world. The United States mined nearly one-half of the world's coal in 1920, having quadrupled its production since 1880, and it had nearly one-half the known coal reserves of the world, one-third of the known iron-ore reserves, one-half the lead and nickel of the world, over a third of the tungsten, and in 1917 nearly three-fourths of the copper (but the opening up of copper areas in South America has diminished that fraction). We had in the same year nearly three-fourths of the world's petroleum supplies, but so rapidly have we drawn upon them that we are

now threatened with the exhaustion of our oil reserves
in less than twenty years. This carries a meaning with
it when we reflect upon what gasoline means to our
industrial life, our motors, our military safety in the air
and on the seas. Our production of oil rose from less
than two billion gallons in 1890 to over twenty billions
today. Our gold reserves were greatly increased by the
discoveries in Alaska, which came soon after the
Populist campaign of 1896 in behalf of the silver
standard. It was argued, then, that gold was not produced in quantity sufficient to serve as the standard of
value and the measurement of debts. Alaskan and
South African mines and improved methods of ore
extraction swelled the world's gold production. Today,
as a result of the disruption of Europe, we have probably
far over half the gold coin and bullion of the world and
are likely to feel the inflation which accompanies it. The
per capita circulation of money in the United States was
less than twenty-three dollars in 1890. In 1920 it
was over fifty dollars. The Populists of 1892 had demanded exactly that per capita circulation.

The wealth of the nation, which was estimated at
sixty-five billions of dollars in 1890, or a per capita of
something over one thousand dollars, has by 1920
become three hundred billions, or toward three thousand dollars per capita. A London authority in 1920
estimated the combined wealth of the United Kingdom,
France, and Germany at considerably less than that of
the United States. Our income was estimated at over
sixty-six billion dollars in 1919. But only ten per cent
of our population have incomes over twenty-four hundred dollars, and it was estimated (less safely, perhaps)
in 1915 that three-fifths of the property of the Union

was possessed by the two per cent of the population who constituted the very rich. In these facts there is food for reflection on the outcome of the pioneer democracy that sought equality as well as opportunity in the American wilderness. There is food for reflection, too, in the fact that in 1908, on the call of President Roosevelt, a conference of governors, scientists, business men, and political leaders met to consider the means of conserving the remaining mineral, timber, and other natural resources of the United States. The call was issued three centuries after Captain John Smith and his men struck the first blows at the American forest and sought for gold among the sands of the James River. By 1920 Professor Graves, former Chief of the Forest Service, declared that we shall feel the pinch of forest exhaustion in fifteen years. The net growth of timber production in the United States is supposed to be less than one-fifth the consumption.

Our agricultural history in the years since the disappearance of the frontier line is very significant. We have come to furnish three-fourths of the corn crop of the world, over one-fifth of the wheat, over a third of the swine, and over half the cotton crop of the world. The opening of new wheat fields and new cattle ranges in the eighties, coupled with the vast development of railroad and steamship transportation, inaugurated an era of cheap food and led to higher commodity wages in the United States. It poured a flood of flour and meat into Europe, fostered the development of industrialism, reduced farmers to ruin there, and was directly influential upon Bismarck's policy of tariffs, state socialism, colonial empire, and sea power, which William II shaped into the military imperialism which ruined

Europe. Europe came to believe that other Americas must be found—new lands whose natural resources could be exploited.

Between 1880 and 1900 there was added to the farms of the United States a region equal to the European area of the combined France, Germany, England, and Wales. The new industrialism of the United States called forth the vast emigration from Europe in the eighties. This inundation, with subsequent tides of foreigners, whose birth rate far exceeded the native-born, negatived much of the gains which labor would otherwise have received from labor-saving machinery, cheap food, and the general improvement of their condition.

Land prices rose as the wilderness supply diminished. The value of farm lands increased about four billion dollars between 1890 and 1900. But in the succeeding decade they increased over twenty billion dollars, and in 1910-1920, nearly thirty-seven billion dollars. Population during these years increased by about the same amount per decade: thirteen millions, except in 1900-1910 (the years of greatest immigration), when it rose by sixteen millions. Wheat production, except for the years of accelerated increase in the World War (when also we ate brown bread that our armies and Europe might be fed), is slowly declining, though per capita consumption increases, while population is increasing more rapidly in the last two decades than wheat production. Iowa farm lands rose from an average of thirty dollars per acre in 1890 to over two hundred dollars in 1920. In the United States as a whole, they rose from about twenty dollars to about seventy dollars. The better lands show an alarming tendency toward holdings by tenancy, which may presage an American peasantry,

or worse. All this means in the long run dearer bread
and meat. But at present the wheat and cattle raisers
are in distress as a result of overproduction in view of
the sudden ending of the European demand, and this
distress is influencing politics and sectionalism as it did
in the days of Grangers and Populists, and as it will
until some reasonable adjustment is reached between the
agricultural and the manufacturing production. But on
the whole there have been great gains. Farming
methods have been revolutionized. Coöperative marketing has extended, and to a considerable extent
coöperative production. Agricultural education has
spread, new machinery, new methods of relating soils
and plants, improved breeds of cattle, have come in.
Irrigation has opened desert lands and developed new
types of farm life. Canneries, the packing industry, and
dairy organization have made important changes in the
life of the nation as well as of the farm. Cost accounting and the application of rural credit facilities have
brought the farmer into relation with the methods of
industrialism. The isolation and the narrowness of
farm life have diminished. If these factors continue
influential we shall have no American peasantry.

I need not remind you that this was the era when
business began to integrate in great trusts and corporations allied with each other—the era of high finance.

Labor in the eighties also felt the forces of change
and began to organize. It was in those years of great
immigration and industrial growth that the Knights of
Labor reached their largest numbers and that great
strikes occurred. They were superseded by the Federation of Labor soon after. This organization has grown
to a dues-paying membership in 1920 of four million.

As the free lands disappeared, and as the immigrant came, the labor movement grew in volume and in the extent of its demands. Within the ranks of organized labor there came to be all grades of conservatism and radicalism, from those like Mr. Gompers who sympathize with the more moderate English type to those, chiefly recent aliens, who interpret America in terms of Russia and adopt the policy of syndicalism. The movement is indicative of labor's reaction to the shrinking world as well as to the tendency of the United States and the world toward industrial democracy. It is also reflective, within limits, of a growing internationalism in labor movements.

In 1880 the American navy was obsolete. Indeed, it hardly existed. But contemporaneously with the rise of our steel industries and the growth of our foreign commerce, the new navy was built. The Naval War College dates from 1885, and the next year Captain Mahan began his lectures there. His *Influence of Sea Power upon History* immediately won European recognition, especially in England and Germany, where it had a pronounced effect upon their rivalry. As we rose after the Spanish-American War to the rank of a world power with an influence in European diplomacy, our navy grew. In 1923 it was recognized as entitling us to an equality in ratio of building with that of England, historically the mistress of the seas.

Thus far I have been recounting some of the larger social and economic forces in the development of the nation since 1889. Obviously, unless ideals keep pace with material growth, these tendencies are as dangerous as they are vast. There is time for but a rapid suggestion of the tendencies in the field of politics and ideals.

For the most part they have been deeply if not causally influenced by the forces I have described. It may be said, however, that philosophy has shown the characteristics of the general trend in the pragmatism that William James expounded and in the studies of which Dr. Stanley Hall became the outstanding leader—the study of the child, and of the changing psychologic forces through adolescence and old age. The study of the influence of the unconscious mind has worked a revolution in psychology and in literature. Our sympathies have deepened and extended. That America has not been uncreative in art, the masterpieces of Saint Gaudens in sculpture, and of John Singer Sargent in painting, attest. But, perhaps, it is in architecture that the American artistic genius of the time has most clearly expressed itself. The skyscraper comes naturally, hugely, and beautifully as its best expression out of the age of steel and concrete, the age of utility, the age of democracy and congestion, the age of aspiration. And the Lincoln Memorial in Washington is an enduring proof of our capacity for sheer beauty. In literature there are no such outstanding original figures as those of the past, but literature is increasingly revealing the common American life in new forms. In an acute examination of recent tendencies in literature, Henry Seidel Canby, in the *Century* for February, 1924, finds a slow swinging-away from discipline and self-restraint, a revolt from the fear of suppression, and a tendency to "rest upon the world prevailingly now, instead of upon ourselves. Our confidence in the alleged conquest of nature has grown until reliance has become a habit." He characterizes the period as "the age of experiment," of "experience at any cost"—"to live fully rather than finely," is the theme. Whatever may be thought of the diagnosis, the generation has shown a logical literary development of the emphasis placed in the eighties upon realism, and a close relation to the tendencies in philosophic thought of which I have spoken.

The ratio of pupils in public schools to the total children of school age has only moderately improved in the period. Such are some of the disadvantages of our immigration, our industrialism, and our imperfect distribution of wealth. But the unexcelled philanthropies of men like Carnegie and Rockefeller have devoted vast new sums to the improvement and extension of education as well as to social amelioration. There is a growing ambition for college education among the children of the common people. While population has less than doubled between 1890 and 1920, there has been a fivefold increase in students in college. Universities now reckon their numbers in thousands where in the eighties they reckoned them in hundreds. In several universities, over twenty thousand students are enrolled in regular courses, correspondence courses, and summer school. But it is a grave question what will be the result of numbers upon quality. The number of women in colleges has increased over tenfold. If the universities can remain the seed plots of ideals as well as of material education, there is promise here of a still better age to follow this.

As the cheap or free lands were taken up and as wealth concentrated in such great corporations as the steel trust and railroad combinations, the reaction toward popular government went on apace, to the destruction of pioneer ideas of individualism and free

competition that had been ascendent before the eighties.
I need only recall the Populist movement and the incorporation of it in a new Democratic party by Bryan,
the Progressivism of the Roosevelt Republicans, the
movements for initiative, referendum, and recall, for
direct primaries, for regulation of corporations, for a
graduated income tax, for diminishing the power of the
judiciary which applied the fourteenth amendment to
corporations as persons and checked state efforts to
control them. Usually these movements began in some
Western state and then, like the weather, took their way
to the East until they won a national position. The
Australian ballot was locally adopted in Kentucky in
1888 and spread across the Union. The Oregon system followed a like course, and today the President is
nominated in about half the states by preferential primaries. The Constitution has been changed, as a result
of these tendencies, by provisions for the income tax,
the direct popular vote for senators of the United
States, by the prohibition amendment, and by nation-
wide woman's suffrage. The presidency has become
more important, the states have lost power to the federal government, and sectional expression in legislation
has correspondingly gained. Perhaps the most significant changes occurred in the alarm over the power of
organized wealth in politics. The farming interests
feared it as endangering their ideals of democracy and
equality. Labor listened to the words of one of the
anthracite-coal owners, in the era of the strike which
President Roosevelt settled, and believed that Mr. Baer
expressed the attitude of the masters of capital when he
said: "The rights and interests of the laboring man
will be protected and cared for—not by the labor agi-

tators, but by the Christian men to whom God in His infinite wisdom has given the control of the property interests of the country." Even less-arrogant men believed that realities should be accepted and that the men who directed the industrial life of the nation should be left unhampered to control politics and to procure the "full dinner pail" of prosperity to the workers. In the words of Chief Justice Taft: "The time came when it was possible in some great corporations for the officers and directors to issue with the same nonchalance and certainty of their being complied with, orders for steel rails or industrial equipment, on the one hand, or for the delivery of delegations in a state, county, or national convention, on the other. In the early years of this century the people became fully aroused to the fact that they were almost in the grasp of a plutocracy."

With the coming of the progressive movements which I have described, there came a whole group of reforming political leaders whose names are merged in the great names of two recent Presidents.

Asking in 1888 why the presidency is not more frequently filled by great and striking men, Mr. Bryce, later Lord Bryce, said: "Since the heroes of the revolution died out with Jefferson, Adams, and Madison some sixty years ago, no person except General Grant has reached the chair whose name would have been remembered had he not been President, and no President except Abraham Lincoln has displayed rare or striking qualities in the chair." Exceptions to the statement will be taken by Americans who remember Andrew Jackson, and James K. Polk and Grover Cleveland. Since Bryce wrote, the United States has given to the world two Presidents whom the entire world has

hitherto controlled the German nation is of the sort here described. It is within the choice of the German nation to alter it." That question, put by an American President while the victorious armies of France, England, Italy, and America, under General Foch, fronted defeated Germany, was followed by the debacle of European emperors and kings. Hohenzollerns and Hapsburgs as well as petty rulers went down in ruin.

Then came the attempt to embody the dream of a reconstituted world, a League of Nations, safe not only for democracy, but for peace on earth. It was perhaps a vision too lofty for a world still smoking with the greatest conflagration of all time. In the process of the construction of the Treaty of Versailles, it appeared that the historic national hatreds and suspicions, the reliance on force and on balance of power, the cynicism of diplomacy, the desire to protect the gains of victory on the European side, had not been burned away, even among the Allies. On the side of the United States, the historic repugnance to anything that might be construed as merging her fortunes with the political system of the Old World, was so great that only the concerted agreement of American leaders could have carried the American people into this new venture, on the wave of great international emotion and sympathy that had swept the country. When the matter became an issue of our party politics, and when prominent leaders spoke words of warning and alarm, the psychological moment of possibility for immediate American participation in the League, as drawn, passed away.

But the vision of a world adjusting its problems by negotiation and by judicial determination in some common organ of decision, will not pass away; or, if it does,

the time will come when the hopes of all mankind will
be blasted in another catastrophe to civilization—the
greater because of the very advances that science has
made possible in the art of war and because the shrinking earth is bringing all mankind into a common destiny.
Woodrow Wilson will then be honored, either as the
prophet of a new dispensation which came too late for
him to see, or as the statesman who vainly pointed out
a way which might have saved civilization. The League
of Nations still lives, though its founder lies dead in
Washington. History forgets the smaller frailties of
men and seizes upon the enduring element, and it does
not forget those who gave life itself to lofty ideals.

In conclusion, I must call your attention to the views
which eminent biologists, geographers, and economists
have been setting forth in recent years as to the tendencies exhibited by the countries of the world, including the United States, toward overpopulation. It is the
striking fact that at the end of the generation since
1890, when the Superintendent of the Census reported
that the American frontier line could no longer be
traced, a whole group of careful and reputable scholars
have attempted to demonstrate quantitatively that
before the year 2000, so great is the increase of
population and so rapid the exhaustion of resources
and such the diminishing production of food relative to
population, our present standards of life must be
abandoned or the birth rate decreased if we are not to
feel the pressure of want and even of universal famine
and war. The World War called out careful examination of the population and the food supplies of many
countries, and now men who participated in those
inquiries are using them to warn the nations. Dr. Baker,

of the Department of Agriculture, whom you are to have the good fortune to enroll in Clark's faculty this year, concludes that, on our present standards and by bringing under cultivation all possible land in the United States and by greater intensiveness of cultivation, we can maintain a population of two hundred and fifty millions. But this would mean taking over poor land as well as good. Professor East, of Harvard, and Professor Pearl, of Johns Hopkins, believe that the saturation point in population will be reached at about two hundred millions, or double our present population; and East concludes that at the present rate of increase this will be reached about the year 2000, and probably the pinch will be felt between 1960 and 1980, or within the lifetime of the students of this university. Nor can the United States expect relief by that time from the outside world, for if these conclusions are correct, that outside world as well will have reached a similar condition of overpopulation relative to food and raw material. If these writers—and European and Australian economists take like views—are even approximately correct, then we are faced with the alternative of a harder world to live in, unless the birth rate of the masses of the people is reduced to an equilibrium with food supply and the materials of industry; and nations must come into some form of association, apportioning the regions and resources of the earth to meet the needs of justice— or war and pestilence will be the lot of all mankind in the struggle for existence. All the sympathies which mitigate the cruelties of the struggle for existence, all the gains in science and medicine which prolong life and increase population, all the social reforms, will only hasten the catastrophe.

Truly a shrinking earth! An earth compelled by irresistible forces to exercise restraint, to associate, agree, and adjust, or to commit suicide. Huxley's friendly comet that should end it all in a burst of light following its impact upon the planet, were a better solution.

For myself, I doubt the rate at which the catastrophe prophesied by these authorities approaches. But in history a few centuries are not determinative. I do not doubt the trend, and to me who have spent much of my life in the study of the movement of peoples into the vacant spaces of the United States, it is a dramatic outcome of a process that began with the first wanderings of the cave man. But I prefer to believe that man is greater than the dangers that menace him; that education and science are powerful forces to change these tendencies and to produce a rational solution of the problems of life on the shrinking planet. I place my trust in the mind of man seeking solutions by intellectual toil rather than by drift and by habit, bold to find new ways of adjustment, and strong in the leadership that spreads new ideas among the common people of the world; committed to faith in peace on earth, and ready to use the means of preserving it.

CHAPTER IX

THE WEST—1876 AND 1926 [1]

Its Progress in a Half-Century

In the extraordinary changes which the nation has undergone in the last fifty years, the West has had a share peculiar to itself. Over much of its spaces it has passed from a wilderness to a settled area. In Eastern consciousness the land beyond the Mississippi, at the beginning of the period, had hardly become a vital part of the economic and political life of the American commonwealth. At the same time, in popular conception, the Old Northwest, the territory situated between the Great Lakes, the Ohio. and the Mississippi, was a part of the West.

Now the latter group of states has become the center of the republic. The West of today may roughly be defined as the lands that lie west of the Mississippi. But that great region is far from being a unity. Made up of the West North Central States, the West South Central States, the Mountain States, and the Pacific Coast, its prairies are to the San Francisco man a part of the East; to the Boston man, the West South Central States are a part of the South.

The domain of this West is more than twice the area of the states that lie east of the river, three times the size of pre-War Germany, Austria-Hungary, and France combined. From St. Louis to San Francisco the traveler must go almost as far as from London to Constanti-

[1] Reprinted by permission from *The World's Work*, July, 1926.

nople. From Minneapolis to New Orleans is a traveling distance equivalent to that from Copenhagen to Rome. In such imperial spaces lies a congeries of geographic provinces, each equal in area to European nations that have made the history of the Old World. Each has passed, or is still passing, from primitive conditions to the varied and complex life of our modern civilization; each has its own environment, its own social traits, interests, and ideals. Generalizations, therefore, upon the West as a whole are apt to be misleading.

By the census of 1880 the trans-Mississippi country held less than one-fifth of the people of the Union. Today this West has nearly one-third of the whole. With its growth in population has come even greater growth in economic and political power. The states and territories west of the Mississippi grew from less than seven million people in 1870 to more than eleven millions in 1880. By 1920 they numbered more than thirty-one millions—a gain of more than twenty millions since 1876. Even in the decade between 1910 and 1920 their gain greatly exceeded that of the old North Atlantic States. The Mountain States have gained nearly three million people since 1870, and the Pacific Coast almost five million.

When in 1870 James J. Hill, who was to become "the Empire Builder" of the New Northwest, visited the northwestern part of Minnesota with his "grub sack" on a dog train, he passed through a wilderness where fourteen years later an almost unbroken wheat field stretched through one hundred and twenty square miles. Between Duluth and the mining camps of the Rocky Mountains were a few military and trading posts. Indian reservations occupied vast portions of the zone.

THE WEST—1876 AND 1926

Over great areas the West is still a frontier; but the West of 1876 has gone. This has been achieved in part by the adventurous railway promoters who in the seventies and eighties paved the way by stretching the "Granger railroads" out into the unoccupied prairies, and the Denver & Rio Grande and the Atchison, Topeka & Santa Fe to the Southwest. By the middle eighties the Northern Pacific and the various lines absorbed into the Southern Pacific had pushed new zones of transportation through to the Pacific, followed in 1893 by the Great Northern. New economic empires had been founded and new bases laid for political power.

The interstate migration to the west of the Mississippi was largely from old American stock or from people who had already undergone a process of Americanization. But Germans and Scandinavians added important elements by immigration. In 1920 the foreign-born in the West North Central division constituted a lower percentage than in the East North Central, while in both New England and the Middle Atlantic States the ratio was twice as great. In all, the West had only a fourth of the nation's population of foreign parentage in 1920, while it had nearly one-third of the total population. Nor, in the southern half of the region of expansion beyond the river, has negro migration kept pace with white. In 1920, only one-fifth of the population of the West South Central States were negroes. It is clear, therefore, that, taken as a whole, the West remains more nearly of the white American native-born than the East.

The Indians who roamed the Great Plains in 1876 were soon eliminated as a serious factor. They were concentrated within great reservations after the Indian wars and the destruction of the buffalo herds. In 1924 every native Indian became a citizen of the United States. Less than 350,000 Indians remain in the Union, two-thirds of them west of the Mississippi. There are only about fifty thousand fewer Indians now than there were fifty years ago.

The West is representative of rural, as well as of pioneer, America. Of the six leading cities of the Union, both in 1870 and 1920, St. Louis alone was included from the West; but by the latter year six of the cities beyond the Mississippi had entered the ranks of the first twenty in the nation—half of the six from the Pacific Coast—and more than half of the twenty were situated west of the Alleghenies.

In 1880 more than half of those engaged in occupations in the West North Central States were in agriculture; two-thirds of those in the West South Central States; only one-fourth in the Mountain group; and less than a third in the Pacific division. In the Mountain section about a third were occupied in the manufacturing, mechanical, and mining industries, and on the Pacific Coast this group was larger than the agricultural. Taken as a whole, about one-half of the population of the West was engaged in agricultural occupations.

Today there are about twice as many in agriculture in the West as there are in manufacturing and mining, including the petroleum and gasoline production. Three-fifths of the farmers of the Union live in the North Central States, east and west of the Mississippi; but, east of the river, the Old Northwest now has twice as many in manufacturing and mining, together, as in agriculture. Less than one-tenth of those engaged in farming in the United States now live in the North Atlantic States. So far as numbers go, however, the manufacturing and mining group takes a larger share of the workers than does agriculture on the Pacific Coast. In the Mountain States those engaged in agriculture outnumber the other group two to one.

The lion's share of the wheat of the nation, in 1880, belonged to the East North Central States, though the single-crop wheat belt, like an irresistible flood, was passing to the virgin soils across the river, leaving the Old Northwest to readjust itself to mixed farming. But already in 1876 a third of all the wheat was raised beyond the Mississippi, only relatively small amounts coming from the Southern and Mountain portions. The population followed the railroads and utilized the homesteads and the cheap railroad lands; the product rose on these new fertile soils.

In the decade before 1874 the United States exported more wheat than in the previous half-century. The deluge of American wheat and meats produced an economic revolution in Europe. Industrialism grew by the receipt of cheap American food. In England and Germany labor was transferred from farm to factory. In both these nations, by reason of American competition, farmers were in distress. In England the small landholder was driven to the wall. Germany enacted protective tariffs and sought equivalent for the vast resources of Western America by building up sea power and colonies.

It might almost be said that the Western farmer was indirectly the cause of the rivalry of the industrial nations of Europe who became engaged in the World War. The Western farms made possible the food sup-

[239]

plies for the Allied nations which fought Germany and for the armies which we sent to join them. Western inventiveness, combined with the scarcity of labor, gave rise to the new age of agricultural machinery, with the ever developing use of gasoline engines. The league-long furrow, the new plow, reaper, thresher, and the tractor, on the plains of the West, made a revolution in agricultural methods, replacing the labor of multitudes of men.

Dry farming and the federal Reclamation Service have won Far Western areas that were classed as untillable when the century began. Writing in 1879, General Hazen, Weather Bureau expert, who had served in the army in those regions, declared that, "Beyond the Red River the country is not susceptible of cultivation." Today the West across the Mississippi supplies more than three-fourths of the nation's wheat; New England is almost entirely dependent on outside supplies; the Middle Atlantic States furnish no more than a third of their own requirements. The "bread basket" for the industrial section is beyond the great river and it still supplies an export which determines its price, on a peace level. In minor part recent agricultural suffering is due to the War-time inflation of land values, on which the cereal farmer makes a vain attempt to figure profitable returns. As fifty years ago, so now he is demanding relief from hard times.

Like the Wheat Belt, the Corn Belt formed and migrated across the old West into the new. But since its significance is rather as a food for livestock than for bread and export, it may simply be pointed out that, both at the beginning and at the end of the fifty years, it was less than half that of the Union, so widely was the industry spread in the East and South. Almost all of this half came, however, from the West North Central States, which, with their neighbors on the eastern side of the central states, constituted the Corn Belt.

The Cotton Belt has also extended across the river. In 1924 two-thirds of the whole crop was raised in this relatively new West. As the scepter of the Cotton Kingdom passed from the seaboard to the new states of the eastern Gulf region before the Civil War, so now it has gone to the Southwestern and South Central states, where cotton constitutes only one of many agricultural activities. Texas now produces more cotton than did the whole South in 1876.

When we turn from these and the many other crops of the West to her livestock, the story of migration is repeated. In 1870, out of the nation's total of around twenty-eight million cattle, ten and one-half million were on farm and range beyond the Mississippi. Then, chiefly in the eighties, came the era of the cowboy of the Great Plains, celebrated in "movie" and fiction as one of the picturesque figures of America's story. Two-thirds of the country's cattle are now grazing in the West. Swine, too, have migrated with the cattle. Three-fifths of the nation's pork supply now comes from this West.

To the United States, the range-cattle industry had a significance beyond its relatively small proportion of the cattle of this class, for it involved the problem of the use of the public lands of the Great Plains and the ranges in the National Forests, when these were reserved. Great companies here and abroad bought outright from Texas (which preserved title to its lands when it entered the Union). Many thousands of acres were held in single, fenced ranches in this state. On the public domain the cattle trails ran from Texas to Dakota and Montana, where the droves moved, as the season decreed, from range to range. The ranchmen, with frontier lawlessness, fenced extensive tracts; and, as the range became occupied, warred with each other and with the sheep men, managed by use of the land laws to occupy the scattered spots where water was to be found, and so extended their effective control to vast surrounding grazing land on the public domain. For a time it seemed that the nation's lands would, by the operation of custom, fraud, and force, pass to the hands of the so-called "cattle barons."

But year after year the farmer pushed his frontier out into their domain, cut their fences, and interrupted their droves. The railroads that made the "cow towns" on the borders of the "drive" were pushed westward and brought with them the flanking movement of the home-seeker, even to the extreme edge of safe rainfall for agriculture, until the great drought of the later eighties checked their advance and brought the Populist movement forward. The farmer's advance destroyed the hope of a broad zone, or cattle right of way, from northern boundary to southern. The great ranches gradually broke up, and the range-cattle industry passed increasingly to the farmer. Meantime, stockyards, the packing industry, the refrigerator car, and the ocean steamer came to supply Europe and to replace the local *abattoir* and meat market in the East. As the cattle country moved west, the packing industry followed, extending from Chicago to Omaha and Kansas City.

The sheep industry, like the cattle industry, crossed the river. By 1870 only a quarter of the nation's

flocks were in this West; but soon the preponderance
changed and, by 1880, more than half of our sheep
grazed west of the Mississippi. Now nearly three-
quarters of them are there, and of these nearly three-
fifths are in the Mountain States. Important influences
upon the Western attitude toward national party politics followed. Protective tariffs were framed by an
alliance between the wool raisers of the West and the
manufacturers of the East.

Before this westward movement the old forests
faded, and on the Pacific Coast new ones, vaster and
nobler in height and breadth, opened. Of lumber produced in the United States in 1880, less than one-sixth
was sawed west of the Mississippi. Even the North
Atlantic States then produced more than Michigan, and
twice as much as Wisconsin and Minnesota combined.
But lumbermen had long been busy in these forests of
the Great Lakes basin, through which railroads were
cutting narrow aisles along their rights of way, and the
tributaries of the Mississippi were bearing rafts through
forests of virgin pine. In Michigan, Wisconsin, and
Minnesota, cutover lands—burnt and dreary landscapes
of man's ravage—are now offered to new homestead
pioneers where those old forests once spread their green
glories over the northern wilderness.

Great central lumber companies like the Weyer-
haeusers moved to the Pacific Northwest, where they
secured imperial forests; others went to the South.
Now, less than six per cent of the lumber comes from
Michigan, Wisconsin, and Minnesota; less than four per
cent from the North Atlantic States; around a third of
the whole from the South; and more than a third from
the Pacific Coast states. The Forest Service sees a

pinch in the timber supply of the country within this generation, although the conservation movement, awakened to practical activity under Roosevelt, stirred by Pinchot's presentation of the facts, resulted in the creation of national forests. These reserves of the Mountain and Pacific states approach one-half the total area of the original thirteen states, not counting their Western claims.

The West has contributed vast wealth in precious metals to the United States since 1876. Now we mine about the same amount of gold as then. The crest was reached in 1915, when it was nearly twice that of 1924. The silver miner's fortunes depended on politics. By 1891, encouraged by legislation at a crisis of discontent over the scarcity of gold as a standard of value, production leaped up, but with the repeal of silver legislation this mining declined for a time. The value of our production in 1924 was only forty-three and one-half million dollars, though in fine ounces it was more than twice that of 1876.

Fifty years ago Great Britain led the United States in the production of pig iron. By 1890 we had passed her, and today two-thirds of the pig iron of the world is produced here—twice the output of the United Kingdom, Germany, and France combined. The opening of the rich, soft hematite ores of Minnesota was the decisive factor in this change, for it furnished supplies upon which the American genius for systematization and improved processes could operate. In 1876 the production of structural steel and iron was so insignificant that it was not given in the census. Now Pittsburgh, situated on the eastern border of what was called the West in 1876, is the vortex of an iron-and-steel industrial activity that has astonished the world, and the United States Steel Corporation is among the world's largest corporations. Minnesota came to mine three-fifths of the iron ore of the nation, and the other ore beds of the Lake Superior basin are really more Western than Eastern in their essential history. Steel rails, bridges, and skyscrapers have come since these fields were opened. The age of steel is a part of the story of the development of the West.

In 1870 Michigan was the leading copper field of the nation, and the Union produced less than thirty million pounds. Now we produce thirty times that amount, and nine-tenths of this comes from west of the Mississippi, chiefly from Arizona, Utah, and Montana.

Petroleum production lay east of the Mississippi in 1876. Now the nation's production has increased one hundred fold, and nine-tenths of it comes from the fields west of the Mississippi. What this has meant to the production of power for transportation by automobile, steamship, and airplane, as well as to farm and factory, is plain. What oil means in the diplomacy of nations has also become evident.

So far, we have been observing how since 1876 the West has been the field of colonization and the field for Eastern investment and industrial development. But we must next take notice of the fact that the West is assuming aspects and developing ambitions like the East. The coöperative organizations of the grangers failed; but since then there has arisen a multitude of producing and marketing associations—fruit raisers, truck farmers, dairymen, and now wheat and cotton raisers, are forming business-like associations. The rise of the canning industry, of cold storage, of the large-scale wheat elevator and flour-mill organizations, of the packing industry, and the power over their product exercised by middleman and speculator, are turning the Western farmer, led by men trained in economics and business methods, to the ways of industrial society.

Manufacturing, of course, was more tardy than farming and mining in moving westward, and as the Northeast grew, as population became denser, and as world commerce and the immigrant sought its ports, it was there that society evolved into the industrial type and there that it became lodged. Of the manufactured product in 1880, the trans-Mississippi country furnished less than one-thirteenth of the value of the total national output. In 1923 the Western section had raised its fraction to one-sixth. The older West, east of the river, even in agricultural districts, has become a mixture of farm and factory, until at present this East North Central group has more than three-fifths that of the North Atlantic's value of manufactured products. Together, these two last-named sections have about two-thirds of the total for the nation.

But now the Mountain States, too, are dreaming of emulating the East in industrialism. Their potential hydraulic power is two-thirds of the nation's total. Their iron and copper and oil, their undeveloped lignite and soft coal, the hides of their cattle, the wool of their sheep, the timber of their forests, call upon the Western imagination in spite of the lack of a labor supply, of capital, and of transport facilities. The recent bill of Senator Gooding, of Idaho, to abolish long- and short-haul discriminations by the railroads was presented, not only as a measure of justice to the

Mountain States, but also to promote a hoped-for manufacturing development, there, in rivalry with the manufacturers of the Middle West. He foresaw the day when the exhaustion of forests and mines would leave these states a restricted agricultural section, at the mercy of the Eastern industrial regions. The bill failed, but it was supported by the senators from all the Mountain States, except those of Colorado, regardless of party, as well as by the west-central states, outside of Minnesota and the Dakotas. The Pacific Coast voted against the measure.

In the political history of the United States since 1876, the West has played a leading rôle. With all his great production in the middle seventies, the Western farmer was having hard times. His indebtedness was given added weight by the contraction of the currency and by high interest rates. Low prices negatived the increase in his crops, so that in many cases rising production meant less income. He resentfully contrasted his low prices for agricultural products with the profits of the Eastern manufacturer and capitalist.

So, in the Granger era, the farmers formed independent parties or made alliances with one or the other of the two great parties in the Middle West of that day, won legislatures and governors in several states of the Old Northwest, and enacted laws fixing maximum rates and restraining discriminations by the railroads. The untrained farmer of the seventies had no preparation for grappling with economic statistics or with legal problems. By the time our survey begins, the crest of the Granger wave had just passed, and in many of the states the agitation turned to the currency question. But among the fruits of the movement were

17 [247]

the decisions of the federal Supreme Court that the states had the right of railroad regulation. The denial that the railroad was a private enterprise and the decision that it was affected by a public interest was made in language more far-reaching than was sustained by later decisions; but it marked a turning point in the history of federal as well as state legislation. The farmers of the West had started a movement that grew with the years.

Every cycle of drought or hard times for the rural creditor classes brought forward new farmers' movements. The Alliance, and similar organizations, with nominal national scope but in reality a combination of the radical farmers of South and West, had their day. The Greenback party found its strongest Western support in those groups of counties which were most heavily mortgaged and where interest on loans was highest. There was never in these fifty years a united Western movement. The interplay of inherited membership in the old political parties; the differing interests of the cereal, livestock, and mining areas among themselves; the responsiveness of Western leaders to promotion in their national-party ranks and their consequent reluctance to affront the Eastern political leaders who exercised control—these and other factors made a more or less confused picture of politics in the years around 1876.

A platform was issued by the People's party in 1892, at Omaha, which painted a dismal picture of "a nation brought to the verge of moral, political, and material ruin." To meet the "vast conspiracy against mankind" which the gold-standard men were charged with organizing, the People's party of Western farmers and miners proposed to join hands with Eastern labor on a programme of free coinage, a circulating medium of fifty dollars per capita, a graduated income tax, postal savings banks, government ownership of railroads, telegraphs, and telephones, restoration to national ownership of the railroad land grants beyond their actual need; and it recommended the Australian ballot, the eight-hour labor law, the election of senators by popular vote, one term for the President, and the initiative and referendum.

It is worth while to recall this list of "visionary" planks, for many of them have since been written into the statute books by Congress. Like the weather, such political innovations took their way from West to East. Demands for initiative, referendum, recall, direct primaries, regulation of corporations, graduated income tax, attacks on the restraining power of the judiciary, and advocacy of woman's suffrage, first won success in the legislation of Western states and then spread over the Union, and in some cases have now been embodied in the Constitution of the United States.

In 1876 the power of the trans-Mississippi West in the Senate was less than a third of that body; now, by the promotion of Western territories into states, this West holds within four votes of half of the Senate, and the electoral college has likewise reflected these changes. New York State, with a population of ten and one-third millions, has only two senators, while the northern zone of "progressive" states westward from the Mississippi boundary of Minnesota and Iowa, with about the same population, has twenty senators, and it also found in the last quarter of the century a militant leader in the late Senator La Follette, of Wisconsin.

When Bryan in 1896 made his definition of the
business man to include the farmer and the miner, and
in the Democratic convention of that memorable year
"defied" the East and issued a declaration of rural
independence, he made himself the spokesman of a new
Democratic party, based on an alliance of West and
South. When Roosevelt in subsequent years, after an
experience as frontier cattleman and "Rough Rider,"
made himself master of the Republican party and the
prophet of a new dispensation and "square deal," he
spoke with the voice of the Great Plains and the
Mountains, and not simply as a New York politician.
In party voting in the presidential election of 1896,
Bryan's plurality in the states west of the Mississippi
was more than half a million. In 1924 Coolidge carried these states by a plurality over Davis of more than
1,961,000; but the combined vote of La Follette,
Progressive, and Davis, Democrat, in these states, was
greater than the vote secured by Coolidge. La Follette
polled over two million votes in this trans-Mississippi
West. His rural strength lay in the Old Northwest
and the zone of Western states running from Wisconsin
to the Pacific: more than one-sixth of the voters of the
Union followed the leader of Western radicalism into
third-party revolt.

The United States, as I have elsewhere urged, is in
many ways a federation of sections, rather than of
states. Politically, this is revealed clearly in congressional votes, where party voting breaks down. In a
vote in the House in 1877 on the free coinage of silver,
only three Republicans and two Democrats voted "No"
from all the states beyond the Mississippi; indeed, but
seven votes in opposition were cast west of the Alle-

ghenies. In the later eighties the East North Central division reflected its changing interests by giving the majority of its votes against free silver. But it swung to the side of its sisters across the river when an attempt was made to repeal the Silver Purchase Act.

From the West came the Insurgency that made it "enemy country" in President Taft's administration and made possible the downfall of Speaker Cannon and the directing group of Eastern "elder senators." The Progressive party of Roosevelt found most of its strength here. Wilson's election was made possible by the West. The farmers' *bloc* of Western Republicans, combined with the Democratic South, evolved from the Farm Bureau movement, growing from local units to state and then to national scope and balking party administrative policies in the period of both Harding and Coolidge. The heart of this revolt of the Republican wing of agricultural states was in the West, rebellious against Eastern control.

In contrast with the Granger era, the Western farmers now have their educated leaders, their experts in the economics of the distribution of wealth, of marketing, of cost accounting, as well as of the science of production. The agricultural colleges, the experiment stations, the powerful federal Department of Agriculture, with an army of experts, are active in the service of the farming interests. The farmer is becoming less "regular" in party ties.

But the existence of many diverse regions in the West makes a political situation that limits its unity in constructive legislation. When the advocates of the Great Lakes-St. Lawrence deep waterway demand an outlet for their land-locked commerce, the Chicago region calls for a Great Lakes-Mississippi waterway and collides with Great Lakes ports in the matter of diverting the waters of these inland seas through the drainage canal. The Mountain States, with allies in the prairies and the plains, vote to prohibit the long- and short-haul discriminations of the railroads, which permit the manufacturing parts of the East North Central States to reach Far Western markets in competition with the Panama Canal. The Mountain West, with its producers of wool, its mine owners (often Eastern capitalists, and powerful in the West), its beet-sugar raisers, and many other interests, is responsive to the protective tariff and to Eastern industry. The Pacific Coast has a maritime and commercial kinship with the Atlantic Coast; but the ports of the Pacific, each with its special hinterland, sharply engage in commercial rivalry. Los Angeles, with irrigated America behind it, makes a harbor where none was; Seattle starts to tunnel the Cascades to connect her "Inland Empire" with Puget Sound; Portland chafes at the Columbia bar; San Francisco from her Golden Gate challenges her rivals. The Wheat Belts are sometimes at odds with the Corn Belt, and neither feels the grievances of the Western Cotton Belt so keenly as its own. It is a complex of sections and parties—this West—and only under stress does it find a community of policy.

Culturally, the West has kept pace with its economic growth and its political influence. In general literacy, at the opening of the half-century, the West North Central States ranked well with New England; and Iowa and Wyoming had even better records. The worst was where the Mexican stock abounded. After half a century the West North Central section's illit-

eracy is only half that of New England; the Pacific
Coast reports a very low percentage; and the illiteracy
of the Mountain States averaged not much greater
than that of New England. Even the West South
Central States made a better showing than their Eastern
sisters in the Old South. Outside of New Orleans,
the large cities of the West were but half as illiterate
as those in the East.

The West receives from taxes, and interest on endowments for higher education, an amount that indicates a
noteworthy future in that section of the Union, even
when we remember the private endowments in vast
sums which have enriched the capital of the universities
of the East. Bringing education to the farming population (so often an ignorant peasantry in Europe) has
been a noteworthy phase of Western life. In 1876
the Commissioner of Education reported only a few
more than one hundred regular students in the land-
grant colleges west of the Mississippi, with half as
many professors and instructors. The day of short
courses in agriculture, farmers' institutes, and agricultural demonstration and extension, had not come. Now
these educational influences have made a new rural
civilization.

Nearly one-fourth of the nation's total of volumes
in universities, colleges, and professional schools are
now found in this new West. The Bancroft Library
in Berkeley, the Henry E. Huntington Library near
Los Angeles, the Hoover Library of war material at
Stanford, are among the most notable collections in
America. Symphony orchestras and choral societies,
art collections, and scientific centers of research, have
given convincing proof that the West is developing a

culture of its own and contributing to American civilization.

The daring initiative and community spirit of the Pacific Coast cities, notably Los Angeles and Seattle, which were but small towns in 1870, in developing harbors and water fronts, in bringing mountain water supplies and power by long-distance electric transmission, and of the Los Angeles suburbs in becoming the center of the moving-picture production, are indications of the Western spirit in municipal life. San Francisco, too, has been among the leaders of the nation in preparation for Asiatic commerce by her developments around the Bay. The opening of the Alaskan wilds furnished a new frontier and frontier spirit to the Pacific Northwest, as well as to the nation, in these years.

The spirit of adventure, of building to the measure of the opportunity, which the Western movement carried into the more spacious and varied provinces beyond the Mississippi, has changed as the surges of migration have passed over these regions. It has been modified by the growing reliance on association instead of individual competition. Self-reliance is still stronger there than in the East; but there has also developed in those regions a "get together" spirit, embodied in social and economic organizations, like chambers of commerce, farm bureaus, coöperative societies, Rotarians and Kiwanians, which carry on with a directness and energy that belong to the Far West. There is a growing insistence on conformity to community public opinion, compared with the days of the frontiersman and the "self-made man."

But the West's old initiative, its love of innovation,

its old idealism and optimism, its old love of bigness, even its old boastfulness, are still here. As yet it has not played the powerful part in the common life of the Union which it will come to play. This land of farm owners, this land trained in pioneer ideals, has a deep conservatism, at bottom, in spite of its social and political pioneering. It may yet make new contributions to America, by its union of democratic faith and innovation with a conservative subconsciousness.

CHAPTER X

THE CHILDREN OF THE PIONEERS [1]

When the East was losing its people to the West, in the middle of the nineteenth century, dire predictions were offered for the future of the children of those families who chose the wilderness in place of settled society. "The West," said the Reverend Horace Bushnell in 1846, "will become the Poland of the United States, while New England will be sprinkled over with beautiful seats and become as a cultivated garden. . . . In the West the first generation can hardly be said to live. . . . They let life go, throw it away for the benefit of the generation to come after them, and these will be found in most cases to have grown up in such rudeness and barbarity that it will require one or two generations more to civilize their habit. Whatever man of family moves to any other country should understand that he makes a larger move also towards barbarism. He has gone beyond the pale of society." This was a typical utterance. Press and pulpit furnished a mass of such warnings.

In a discussion of ability in the United States, the late Senator Henry Cabot Lodge printed in the *Century* for September, 1891, the results of a careful statistical study made by him of the names listed in Appleton's *Cyclopedia of American Biography*. The result gave New England natives 5,486; Middle States, 5,021; Southern, 3,125; and Western, including all the rest,

[1] Reprinted by permission from *The Yale Review*, July, 1926.

[256]

only 641. Of the names, Massachusetts, New York, and Pennsylvania furnished half, or New England and the Middle Atlantic States together, three-fourths, "of the ability of the entire country."

As a descendant of the New England stock, I regret to say that there were certain flies in this statistical ointment. Mr. Lodge himself, in a brief sentence, admitted limitations to the conclusions, due to the recent settlement of Western states, but so far from applying this deduction to his statistics, when he found that Ohio (by far the earliest settled of the North Central group) had a long lead in ability in that section, he explained that it must be due to the character of the early settlers. It is not unlikely that by them he meant the little band of New Englanders at Marietta and the Connecticut settlers of the Western Reserve, and there is something to be said for that view; but the majority of the pioneers of Ohio were, so far as we can get at it, from the Southern and Middle states.

At any rate, the preponderance of Ohio natives in the Western men of ability might well have suggested that the older states had an advantage over the newer-settled states so great as to vitiate his statistics as an accurate survey in detail. New England had been a going concern since 1620 or 1630, according to whether you are a Cape Codder or a Hub man, while the North Central States were chiefly a land of buffalo, deer, moose, and Indians, who could hardly hope to be embalmed in Mr. Fiske's biographical dictionary for the whole period of colonial and revolutionary history, during which the Old Thirteen were furnishing names to the encyclopedia. The native-born of Wisconsin, for example, so late as 1850, were only seventeen per cent of the total population of that state, and it is probable that most of them were so youthful that in spite of the well-known "spirit of Wisconsin" they could hardly have broken into a dictionary published in 1887. Later statisticians, however, eliminating some of the defective methods, have also reached conclusions favorable to New England.

Some scholars in the service of eugenics have assumed that "while the better of the middle classes might have joined the emigrant trains, the intellectual aristocracy did not," hence the later modern deficiency. It would be an interesting study to ascertain how far, in all the fields of New England predominance, her "intellectual aristocracy," as existent in the migration years, really furnished the children who became the distinguished representatives of the section in later times; and how far these children came from the same little towns and social classes from which her pioneers went to the West. The "goers" were by no means mere materialists, as critics have assumed; they were not only the younger sons of families which had outgrown the farm, seeking new fields of business and the cheaper and more fertile soils of the West, but they were also the ambitious youth generally, revolting against the domination of age and the crystallization of custom.

To the thinker and idealist who hesitated to challenge the society in which he lived, there was a real obstacle to originative thinking and action in the intolerance of the village life, the suffocating atmosphere of a "completed society." And among the farmers of interior New England who sent their members to the new land of the West to build new societies, in the hope of making for their children a better life than the one they lived, there were books, schools, colleges, the love of learning and of religion. These were far from being extinguished even amid the hardships of pioneer life.

Young men saw in the West the opportunity for careers, not only as farmers, but also as journalists, public men, teachers, preachers, and men of vision generally. It is possible also to exaggerate the numbers of the intellectual élite in Boston. Are the eminent children of New England's literati numerous?

In *Who's Who* for 1918-19, New England's natives still had much the larger share in proportion to her population. But the North Central States were rising so rapidly in the scale of distinguished children that it seemed not unlikely that the prediction made by Professor E. L. Clarke, in his *American Men of Letters*, might come true. He concluded that in the decade 1841-50, "when were born the writers of about 1890 to 1910," New England's lead had been appreciably reduced and that the East North Central States showed the least relative decline in literary fecundity—a fact which may indicate, he said, that the future literary leadership of the country is to be theirs.

The case would be still stronger if the babes and young children who were brought by their pioneer parents into the West were reckoned as Western—a designation which belongs to them if, as Clarke thinks, not heredity but social environment is the leading factor in determining literary ability. This author limited his study to those born before 1850, which of course cuts out the larger share of the pioneer children of the North Central States.

The people listed in *Who's Who* for 1923-24 probably represent average birth years between 1860 and 1875. On the basis of ratio of ability to population, New England is still in possession of a two-to-one lead over the North Central States; but as a whole the latter section furnished almost 7,000 against about 4,000 for New England. Thus, by the weight of population at least, the Middle West is outstripping New England in the production of the nation's men of ability. It has gained also in its relative position compared with the previous decade.

Educational statistics are also favorable to the West. Dakota has the same percentage of illiterate white natives of native parents as has Massachusetts. Connecticut's record is no better than that of Wisconsin, Minnesota, and Nebraska. Ohio and Illinois are as well off in this respect as Maine and Vermont. There is less illiteracy for all classes in the North Central States than in New England and in the Middle States. Judged by the support of such idealistic reforms as prohibition, the West North Central section has a sterner Puritanism than exists in its home section.

What I shall aim to do is to present the results of an examination, in leisure hours (by means of biographical dictionaries, *Who's Who,* current newspapers, magazines, and lists of successful men and women in various fields), of the problem of how far the expectations quoted at the outset of this article, in regard to the children of the pioneers, proved well founded. Did the pioneers produce "young barbarians, all at play"? Were the children of the so-called "materialists" who built up the West, exiles from the Eden of ideals, of literature, of science, of art? In particular, were they obliged, in the field of scholarship, of creative business, of enlightened politics, of finer social organization, to find their leaders in the families who remained in the East?

I shall devote my attention chiefly to children of the North Central States pioneers, with occasional mention of those who migrated as young children to the region, and with a few references to farther-western states. If others find striking evidences of ability in other sections, I shall have nothing but pleasure in the result.

The men and women who settled in the North Central States long before the Civil War period, may well have been the parents of children born so late as in the middle seventies. I shall, therefore, somewhat arbitrarily, treat as "children of the pioneers" those born as late as at that time. For an older state like Ohio, to which the pioneers began to come in large numbers in the first years of the nineteenth century, this may seem to prolong the pioneer period unduly; but when Lyell, the English geologist, traveled from Cincinnati to Cleveland in the forties, he saw in the middle of the state a succession of new clearings where the felling, girdling, and burning of trees was still going on, and he "lost sight of human habitation for many leagues, save where empty movers' houses enabled the pioneers to pass the night." (The word "pioneers" is his.)

The injustice to Ohio in the drawing of a late terminus is no greater than would be done to the rest of the section by an earlier date. Through the whole Middle West, moreover, pioneer ideals of society, pioneer traditions and prepossessions long survived. Even the children born in Ohio so late as 1870 might have had fathers who came before the middle of the nineteenth century.

Obviously, it would be out of the question to determine accurately how largely each of the varied stocks which made up the section was represented in the men of talent. I shall select, from a mass of items, some, and only some, of the children of the pioneers in the North Central States who have won distinction, especially in sections other than those of their birth.

From what has been said, it would be expected that the children of the pioneers in the Middle West would succeed in business, and that this would be a strong argument for the materialist theory. The most distinguished of such children were of the New York-New England stock. But the men who became captains of industry in the West had vision and idealism respondent to the undeveloped spaces, the unexploited wilderness, and the tremendous opportunities which opened to their imagination as well as to their will power. With faith they stretched railroad lines out onto the open prairie in advance of settlement. Industrial leaders were created whose daring organization made a new business era. These descendants of the pioneers operated under squatter ideals, free from the restraints of custom and carrying a combination of individual initiative and association.

They had the frontier belief that social creation was more fundamental than formal law, and the results of their work have been profoundly influential upon American industrial history and upon political development. In the group of oil magnates born or brought up from early youth in the Middle West, were Rockefeller (who was born in New York, but who came as a child to Ohio) and several of his associates, as well as Doheny, a native of Wisconsin. Henry Ford, born in the oak openings of Michigan in 1863, exhibited characteristic Western traits when he brought to the masses the automobile in vast quantities at low prices, and with other children of pioneers made Detroit the metropolis of a new industry, and revolutionized rural life and the streets of our cities. Edison, the creator of the incandescent lamp, around whose inventions were built up huge electrical corporations, was born in Ohio in 1847 and went as a boy to Michigan. In the packing industry, J. O. Armour and the Cudahys were of Milwaukee birth. "Bet you a million" Gates, the organizer of the wire-fence industry in the form of the American Steel and Wire corporation, a multimillionaire, was born on an Illinois farm. His secretary, Judge Gary, another child of pioneers, became the head of the billion-dollar Steel Corporation. Cyrus McCormick moved from western Virginia, to develop the harvester industry in Chicago, in 1847, and his son became the head of the International Harvester Company. George W. Perkins was born in Chicago and helped to organize this company. Frank Vanderlip came to the Morgan partnership from Illinois; G. E. Roberts (Iowa), C. D. Norton (Wisconsin), and many others who have brought to the great banks of New York vigor and imagination of Western men, are significant financial types.

The head of the traction interests in New York City, Gerhard Dahl, is a native son of Norwegian pioneers in Wisconsin; John D. Ryan (of copper fame), born in Michigan, was a child of pioneers. Jay Cooke, born in Ohio in 1821, first popularized the sale of government bonds in small denominations, and afterward applied the system to financing the Northern Pacific. George Hearst, who became a leader in the Pacific railroads, was born in Missouri in 1820, of South Carolina stock, and was thirty years old before he moved to California. Julius Rosenwald (born in Illinois in 1862), as manager of a great catalogue merchandising house, as a leader in bringing big business interests to the aid of the government in the last war, and as a philanthropist, illustrates the activity of Hebrew children of the Middle West. German-born youths who came at an early age to the Middle West and grew up under its influences as business men are represented by Weyerhaeuser, the late lumber king; and by brewers like Busch, Pabst, Schlitz, and Seipp, who transformed the brewing interest from small, local enterprises to the great proportions and influence which the industry had before it was prohibited.

There was a contrast between the masters of capital who grew up in the East and those of Western training. Eastern financiers like the Vanderbilts, Goulds, Morgans, Belmonts, the later Astors, and other millionaires, built up fortunes which they had inherited, or amassed new ones, more by the ways of the speculative investor of capital in existing enterprises than by constructive activity. The Western group is not without similar traits, but on the whole it has been interested in finding new opportunities to develop enterprise, and it has been more democratic in its visions, its creations, and its endowments. The concentrations which this group brought about rested primarily upon a full realization of the opportunities presented by undeveloped resources, on the one side, and massed production on the other. In the promotion of art collections, some of the pioneer capitalists, like Clark and Hill, were nationally prominent.

It seems natural, also, that the Middle West, with the Chicago area as its center of energy, should produce for all sections the larger proportion of great railroad presidents. Listing such children of pioneers, or those who entered the Middle West as children, we find that almost all of the large railroad systems, Eastern as well as Western, have, at one time or another, been under the presidency of a child of pioneer parents.

As counterfoils to such builders of transportation routes, whose imagination was joined with the will power which made new industrial commonwealths, were such idealistic labor leaders, born in Indiana, Illinois, Iowa, or Ohio, as Eugene Debs, Garretson, once head of the Brotherhood of Railroad Conductors, Stone of the Brotherhood of Locomotive Engineers, Lee of the Brotherhood of Railroad Trainmen, John Mitchell, who led the coal strike in Roosevelt's administration, William Green, the successor of Gompers as president of the American Federation of Labor; and a younger generation is represented by John L. Lewis, president of the Mine Workers and leader of the anthracite strike in 1925. Socialistic writers like Wayland, Russell, Darrow, Simons, Benson, and others, were children of Middle Western pioneers. Others, like Jane Addams, who was born in Illinois in 1860, have carried into their writings attitudes towards social and political reform and international peace movements which have had a strong influence.

There is a long list of noted magazine writers, characterized by Roosevelt as the "muckrakers," almost all of whom have a similar origin in the Middle West.

It was to be expected, also, that the Middle West would produce political leaders. Among the many reasons why this was natural, was the American system of apportionment of political power by states, and the desire of parties to "recognize" geographical regions and to cultivate pivotal areas. But while this must be considered, it seems also true that out of the discipline of pioneer life, the training in leadership, the need of knowing how to "mix" in that seething "bowl," and out of the pioneer's hope to create a new and finer type of society in the midst of his free opportunities, came qualities that fitted Western men for leadership in a democracy. Ohio was the birthplace of Presidents Grant, Hayes, Garfield, Harrison, McKinley, Taft, and Harding. Secretaries of State like John Hay and John W. Foster showed more than a mere sectional recognition of political power. William Jennings Bryan at least falsified the fear expressed in 1896 by Charles Eliot Norton that the West would precipitate the coast in wars—that "a chance spark might fire the prairies."

Such insurgents, progressives, and independents as Altgeld (brought as an infant from Germany), Weaver, Bryan, La Follette, Borah, Dolliver, Beveridge, Folk, Tom Johnson, Walsh of Montana, indicate a certain quality in leadership by children of the pioneers that becomes marked as one passes from the older-settled portions of the North Central States to the states more recently occupied by pioneers. From Mark Hanna, McKinley, and Harding to Bryan, La Follette, Borah, Knute Nelson, and Townley, is a long step; but there are qualities common to them all. "Joe" Cannon, who came as a child to Illinois from North Carolina, and the "insurgents" who resented his use of the power of the speakership, were deeply shaped by pioneer experience.

To enumerate the children of the pioneers who have distinguished themselves in science would perhaps fatigue the general reader, for it is a long one. In the living membership of the National Academy of Science, chosen for especial distinction out of the scientists of the country, there were in 1924 over twice as many of North Atlantic as of North Central birth, although in 1870, the average birth year, the latter section had a somewhat larger population. Nevertheless, as Mr. Cattell pointed out in his *American Men of Science* (1921), the "central" states showed striking relative gains. Of the twenty-two native-born living medalists of the Academy, nine were children of pioneers of North Central states. Of the presidents of the Association for the Advancement of Science living in 1908, eleven were children of pioneer parents. Of the heads of the Carnegie Institution of Washington, formed for the promotion of research, the first president, Mr. Billings, was born in Indiana; his successor, Mr. Woodward, was born on a farm in Michigan; the present head is J. C. Merriam, born in Iowa. Of the staff, Bower, the magnetician, was born in Cincinnati; Benedict, the nutrician, in Milwaukee; Hale, the astrophysicist, in Chicago.

Of course the pioneers and their offspring became distinguished in agriculture, but not merely as materialistic farmers. They have played a prominent rôle in the raising of agriculture to a science and in exploring the mysteries of our nourishing Mother Nature. In botany, too, there are distinguished names, among them Lester

Ward, the paleobotanist, Robinson of Harvard, and Harper of Columbia, not to mention eminent leaders in the West. Among the sons of pioneers whom entomology attracted, were Comstock of Cornell, Howard, head of the national Bureau of Entomology, and Wheeler of Harvard.

Not only the flowers and insects of the prairies caught the imaginations of the pioneer boys. In zoölogy and biology they came to professorships in some of the greatest Eastern universities: Castle and East of Harvard, Conklin of Princeton, Calkins of Columbia, Jennings of Johns Hopkins, and Hornaday, director of the New York Zoölogical Park, were pioneer children.

Very remarkable contributions of the pioneers, through their sons, to science have been made in geology and geography. Perhaps the borderland where prairie ran into driftless area had an influence in awakening their minds to the problems of the earth beneath their feet, for many of them came from that region of northern Illinois and southern Wisconsin. Perhaps the large-scale simplicity of nature in the Middle West opened their eyes. The North Central States gave birth to Major Powell, John Muir,[2] Chamberlin, Van Hise, Salisbury, Leith, Crosby, Goode, Scott, and many younger, or less famous, men. Of the twenty-one presidents of the Association of American Geographers, nine were of Middle Western birth.

The heavens as well as the earth appealed to these children, for the pioneers gave birth to probably the greatest of recent astronomers: Hale and St. John, of Mount Wilson Observatory; Campbell, Holden, and

[2] Born in Scotland, brought as a child to Wisconsin.

Aitkin, of Lick; Slipher, of the Lowell Observatory; Curtis, of the Allegheny Observatory; and others of international fame, many of whom were born in Michigan and trained there. Moreover, in this connection should be mentioned the work of Chamberlin, who developed a new hypothesis of the origin of the earth, and of Huntington, whose investigations of climatology have carried him into daring hypotheses as to the relation of the sun and planets to the weather.

In physics are Hilgard and Tittman of the Coast Survey, Stratton, who went from the headship of the Bureau of Standards to the presidency of the Massachusetts Institute of Technology, Pritchett, once president of the same leading Eastern institution and now president of the Carnegie Foundation, the late Dean Sabin of Harvard, T. C. Mendenhall, Barus of Brown, D. C. Miller of the Case School, and—most noted of all, perhaps—Millikan, the finder of the electron and of the new ray.

In chemistry are such names as Noyes, Franklin, and Hulett; and in mathematics are leading professors, including Moore and Dickson.

Among engineers are Herbert Hoover, born in Iowa, whose work in Belgian relief, as Food Director in the War, and as Secretary of Commerce (where he has been the power behind important movements for eliminating waste, combining power projects, and treaties between states for the use of water); Shonts; Wallace, of the Panama Canal; Hubbard and Hayes, of the Telephone and Telegraph Company; Mead, of the Reclamation Survey; Dean C. A. Adams, of the Harvard Engineering School; and a distinguished group of hydraulic engineers who took captive the

Sierra waterfalls and made possible long-distance transmission of water power. These developments in turn may result in new giant power coördination of hydro-electric plants, and possibly in giving legal existence to regions as well as states as a factor in government. The builder of the Muscle Shoals plant for nitrogen extraction, Washburn, was an Illinois son. There were subway engineers, like Boyd of New York and of the Boston Elevated. Irving T. Bush of the Bush Terminal is the son of a pioneer who migrated in his youth to Michigan.

To the Middle Western Yankee and his neighbors, invention came naturally. Among those who were of Western birth or who were youthful pioneers, were Marsh and Appleby, who, on the frontier of wheat cultivation, invented farm machinery; Glidden, who invented barbed wire; Norton, who developed the sheet-metal industry. Hayes, whose work on tungstenchrome steel became so important to the automobile industry; Hyatt, the maker of celluloid; Cowles, whose work on electrical furnace reduction was important; Stevens, who developed the roller flour mill; Hurley, the inventor of pneumatic tools; Lillie, who constructed the first electric railroad; and Gillette, of the safety razor—all belonged to this list. But the leading Western inventors are Brush, of the arc light, born on a farm in Ohio in 1869; Wilbur and Orville Wright, who made the airplane possible; and Thomas Edison—born in Ohio in 1847—who went as a boy to Michigan. Of the eleven winners of the Edison gold medal up to 1924, four were foreign-born, four were natives of the North Atlantic States, and three were born in the North Central States of pioneer parents.

THE CHILDREN OF THE PIONEERS

To medicine and surgery the Middle West has contributed such eminent men as the Mayos, born in Minnesota; Dr. J. D. Bryant, long a leader in New York; Harvey Cushing of Harvard; Benedict, the head of the nutrition department of the Carnegie Institution; Dean Vaughan of Ann Arbor, who was chairman of the division of medical sciences of the National Research Council during the War; and a notable group of Chicago surgeons and physicians, living and dead.

At first sight, the lists above given may seem, to some, to sustain the conclusion of those who assigned to the children of the pioneers a career of action and of devotion to materialism rather than to spiritual interests. But the world now recognizes that there is idealism, vision, and humanity in the work of men like these and that the humanities, so-called, are not the only fields of culture, of improved social relations, of the elevation of the mind of man. Certainly it can hardly be said that reversion to barbarism has been the fate of such pioneer children.

Let us turn next to the humanities themselves. Although the frontier proper is not the soil on which the finer life of the spirit would be expected to flourish, and although the first rough forest choppers or huntsmen were not of the sort to breed scholars and men of letters, there were in all the new Western states centers where refinement and a social élite were to be found. Sons and daughters of families distinguished in the East did go to the West. There were centers of aristocracy, in the better sense of the word, in pioneer regions, which kept alive the traditions of culture. Among the immigrants, particularly of German and Scandinavian stock, were also men of learning, lovers

[271]

of art, music, and literature.

We find painters like W. M. Chase, a member of the American Academy, born in 1849 in Indiana; Gari Melchers; Carroll Beckwith of the National Academy of Design, born in Missouri; Kenyon Cox; and such exponents of animal folklore as Dan Beard, F. S. Church, and Peter Newell. Musical critics, like Krehbiel, came from this pioneer environment to the metropolis. St. Louis, Cincinnati, and Milwaukee, especially, fostered the love of music, because, perhaps, of the German element.

In sculpture, America has not had many distinguished names, but most of these belong to pioneers and their children. Hiram Powers was a youth of fourteen when he came to Ohio from Vermont in 1819 and learned his art of a Cincinnati German. J. Q. A. Ward was born in Ohio in 1830, and his "Indian Hunter" in Central Park, New York, is more characteristic of America than is Powers's "Greek Slave." Lorado Taft was born in Illinois, and he has used Middle Western themes for his material. His Columbus monument in the Union Station in Washington is also well known. Niehaus, who did various statues in Washington, was a native of Cincinnati. Cyrus Dallin of Boston was born in Utah of distinctly pioneer parents, and his Indian in front of the Boston Art Museum carries the breath of the pioneer West into the old center of culture. Gutzon Borglum was a native of a pioneer Mountain state, but was educated in Kansas. Barnard (sculptor for the Pennsylvania Capitol), although born in Pennsylvania, spent his boyhood in Iowa. Janet Scudder, perhaps the most widely known of women sculptors, maker of elfin fountain figures, was of Indiana birth.

Middle Western quality shows itself unmistakably in architecture. Daring and massiveness came naturally from the pioneer section. Architects and builders experimented there with skyscrapers—probably the most noteworthy contribution of the United States to that art. Burnham is recognized not only here but abroad as a city planner and an architect. His guiding hand in the gathering of a great group of architects to produce the World's Columbian Exposition at Chicago, marked an epoch in the development of architectural taste in the United States. Such of his buildings as the Flatiron in New York and the Union Station in Washington and such re-planning as at Chicago and West Point, are well known. Coming to Chicago as an eight-year-old boy, he grew up with children of New England pioneers, like Charles L. Hutchinson, president of the Fine Arts Institute, ready to give wealth and energy to making real their dreams of a "city beautiful." Henry Adams relates how he sat down before Richard Hunt's dome at the Chicago Exposition in amazement, and concluded that "Chicago was the first expression of American thought as a unity."

Burnham's words carry a message from the pioneers who made the Middle West: "Make no little plans, they have no magic to stir men's blood and probably themselves will not be realized. Make big plans; aim high in hope and work." These words, it is true, are from a native of Massachusetts, but they find their driving force from his whole life in the wilful and masterful city of the Middle West. They speak the language of Chicago, not of Boston. Cass Gilbert, born in Ohio and educated in Minnesota, designed the Woolworth building, perhaps the most famous achievement in New York's distinctive architecture. Henry Bacon (Illinois) produced that noble example of sheer beauty, the Lincoln Memorial in Washington; Charles Moore, the chairman of the National Fine Arts Commission, was born in Michigan.

In the drama also, in spite of its lack of urban centers, the pioneer Middle West contributed such men as Augustus Thomas, born in St. Louis.

In addition to the grinding necessities of pioneer life and the appeals to ambition in material endeavor, the development of general literature suffered at first in the Middle West from the relative lack of schools and of competent colleges and from absence of the atmosphere of a settled and cultivated society. This stimulates literary expression and enriches and criticizes the author's work. The Middle West, moreover, as we have seen, was far from being homogeneous—a factor which seems important in literary expression.

But the children made striking contributions to American literature. The pioneers started with artificial and formal imitation, but the children came to express the Middle Western scene and its spiritual quality in a way that attracted the interest of the nation and, indeed, shaped the form of what some Eastern and European critics have called the distinctly American literature. In so large a nation with such varied sections, a national, rather than a new, type of literature is perhaps not to be expected. But of the seven first members to be chosen to the American Academy of Arts and Letters, by the National Institute of Arts and Letters, three were children of the pioneers, and so are one-fourth, at least, of the present members. Their membership in

THE CHILDREN OF THE PIONEERS

the department of literature of the Institute is one-sixth. The Pulitzer prize for fiction has fallen for three-fifths of its awards to children of the pioneers.

Ohio was the birthplace of William Dean Howells, who came to be the dean of American literature, editor of the *Atlantic Monthly* in Boston and of *Harper's Magazine* in New York. He led the movement away from the romantic to the realistic and substituted the American scene for the English. Ohio also gave birth to Albion Tourgée, Mary Catherwood, Edith Thomas, Mary Watts, Brand Whitlock, Sherwood Anderson, Irving Babbitt (whose critical essays are hardly a reflection of the Western spirit). Indiana was the birthplace of James Whitcomb Riley (whose poetry springs from the very soil of Hoosierdom), Joaquin Miller, John Hay, Piatt, Edward Eggleston, Maurice Thompson, Lew Wallace, David Graham Phillips, Booth Tarkington, Meredith Nicholson, William Vaughn Moody, Theodore Dreiser, as well as George Ade, Zane Grey, Gene Stratton Porter, George Barr McCutcheon, and Samuel Merwin. From Illinois came Mary Austin, Elbert Hubbard, Harriet Monroe, Edward R. Taylor, Henry Fuller, Ernest Poole, H. K. Webster, Frank Norris, Vachel Lindsay, Edgar Lee Masters, Carl Sandburg. Wisconsin was the birthplace of Hamlin Garland, whose novels and autobiography present a classical picture of the pioneer period; and of Zona Gale. From Missouri came Eugene Field, producer of a new type of newspaper humor, Rupert Hughes, Winston Churchill, and Paul Elmer More (who stands out with Irving Babbitt as preëminently representative of Eastern culture). Iowa was the birthplace of Emerson Hough, and of Herbert Quick, whose trilogy of

novels brilliantly exhibits the movements of Western
pioneers.

No contribution of the West to literature was more
characteristic than that of its humorists. Mark Twain
was born in Missouri in 1835; Bill Nye was brought
as a baby by his Maine parents to the pineries of Wisconsin; Petroleum V. Nasby learned the trade of a
printer while a boy in Ohio; Robert Burdette came as a
boy to Peoria, Illinois; Abe Martin was born in Ohio;
Peter Dunne, the creator of Dooley, in Chicago.
Eugene Field and George Ade have already been
named. New Englanders like Artemus Ward drifted
early to Ohio, and Josh Billings came under the same
influence.

On a border-line, in a class of their own, are the
cartoonists who have revealed the quality of American,
and particularly of Middle Western, life by their char-
acterization of the faiths and foibles of the common
people. Among them perhaps the best known are
McCutcheon, Briggs, and Bud Fisher, but there is a
large group of these men, almost all of them the children of the pioneers.

Percy H. Boynton in his recent book, *Some Contemporary Americans,* gives especial attention to ten
authors, of whom four are children of the North Central pioneers and the fifth is Willa Cather, whose
youth was spent in Nebraska.

The leading names in the humanities in the universities of the country, Eastern as well as Western, would
have surprised the writer in *Blackwood's* who in
1819 predicted barbarism for pioneer children and
grandchildren. Among the prominent scholars in the
study of ancient classics in this country, are or have

been many of the sons of Western settlers. In Greek, Paul Shorey of Chicago, Capps of Princeton, T. D. Seymour of Yale; in Latin, Hendrickson of Yale, Slaughter and Showerman of Wisconsin—are examples of a considerable group of Western-born classicists. With them may be associated the professors of classical history at Columbia—Botsford and Westermann; Frank of Johns Hopkins; and the Egyptologists, Reisner of Harvard and Breasted of Chicago. In modern languages, the West has furnished to Eastern universities many of their leading professors of German, such as Thomas of Columbia, Hewitt of Cornell, and Palmer of Yale. In philosophy, Ladd, Thilly, and Josiah Royce are striking examples.

The Middle West was particularly fecund in the production of historians from among these pioneer boys. Ohio produced Rhodes, H. H. Bancroft, Sloane, Beveridge, Chalfant Robinson, Schevill, Spears, and many others. In Indiana were born Abbott of Harvard, Rives, Harding, Woodburn, Bowers, and others; in Illinois, James Harvey Robinson (formerly of Columbia), McLaughlin, Goodspeed, and Breasted, of Chicago; Nicolay came to that state as a child. Michigan was the birthplace of Avery, Van Tyne, Knight, and Charles Moore. To Wisconsin came as boys G. B. Adams and Thwaites; and it was the native state of J. B. Perkins, H. E. Bolton, Schafer, and F. J. Turner. A country town in Iowa gave birth to Becker of Cornell and E. D. Adams of Stanford.

The list is too long for complete presentation. It shows a common quality on the part of these men, not only in striking out new lines of investigation, but in interest in the common people; in the emphasis upon economic and social, geographical and psychological interpretation; in the attention to social development rather than to the writing of narrative history of the older type, wherein the heroes were glorified. To the children of the pioneers, if not to their fathers, history was not the lengthened shadow of the great man; it was not the romantic tale, nor the mere effort to set forth bald annals.

Economists born of Middle Western pioneers include Taussig, Gay, Carver, and Young, of Harvard, Johnson of Pennsylvania, Seager of Columbia, Droppers of Williams, Fetter of Princeton, Laughlin of Chicago, Adams of Michigan, Commons of Wisconsin, Meyer of the Interstate Commerce Commission, Koren, the statistician, Victor Clark, and many others.

In sociology, are Ward, Ross, and George Vincent, now president of the Rockefeller Foundation; among ethnologists and anthropologists, Holmes, Moore, Dorsey, McGee, A. B. Lewis, and Moorehead.

If one takes the choice of university presidents as a test of sectional contributions to culture, one finds the children of the pioneers well represented, for among them are Presidents Hibben of Princeton and Angell of Yale (he came to Michigan as a small child), ex-President John Finley of the State University of New York, Hutchinson and Murlin, both ex-presidents of Boston University, Nichols, formerly president of Dartmouth, and Atwood of Clark. Ex-President Charles Kendall Adams, of Cornell and of Wisconsin, came as a young man to an Iowa farm. In the West (which has in the past chosen its presidents so generally from the East), there have come from the sons of pioneers: Harper of Chicago, Van Hise of Wisconsin,

Campbell of California, and Scott of Northwestern. Chicago and Wisconsin have likewise chosen their present presidents from Middle Western natives— Mason and Frank. But these young men might more properly be classed as grandsons, than sons, of pioneers.

Many of the deans of schools and colleges of the important Eastern universities, including Harvard and Yale, had pioneer fathers; and a long list of prominent educators could be given, whose early youth was passed in country towns of the pioneering states. They include such men as Monroe and McMurry of Columbia, Hanus of Harvard, the late R. G. Boone, De Garmo of Cornell; and Ella Flagg Young, once Superintendent of Schools of Chicago. Librarians include Spofford, who went as a boy to Ohio and whose work was foundational in developing the Library of Congress, Anderson of the New York Public Library, and Bolton of the Boston Athenæum.

In law, the children of the pioneers have won the highest honors at bench and bar in their own section and have contributed such distinguished jurists and reformers of law as Chief Justice Taft (Ohio); Dean Pound (Nebraska); and Wambaugh and Hudson of the Harvard Law School; such leaders as the late John C. Spooner in constitutional law; Professor Kirchwey, the authority on penology of the New York School of Social Work; many important members of New York firms; and Judge Gary, head of the Steel Corporation.

In the matter of law and the Constitution, the attitude of the pioneer children is indicated in the following which such political leaders as Bryan, Roosevelt, and La Follette acquired in the West. Movements for the initiative, referendum, and recall, for direct primaries, for regulation of corporations, for diminishing the power of the judiciary to check state innovations in legislation, usually gained their first considerable strength in states controlled by children of the pioneers, and then, like the weather, cycloned their way to the East and won national acceptance. Today the President is nominated in about half the states by preferential primaries; the Constitution has been amended by provisions for the graduated income tax, by the direct popular election of senators of the United States, by prohibition, and by nation-wide woman suffrage. There are those who will regard this record as a proof of barbarism; but it is hardly the product of mere materialism.

Among the political scientists, familiar names are Beard, once of Columbia, Corwin of Princeton, Merriam of Chicago, Reinsch, once Minister to China, and Ogg of Wisconsin.

Included in a list of twenty-five preachers voted the most influential in America by a poll of about 25,000 preachers of every Protestant denomination, one-third of those selected were children of the Middle West.

When the World War came on, with its call for action and effective organization, the Middle West furnished, out of the men born in its pioneer period, far more than its share of the principal administrators in the organizations which assisted the government. Such names as those of Herbert Hoover of the Food Control, Garfield of the Fuel Control, Hurley of the Shipping Board, Gay of the Commercial Economy Board, and Carrie Chapman Catt, Anna H. Shaw, and Eva P. Moore, as representative of women, serve to indicate the part of the children of the pioneers. The army was commanded by General Pershing, born in Missouri in 1860, and the conscription was effected under General Crowder, born in Missouri in 1859. General Dawes, a native of Ohio, was head of supplies of the American Expeditionary Force and was later the head of the Dawes Commission which opened the way for a rehabilitated Europe.

Some of the most prominent editors and publishers of daily newspapers, moulders of ideas, in the East as well as in the West, have been children of pioneers, or emigrants to the West in their early youth. Reid and Hay of the *New York Tribune;* White and Gay, formerly of the *Evening Post;* Ochs, publisher, Finley, of the editorial staff, of the *Times;* Hearst (son of a Missouri pioneer who has lived in California) of the *American* and the nation-wide string of "Hearst" papers; Frank Cobb, editor of the *World* for many years, called the strongest writer on the New York press since Horace Greeley; Allan Dawson, of the defunct *Globe*—were all children of pioneers. Pulitzer, who bought the *World,* was himself a later emigrant to the West, but over one-third of the principal writers on the staff of that metropolitan daily were (two years ago, at least) of Western birth. Besides the New York list, there were such prominent editors as Murat Halstead, W. R. Nelson of the Kansas City *Star,* Scott Bone of Seattle, M. H. DeYoung of San Francisco, Harrison Gray Otis of Los Angeles, Casper Yost of St. Louis, William Penn Nixon of Chicago, and William Allen White of Emporia.

It was Melville E. Stone, born in Illinois in 1848, who established the Associated Press; and a large number of his principal lieutenants were drawn from the same section. G. G. Bain founded the Illustrated News Service, and M. A. McRea, the Scripps-McRea service. In. such institutions we see characteristic Middle Western quality in their organizing capacity and their effort to reach the people.

The list of leading editors and writers for the periodicals, who had a similar origin, is too long to enumerate. It embraces, not only the "muckrakers," but such writers as Howells of the *Atlantic* and *Harper's;* Shaw of the *Review of Reviews;* S. S. McClure, who founded *McClure's* (but who was a native of Ireland); Robert Underwood Johnson of the *Century* (he came as a youth to Ohio); Alvin Johnson of the staff of the *New Republic;* Kellogg of the *Survey;* Wheeler of the *Literary Digest* and *Public Opinion;* and Siddall of the *American.*

The hardships that fell upon pioneer children must have rested with peculiar force upon the daughters, for they were obliged to occupy themselves largely with household duties, in isolation from the social environment that helped to stimulate thought, and, for the most part, without the opportunities of higher education which their ambitious brothers could secure. Such a home life is portrayed in the volume entitled *The Pioneer,* by Anna Howard Shaw, who came as a four-year-old child to the oak openings of Michigan in 1851 and rose to leadership in the feminist movement. Among other distinguished daughters of the pioneers are Carrie Chapman Catt, May Wright Sewall, Edna South Davis, and Elizabeth Jordan, natives of Wisconsin; Ida Husted Harper of Indiana; Frances Willard (brought as a girl to Illinois), Jane Addams and Julia Lathrop, who were both born in that state; Victoria

Woodhull and Mabel Boardman, of Ohio. In old centers of culture, like Boston, a daughter of the pioneers is at the head of the League of Women Voters. Of the twelve selected last year as "the greatest women of America," one-third were children of pioneers.

Though such a list (incomplete as it is) as this which we have been making may appear as tiresome as a catalogue of ships in Homer, it is perhaps the only way in which one can effectively set forth the part played in recent American civilization by distinguished children of the Middle Western pioneers. The pioneer's own contributions were rather in the upbuilding of new communities and in laying the foundations for a new type of society, in providing for a better future for his children. That the children themselves were not intellectually stunted by this transplantation of the parents into the wilderness, would seem to be proved.

That a few of these names were those of men who could only be classed as children of the pioneers by liberal construction of the phrase, is probable. In such varying states as those that made up the North Central group, there must be some men listed who were grandsons of the typical pioneers, especially in Ohio; or who were born of mature parents who had come at the very end of the period of pioneering. This would apply with peculiar force to cities like Cincinnati, St. Louis, and Chicago.

But it has not been practicable to carry the analysis far enough to determine who should be eliminated because of this consideration. As was said in the beginning, pioneer spirit and conceptions prevailed even in these cities, long after the era of especial hardships of pioneering passed away. The author has been impressed with the high proportion of these men of ability who first saw the light on pioneer farms of states settled later than Ohio. This is particularly the case with the most striking examples of ability among them. And these eminent men will bear comparison with the best of New England, of the Middle States, or the South, chosen on the same basis.

It must be borne in mind that the result was partly due to the fact that to the little Western colleges had come faculties recruited largely from the East, and that Eastern preachers, editors, and teachers came to live in practically every Western community. But this is merely to say that not all the pioneers were the materialists that they have been supposed to be by Eastern critics. It is probable that in many ways the West, with its pioneer environment, shaped the thinking of these men quite as much as they shaped their social environment. Many of them came because they preferred the kind of society which the West furnished; and not a small proportion of those who came with the missionary spirit, to carry to the section the New England type of society, found after a few years that they had so lost their loyalty to the East that the idea of returning was repugnant. Indeed, some of them became even more ardent Westerners than those who had not originally gone forth to "save the West."

Allowance must also be made for the fact that so many of the various scholars and writers of the section returned to the East in their young manhood for their higher education and then became enamored of the academic life and thus went on to leadership in their profession. Nevertheless, the Western quality, as has been said, is generally visible in their work, and the initiative, the exploring instinct, the talent for work, which were born of pioneer customs and ideals, help to explain why, in so many cases, the leadership in things academic, as well as in the professions in general, fell to them. And it must always be remembered that the pioneers sacrificed much to send their sons to college. They were not such contented materialists as to let their children fall into barbarism. They and their children built up the great state universities of the West, and very many of the distinguished children of the pioneers were trained in them.

When the man from the Mississippi Valley walks the streets of New York City, he is, in a sense, at home. He sees the electric lights, the architecture that shapes its famous Babylonic sky line, and the idealism thereof —which made Lowes Dickinson pause in his designation of the common man of America as "all too common," when he looked upon the glowing lights, the silhouettes of massive climbing structures, seen from his Brooklyn room, and exclaimed: or is it "all divine? Divine somehow in its potentialities?" These are the works of engineers and architects for whom the initiative came from the Middle West, many of them children of the pioneers, changing their expression from the horizontal to the vertical, as the frontier expansion ends and urban congestion takes its place.

Drawn into that metropolitan vortex came as children of pioneers most of the editors who have shaped the nation's thinking from their New York offices in recent years; the writers who have given the city publishers their fame; some of her leading playwrights, of her scholars, of her reformers, even of her preachers.

In every field the children of the Middle Western pioneers have shown varied traits, but generally speaking there runs through all of their work the Lincolnian quality—the interest in the common man, the attempt to serve him by mass production, by opening new areas, and by accelerating and cheapening communication by rail, by "auto," by airplane. The novelists have aimed to express realities and to portray the life of the average man; the historians have been interested less in heroes than in the masses, in economic and social history; the reformers have been "too helpful" to suit the native Knickerbocker. There has been a breaking away from the past by the constructive capitalist, with his large combinations, and by socialist labor leaders.

But in all this interest in the mass there is a danger of the loss of individuality, originality. If the grandchildren of the pioneers aim to standardize us all to the measure of the average man; if they cease to look upon universities as levers, and come to think of them as social mirrors; if they strive to exile the rare man, the dissenter from majority opinion, they will be false to the spirit of the pioneer.

CHAPTER XI

IS SECTIONALISM IN AMERICA DYING AWAY?[1]

A satisfactory discussion of whether American sectionalism is dying away, demands inquiry into what
sectionalism has been in this country, and what are its
bases; after this has been attempted, prediction will
find a ground on which to act. Mindful of the traditions
of the historical craft, I shall offer some suggestions on
the preliminary questions and shall not venture far in
the uncertain sea of prophecy.

The student of American history since the Civil War,
and especially in the last decade, seeing the sweep and
power of the nationalizing movement, may readily agree
with Secretary Root that "our whole life has swung
away from old state centers, and is crystallizing about
national centers." From this it might also be assumed
that sectionalism is passing away with the decline of the
state. But the state has shown marked vitality since
these words of Mr. Root, and, in fact, history does not
justify us in laying so much stress upon the state as the
anti-national factor in our development. From the point
of view of constitutional law and the division of legislative functions, the rôle of the state has, of course,
been highly important. But, after all, the deepest significance of state resistance to the nationalizing process
has lain in the fact that state sovereignty was the sword
wielded by sectionalism. It is because the state was one

[1] A paper read before the American Sociological Society, Madison, December 28, 1907. Reprinted by permission from *The American Journal of
Sociology*, March, 1908.

of a group with common interests menaced by federal action, that its protests had power. When we look at underlying forces of economic and social life, and at the distribution of political power in the Union, we find that sectionalism antedated nationalism, that it has endured, though often concealed by our political forms, through the whole of our history, and that it is far from certain that it would pass away though the state should be extinguished; indeed, it might gather new vitality and power from such an event.

There are degrees of sectionalism, varying from that exhibited in the struggle of North against South over the slavery issue, culminating in war between the sections, to the lesser manifestations of resistance to national homogeneity and to the power of a national majority. I shall recognize as tests of sectionalism all of those methods by which a given area resists national uniformity, whether by mere opposition in public opinion on the part of a considerable area, or by formal protest, or by combining its votes in Congress and in presidential elections; and also those manifestations of economic and social separateness involved in the existence in a given region of a set of fundamental assumptions, a mental and emotional attitude which segregates the section from other sections or from the nation as a whole. Sooner or later such sectional influences find expression in politics and legislation, and they are even potential bases for forcible resistance.

Geographical conditions and the stocks from which the people sprang are the most fundamental factors in shaping sectionalism. Of these the geographical influence is peculiarly important in forming a society like that of the United States, for it includes in its influence those factors of economic interests, as well as environmental conditions, that affect the psychology of a people.

The United States is imperial in area. If we lay a map of Europe upon a map of the United States constructed to the same scale, the western coast of Spain would coincide with the coast of southern California; Constantinople would rest near Charleston, South Carolina; Sicily, near New Orleans; and the southern coast of the Baltic would fall in line with the southern coast of Lake Superior. Thus, in size, the United States is comparable, not with a single nation of Europe, but with all of Europe, exclusive of Russia. It is also comparable with Europe in the fact that it is made up of separate geographic provinces, each capable, in size, resources, and peculiarities of physical conditions, to be the abode of a European nation, or of several nations. American history is in large measure still colonial history—the history of the exploration, conquest, colonization, and development of these physiographic provinces, and the beginnings of a process of adaptation of society to the section which it has occupied. The movement is too new, too incomplete, to allow us to affirm that the influences of diverse physical sections have as yet worked out their effects upon the American nation.

American society has spread westward into the wilderness. It has shown a sectionalism arising from the opposition of interests between the outer edge of this advance, where nature reduced man to the primitive conditions of the frontier, and the older areas of occupation, where social development had progressed farther. The sectionalism of East and West has been a migrating sectionalism in American history, for regions once typically Western have later, under a process of assimilation, become characteristically Eastern, with all the phenomena of complex and developed society, economic and social. Thus the sectionalism due to the movement of American settlement into the wilderness is a declining sectionalism. It is by no means in immediate prospect of extinction, and in view of the persistent effects of social habits and ideals this process will be influential as a sectional influence long after the westward movement of American society itself has ceased.

But, in the long run, as American society loses the mobility stimulated by the artificial and transient opportunities of free land and the demand for labor in sparsely occupied areas, the sectionalism due to physiographic conditions, economic interests, and constituent stocks of settled societies, will persist, if sectionalism persists at all.

How far have these factors already produced sections in the United States, and how far have these sections given way to a movement of national uniformity?

Writing in the middle of the eighteenth century, Thomas Mitchell proposed that the English colonies be divided into northern, middle, and southern unions— "three distinct and different countries, separated from one another by natural boundaries; different in situation, climate, soil, products, etc., while the several colonies included in these divisions, which we look upon as separate countries, are all one and the same country in these respects." This early recognition of these separate colonial divisions, while the settlements were still limited to the seaboard, is significant of the fact that physical conditions and component stock had, almost from the beginning, produced three coastal sections—New England, the Middle Region, and the South. I shall not take the time to characterize them, nor to point out how their separate economic interests controlled the history of politics and legislation in the later colonial period, the Revolution, the Confederation, and the era of the dominance of the Federal party. It was only in the presence of superior danger that these mutually repellent groups were drawn into union; only by sectional compromises that they achieved a constitution; only by the fact that the Middle Region was a buffer area, a fighting ground, and consequently afforded an opportunity for breaking the impact of sections and of affording a means of accommodating rival interests and shifting the balance of power, that the union held together in those early years. The fierceness of resistance of the Jeffersonian Democracy of South and West to the Federalism of commercial New England, is well known. The Virginia and Kentucky resolutions constituted a platform for sectional defense. The equal fierceness of New England Federalism's opposition to the triumphant Jeffersonian Democracy, is equally well known. The Hartford Convention was the expression of the revolt. Parties in this era were distinctly sectional, as anyone may see by examining the maps of presidential elections, or of votes in Congress on test issues. The existence of sectional differences between New England, the Middle Region, and the South, today, will not be denied.

On the whole, however, as capitalistic development progressed, foreign immigration swarmed in, urban populations widened their influence and absorbed the country places for their playgrounds; and, especially as the traditional spiritual faiths and moral convictions tend to pass away, the similarities between New England and the Middle Region tend to increase; while the seaboard South finds itself in continued contrast with these Northern sections, but increasingly absorbed into the interior Southern section. And yet, in spite of the blurring of these old divisional lines, it may well be a question whether New England, with its only opportunity for sectional expansion in the direction of Canada, with its industrial life threatened by the transit of manufacturing toward the areas of production, might not at some indefinite future find its interests in closer relations with the adjoining Canadian area, and develop a new economic sectionalism under a conceivable political union of eastern Canada and the United States, or of Canada and New England.

I turn from conjecture to ask attention to another type of section, significant because it is concealed by the way in which it lies within, but not identical with, the lines of several different states. There are many such sections which have had real influence upon our history but which the historian, with his eyes fixed upon nation and on state, has largely overlooked.

The Piedmont Plateau, or upland area of the South, reaches from the fall line, behind the old tidewater, southwestward to the Allegheny Mountains, in a long belt running from Pennsylvania to Georgia. It is familiar to the geologist, less so to the historian—and yet important, and illustrative of what is occurring elsewhere at present. Historically, it was closely associated with the Great Valley of Pennsylvania and its continuation, the Shenandoah Valley, as well as with the Allegheny Mountains. The section comprised in these physiographic provinces runs like a peninsula from Pennsylvania southward to the rear of tidewater, until it touches the northern edge of the Gulf Plains. Cut off from tidewater, not only by the falls of the rivers (the head of navigation), but also by a parallel strip of pine barrens through much of its length, this region was in many respects a projection of the Pennsylvania type into the very midst of the South. It was settled in the middle of the eighteenth century, largely by migrations from Pennsylvania of Scotch-Irish, Germans, and English pioneers, having little contact with, or resemblance at first to, the seaboard life, either economically, politically, or socially. It was the first distinctively Western region, nonslaveholding, grain and cattle raising, a land of dissenting sects, of primitive democratic conditions, remote from the coast, and finding the connection with Baltimore, Philadelphia, and the Pennsylvania valley, both in spiritual and economic life, more intimate than with the tidewaters of Maryland, Virginia, North Carolina, and South Carolina, within whose boundary lines it chiefly lay. In every one of these states, contests occurred between this upcountry and the coast. Indeed, the local history of each of these colonies and states, in the period from 1750 until about 1830, is perhaps dominated by the antagonisms of the upcountry against tidewater. In every one, the tidewater minority area, where wealth and slaves preponderated, ruled the more populous primitive interior counties by apportionment of the legislatures so as to secure the effective majority of the representatives. Unjustly taxed, deprived of due participation in government, their rights neglected, they protested, vainly for the most part, in each of these colonies and states. But all this long struggle of a

section with definite social and economic unity and separate interests, and with enduring influences upon the
history of the interior, must be worked out from fragments in the monographic treatment of the individual
states. A whole section was engaged for nearly three
generations in a struggle for its interests. Since the section acted in separate states, the movement was obscured. But it was the existence of this section that gave
Jefferson his power. It produced the men themselves, or
the ancestors of Andrew Jackson, James K. Polk, and
Abraham Lincoln, and gave to them the traits and the
following that made possible their careers and their
contributions. We can infer the influence of the section
as we see the towns for retail trade develop along the
fall line at the edge of the Piedmont, gradually relieving
the country from direct commercial colonial bondage to
England. We note its increasing political power, by
such evidences as the advance of the capitals to its eastern edge—as that of Virginia from Williamsburg to
Richmond in 1779; South Carolina's to Columbia in
1790; North Carolina's to Raleigh in 1791; Pennsylvania's to Lancaster in 1799 and to Harrisburg in 1812.
From the Piedmont came the men who demanded statehood for the Western settlements in the Revolution,
basing their demand on the antagonism between their
interests and those of the coast.[2]

The significance of the Piedmont area was diminished
when the cotton plant crossed over to the section, bringing slavery with it, in the period from about 1800 to
1830. Just prior to the completion of the ascendency
of slavery over the Piedmont, this section showed a
sharp contrast with the tidewater South, in its friendly

[2] Cf. Chapter 4.

attitude toward federal internal improvements and tariff and, in general, its responsiveness to loose-construction legislative programmes. Even in the matter of slavery, there was a final struggle between this section and the coast, in each state, for some means of ridding the South of this labor system. The independence of the state of West Virginia is an enduring evidence of the antagonism of interests between the interior and the seaboard, and the attitude of the other mountain districts in the Civil War was a grave disadvantage to the South. Helper's *Impending Crisis* was an exposition of ideas not uncommon in this whole interior section.

The section, however, became far larger than the hill and mountain region of the Piedmont and Allegheny system. As the pioneers of the Piedmont had pushed into Kentucky and Tennessee in the period of the Revolution, so their descendants, in the years when slavery was transforming the upcountry, moved across the Ohio in great numbers, and up the Missouri and into the northern portions of the Gulf Plains. The whole area occupied by the nonslaveholding poorer Southern pioneers had a community of prejudices, traditions, fundamental assumptions, religious tendencies, ideals, and economic and social interests, and these are still clearly traceable and influential.

In the Mississippi Valley the colonization of different stocks resulted in interesting sectional groupings, which may next be considered as a means of illustrating how such groupings affect political history. I have just spoken of the settlement of the Southern pioneers in the hilly and forested areas of southern Indiana and Illinois and the similar regions of Missouri. In the Old Northwest this movement continued till it reached the non-forested prairie lands, which were almost untouched by 1830. In the Southwest the same kind of population passed from Kentucky and Tennessee and from the parent Piedmont region into northern Alabama, eastern Mississippi, and into Arkansas and Texas.

A different stream entered the Northwest about 1830 and continued to flow with little interruption until the Civil War. This stream had its original source in the hill country of western and northern New England. Between 1800 and 1820 colonies of these people occupied central New York and the margin of the Great Lakes in that state and in Ohio, especially in the Connecticut Reserve. A combined New York and New England stream poured into the prairies in the succeeding generation, taking up the work of colonization of the northern Mississippi Valley at the boundary where the Southern element had met the prairies and had stopped. Between the settlers of the northern region and those to the south were sharp antagonisms, which showed themselves in many ways.

In the Southwest, in the years between 1820 and 1860, the planters entered the Gulf Plains in increasing numbers, bringing cotton culture and slavery to this section as they had before brought them to the Piedmont. They sought especially western Georgia and the black soils of central Alabama, and the alluvial lands of the Yazoo district along the Mississippi River. We have, thus, five zones within the Mississippi Valley: (1) the New England-New York area; (2) the Southern settlers north of the Ohio River, in free states; (3) the Southern settlers in the border area, including West Virginia, the hill country of Kentucky and Tennessee, Missouri and Arkansas, where slavery was a subordinate element; (4) the uplands of northern Alabama and Georgia and northern and eastern Mississippi; and (5) the Cotton Kingdom of the Lower South.

I will next ask your attention to the accompanying maps,[3] which show how clearly party action has reflected the influence of these sectional groupings.

In the first series of maps, Democratic pluralities in presidential elections are shown in black for the counties of Ohio, Indiana, and Illinois, 1856 to 1900. It is seen that the New England-New York area is consistently Republican, and that the Southern zone, especially in Illinois, shows Democratic majorities. So clearly marked is this, in the latter state, that the map might almost serve for one exhibiting the areas of the forests extending like a huge delta along the Illinois River, in contrast with the prairie lands. So deeply seated is political habit that, in election after election, almost the same party sections are seen in all these states. On the whole, the explanation for this grouping would appear to be that the different stocks followed their different habits; and that psychological tendencies, rather than the physiographic fact of prairie against forest, determined sectional alignment. But the physical conditions determined the location of the stocks, and they continue to exert an influence.

In the next map[4] are to be seen the votes of the Gulf States in the election of 1836, when Van Buren and White were contestants. The relation of the Whig vote to the cotton soils, and consequently to the areas of densest negro settlement and of wealth, is obvious and

---

[3] See Plate I. The elections chosen are typical. If the whole series were given, the similarity in the sectional subdivisions would be made even more striking.

[4] See Plate II.

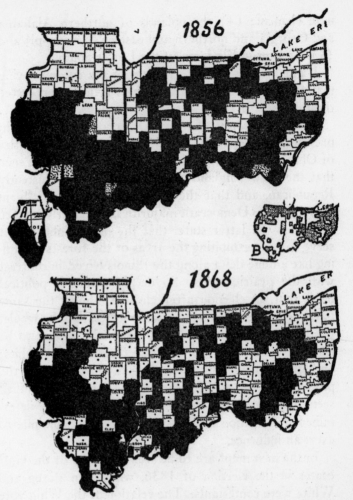

PLATE I. PRESIDENTIAL ELECTIONS IN (

The Democratic counties are shown in black, the Repub
Map A shows in black the settled area of Illinois at the
the forested area, leaving the prairies to be taken by the Nor
Map B shows the Free Soil vote in 1844, after the Nort
cent or more of the total vote.
Map C shows the location of the Western (or Connectic

1888

L. ERIE
C
Cleveland
WESTERN RESERVE

1900

, AND ILLINOIS, 1856, 1868, 1888, AND 1900.

riod of Southern settlement; it shows also that the South occupied
gan to flow. The area shown is that where the vote was 1 per
Ohio, a new England area, consistently Republican.

interesting, while the Democratic area is equally striking confirmation of the attitude of the region of the poor whites.[5] In this election the party alignment in the Old

PLATE II. PRESIDENTIAL ELECTION, 1836.

■ Whig Counties
□ Democratic Counties
◩ No returns, territories, etc.

Northwest is somewhat confused by the candidacy of Harrison, a favorite son of the section, on the Whig

[5] See maps of cotton-soil areas of the Gulf States, in *Census of 1880,* Vol. VI, Cotton Culture, I, ii.

ticket. New England and New York, moreover, had not at that time reached Illinois in force.

These maps may be taken as typical. In all elections in the United States, clearly marked sections appear.[6] For the most part, there is a tendency for similar regions to reappear through long periods. The subsections—if I may use the term—appearing within the larger sections, are limitations upon the unity and permanence of sectional existence. The majorities are but slight, as a rule, and are therefore in danger of reversal. But the existence of these heterogeneous subsections renders the section as a whole less stable and its action less inevitable, except in cases where unusual issues arise, stirring up moral stimuli or direct interests. As a rule, party discipline is sufficient to exercise a desectionalizing and restraining influence, because the party following is, as Professor Giddings[7] has pointed out, made up of varied and more or less antagonistic groups held together by adjustments of interests, and the party must therefore avoid extreme policies if it would hold its majority together. Were parties, however, broken into numerous small factions, as they may be in the future, each representing special interests, the shock of opposing sections might be more direct and obvious.[8]

Next let us observe the physiographic areas of the Mississippi Valley. In many respects, the region is a single section in economic interests and in the traits of the people. It is a region certain to have a profound

[6] See maps for 1876, 1888, 1892, and 1904, in Plates III (1), (2), (3), (4).
[7] "Conduct of Political Majorities," *Political Science Quarterly*, I, 116; see also his *Inductive Sociology*, pp. 285, 293.
[8] On the conflict of interests as a fundamental process in social development, see Small, *General Sociology*, pp. 209, 248, 280, 282, 305, 307. A. L. Lowell, in *Report of American Historical Association, 1901*, I, 321, shows that party voting in legislation is less common than is popularly supposed; A. Johnson, in *Yale Review*, November, 1906, points out the nationalizing tendency of party organization.

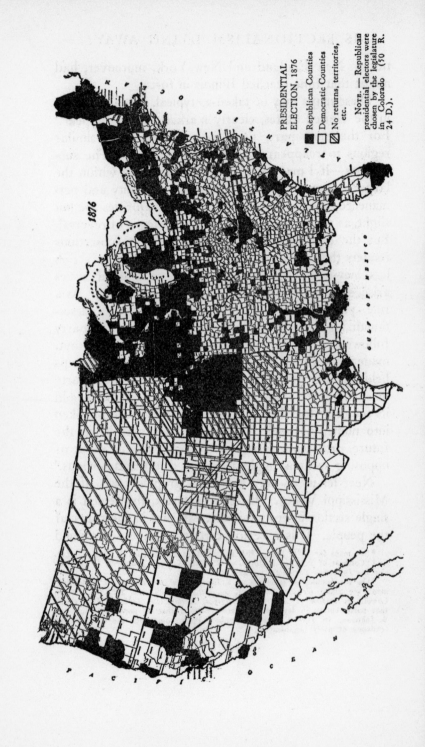

PRESIDENTIAL
ELECTION, 1876

■ Republican Counties
□ Democratic Counties
▨ No returns, territories,
etc.

NOTE.—Republican
presidential electors were
chosen by the legislature
in Colorado (50 R.
24 D.).

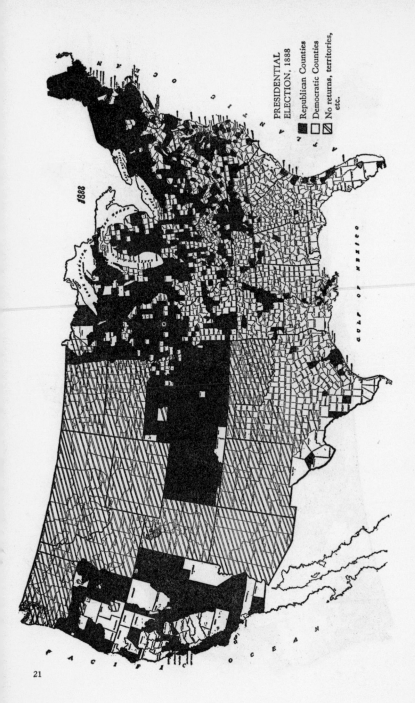

PRESIDENTIAL
ELECTION, 1888

■ Republican Counties
□ Democratic Counties
▨ No returns, territories,
etc.

21

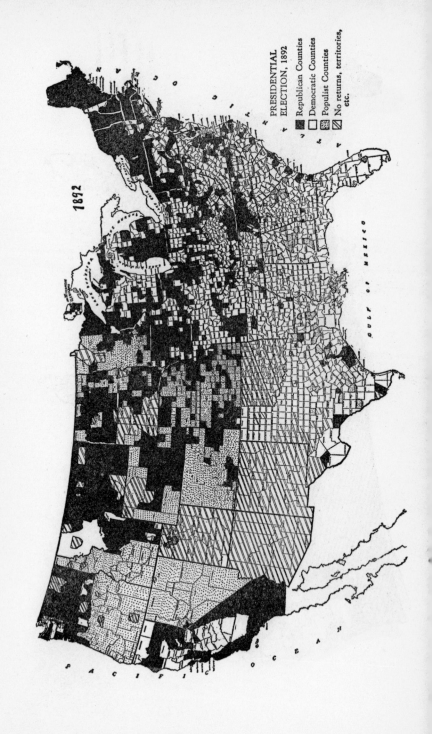

1892

PRESIDENTIAL
ELECTION, 1892

■ Republican Counties
□ Democratic Counties
▨ Populist Counties
▨ No returns, territories,
etc.

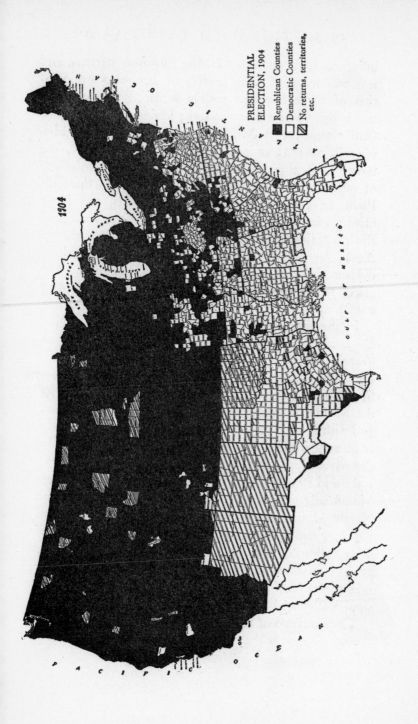

1904

PRESIDENTIAL
ELECTION, 1904

Republican Counties
Democratic Counties
No returns, territories,
etc.

influence, for it could hold many European nations, and it is credited with being capable of sustaining a population of three hundred million souls. Physiographers divide this empire into the Lake Plains, Prairie Plains, Gulf Plains, Ozark Mountains, and Great Plains. Historically, the Lake and Prairie plains (roughly, the North Central group of states) have had a community of experience and influence, while the men of the Gulf Plains have been for the most part rivals, and for a brief period bitter foes, of the men of the Lake and Prairie plains. Part of this opposition is the result of climatic contrasts, part of it is the secondary result of differences in economic interests, but the most of it arises from the presence of the negro as a governing consideration in politics, industry, and social structure.

In the course of this rivalry, the New York-New England element of the North, aided by German immigrants, established its control over the section of the Lake and Prairie plains. It made alliances, in economic life, politics, and education, literature and religion, with the Middle Region, especially with western New York and with New England. Railroads extending across the same zone broke the ascendency previously exercised by the Mississippi as the avenue of transportation for the Lake and Prairie plains and the Ohio Valley. A section of mutually interdependent states was established in the North, at the same time that similar relations bound together the various sections of the South. The Civil War followed, and the men of the Lake and Prairie plains controlled the government while they fought the men of the Gulf Plains for the possession of the Mississippi Valley and the preservation of the Union.

The survivals of this sectionalism between North and

South seem slowly to be giving way. But the negro is still the problem of the South and while he remains there will be a Southern sectionalism.[9] If the negro were removed, it seems not unlikely that the unity of the Mississippi Valley would once more have free play in presenting common interests in the greatest of all our

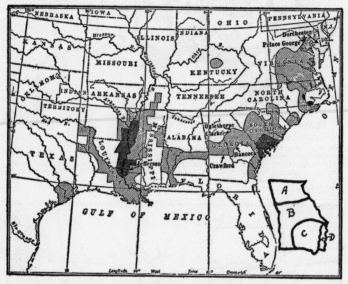

PLATE IV. THE BLACK BELTS IN 1850.

NOTE.—Reproduced from article by Professor U. B. Phillips, in *American Historical Review*, XI, 810. The shaded areas show where the negro equaled or outnumbered the whites; in the darkest they were 75 per cent of the total population. The sketch map of Georgia at the side shows: (A) Northern Georgia, grain raising; (B) Cotton Belt; (C) Pine Barrens, mixed agriculture; (D) Coast, raising sea-island cotton and rice. See *Report of American Historical Association*, 1901, II, 140. Compare Plate VI, *post*.

sectional areas. Such a movement as that lately promoted by President Roosevelt in favor of a vast system of internal improvement of the Mississippi and its tributaries and their connection with the Great Lakes, taken

[9] Cf. maps in Plates III, etc., for evidence of the persistence of the negro as a sectionalizing force.

IS SECTIONALISM DYING AWAY?

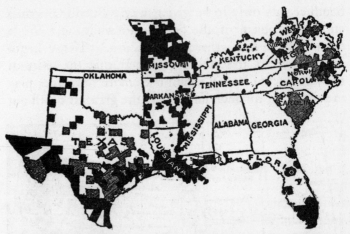

PLATE V. WET AND DRY MAP OF THE SOUTHERN STATES, 1908.

NOTE.—The white sections represent Prohibition territory; black, licensed-saloon territory; shaded, modified-license territory, dispensaries, distilleries, etc., or territory which is partly wet and partly dry. Georgia and Alabama have state prohibition; therefore the areas favoring the saloon do not appear in those states. Compare the election of 1876. For Missouri and Arkansas compare Plate 55, *Census Atlas*, 1900, showing density of negro population. See the map below.

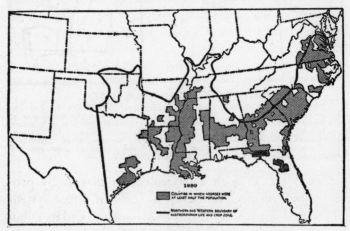

PLATE VI. DENSITY OF NEGRO POPULATION, 1880.

NOTE.—From Twelfth Census, *Bulletin Number 8*. The map of 1880 does not greatly differ from that of 1900, and it serves also to illustrate the presidential election of 1876 (Plate III (1), *ante*).

together with the effect of the Panama Canal in building up the Gulf ports, would tend to restore the old significance of the Mississippi and the railroads parallel to it as trunk lines; and it would so emphasize the natural unity of the Valley, and so press forward its interests in national appropriations, that the remoter outcome might be a new sectionalism over an area vaster than any previous section. Such a section, however, would in truth be the nation; and the Atlantic and Pacific coasts would then constitute peripheral sections. While the negro problem exists, it is doubtful whether transportation and commercial interests alone can give the Mississippi Valley a sectional consciousness, though they are certain to create sectional alignments in congressional votes upon appropriations.

Other great sections must be considered in estimating the permanency of sectionalism. The Pacific Coast is so obviously isolated by the mere fact of distance from the regions which permit dense settlement, as well as by the barrier of mountains and deserts, that a sectional attitude may be expected to increase rather than diminish, there, as society settles to stable conditions in the United States. More important even than this, perhaps, is the Asiatic problem. Fronting the Orient, the Coast is certain to develop its separate point of view in reference to the problems of the Pacific Ocean, Oriental trade, and Oriental immigration. What the negro is to the South, as a sectionalizing influence, that the Mongolian stock is to the Pacific Coast. On race issues, the two sections may form political alliances and thus strengthen the resistance of each to what may be the tendency of national legislation and diplomacy. If the nation, in the interest of its foreign relations, should attempt to impose upon the Pacific Coast a policy of the open door to Oriental immigration, the sectionalism of that province would show no signs of dying out. However, in many respects—industrially, commercially, socially, as well as geographically—the Pacific Coast is itself divided into sections, more or less inharmonious. But there is a distinct tendency to draw together in intellectual life. Such organizations as the Pacific Coast Branch of the American Historical Association has a sectional significance as well as a national aspect.

Passing over other extensive natural sections of the West, such as the region known as the Inland Empire of the Far Northwest, with its sectional self-consciousness, shown in trade relations, educational and religious conventions, and so on, I wish to allude to the important bearing upon American sectionalism of the arid region. The activity of the federal government in the Reclamation Service is a striking illustration of how old individualistic principles and the *laissez faire* conception of government, may give way to a semi-socialistic policy. The general government as land owner has become, for the vast spaces of the arid region, the builder of huge irrigation works. By the conditions on which it disposes of the land and the water privileges, it preserves a parental control over the social and economic conditions of the section. It owns and operates quarries and coal mines for its uses. It experiments with new crops, tells the farmers what and when and how to plant, and even contemplates the rental of the surplus water and steam power, generated by and for irrigation uses, for the purposes of manufactures.

This aspect of sectionalism is, however, an illustration of how sectional conditions may affect a national transformation and increase national power, rather than the reverse. Its bearing upon the possible production of sectional resistance to these new national tendencies on the part of the older regions, where capitalistic exploitation has had such important power in shaping national action, is obvious. Just as the Eastern section of wealth and commercial and manufacturing interests today resents the present policy of the administration in economic matters, so, later, the development of national power in dealing with the arid area and the Mississippi system is certain to produce sectional reaction in those older regions that have formerly shaped nationalism.

The nationalizing tendencies are at the present time clearly in evidence. The control of great industries has passed to a striking extent into the hands of corporations or trusts, operating on a national basis and centered in a few hands. Banking and transportation systems show the same tendency to consolidation. Cities are growing at a rate disproportioned to the increase of general population, and their numerical growth is only a partial index of their influence upon the thought as well as the economic life of the country. On the whole, in spite of rivalry, the business world of these cities tends to act nationally and to promote national homogeneity. The labor organizations are national in their scope and purposes. Newspapers, telegraph, post-office—all the agencies of intercourse and the formation of thought—tend toward national uniformity and national consciousness. The coöperative publication of news furnished by national agencies, the existence of common ownership and editorial conduct of chains of newspapers, all tend to produce simultaneous formation of a national public opinion. In general, the forces of civilization are working toward uniformity. Even the religious life and organization take on the national form.

Nevertheless, I, for one, am not ready to believe that it is clear that sectionalism is to die out. To take the matter of transportation as an illustration: any attempt at political control of rates by direct national legislation would produce injustice to some sections and undue advantages to others.[10] Sectional alliances and conflicts would appear in congressional votes. If, on the other hand, such transportation control is left in the hands of a board, either the board will recognize the existence of sectional necessities on some basis of justice —not easy to find—or it will itself reflect sectional combinations to the disadvantage and exploitation of the minority section. The factor of distance from a market, as well as the factor of a sectional distribution of crops, and other economic activities, will always tend to produce sectional diversities and conflicting interests in the vast area of complex geographical provinces which makes up the United States. It will be many years before the sectional distribution of the stocks, with inherited customs, institutions, and ways of looking at the world, will cease to be reflected in the sectional manifestation of public opinion and in the sectional distribution of votes in Congress.

The sectional influence in the selection of the President is a case in point. As economic and political power passes from section to section, the presidency has in the past tended to fall to the area of greatest energy and power. Thus the era of commercial influence of

[10] Cf. W. Z. Ripley, in St. Louis *Congress of Arts and Science*, VII, 95-114.

the Northeast saw the presidencies of the two Adamses. But the rival, and for the most part dominant, influence of the agricultural section led by Virginia, brought in the rule of the Virginia dynasty. The transition of power to the trans-Allegheny lands witnessed a struggle between Clay, of Kentucky, and such Tennessee leaders as Jackson, White, and Polk, for leadership of these lands. There was a distinct era of influence of these two states, exercised through their widespread colonies in the West, when Benton, Grundy, Bell, and others had the reins of government. The transition of power to the Cotton Kingdom was marked by a tendency on the part of the leaders of that section to select Northern men to serve their purpose; but the real center of power was in the Lower South in the decade before the war. The war, and the period immediately following, showed the passage of political energy to the Old Northwest, whence came Lincoln, Grant, Hayes, Garfield, Harrison, and McKinley, and a host of other leaders in the cabinet and in Congress. More recently the formation of a new sectional influence is shown in the importance of the movements led by Bryan, and by Roosevelt, who is deeply affected in his point of view by his sojourn in the newer lands of the trans-Mississippi West. So it is likely to continue. The sectionalism that continues to shape political action underneath the forms of nationalism is not dying out.

In conclusion, divesting myself of the historical mantle, in order to venture upon the rôle of prophet, I make the suggestion that, as the nation reaches a more stable equilibrium, a more settled state of society, with denser populations pressing upon the means of existence, with this population no longer migratory, the influence of the diverse physiographic provinces which make up the nation will become more marked. They will exercise sectionalizing influences, tending to mould society to their separate conditions, in spite of all the countervailing tendencies toward national uniformity. National action will be forced to recognize and adjust itself to these conflicting sectional interests. The more the nation is organized on the principle of direct majority rule, and consolidation, the more sectional resistance is likely to manifest itself. Statesmen in the future, as in the past,[11] will achieve their leadership by voicing the interests and ideas of the sections which have shaped these leaders, and they will exert their influence nationally by making combinations between sections and by accommodating their policy to the needs of such alliances. Congressional legislation will be shaped by compromises and combinations, which will in effect be treaties between rival sections, and the real federal aspect of our government will lie, not in the relation of state and nation, but in the relation of section and nation.

[11] By way of illustration, reference may be made to my *Rise of the New West (American Nation,* Vol. XIV), wherein I have attempted to exhibit the play of sectional forces in the period 1820 to 1830. [Professor Turner's forthcoming work, "The United States, 1830-1850: The Nation and Its Sections," deals with those two decades from a similar point of view.]

CHAPTER XII

SECTIONS AND NATION [1]

We are apt to think of the United States as we might think of some one of the nations of the Old World, but the area of the Union is almost that of all Europe, and this vast country is gradually becoming aware that its problems and its difficulties are not altogether unlike those of Europe as a whole.

It may readily be admitted that bigness is not greatness. But room for population and ample resources for development are important in the life of all nations. England, France, and Italy could be placed within the boundaries of the old thirteen states along the Atlantic Coast, with which this nation began. The Middle West (the North Central States) could find room for all the European powers which joined Germany in the World War in her efforts to conquer Europe.

So considered, the American section takes on a new importance and a new dignity. The various sections of which this country is composed, are thus seen as potential nations. We are led to wonder why the United States did not in fact become another Europe, by what processes we retain our national unity. The imagination stirs at the possibilities of the future, when these sections shall be fully matured and populated to the extent of the nations of the Old World.

We must also remember that each of the sections of this continental nation—New England, the Middle

[1] Reprinted by permission from *The Yale Review*, October, 1922.

States, the Southeast, the Southwest, the Middle West, the Great Plains, the Mountain States, the Pacific Coast —has its own special geographical qualities, its own resources and economic capacities, and its own rival interests, partly determined in the days when the geological foundations were laid down.

In some ways, in respect to problems of common action, we are like what a United States of Europe would be. It is true that the differences are not by any manner of means so marked here as in Europe. There are not in the United States the historic memories of so many national wrongs and wars, nor what Gilbert Murray calls the "Satanic spirit" of reliance upon force. There is not here the variety of language and race nor the sharp contrast in cultural types; there has not been the same bitterness of class conflicts; nor the same pressure of economic need, inducing the various regions to seek by arms to acquire the means of subsistence, the control of natural resources. The burden of history does not so weigh upon America. The section does not embody the racial and national feeling of the European state, its impulse to preserve its identity by aggression conceived of as self-defense. But there is, nevertheless, a faint resemblance.

The American section may be likened to the shadowy image of the European nation, to the European state denatured of its toxic qualities. In the relations of European nations with each other, making due allowance for the deep differences, we may find means of understanding some of our own problems. Perhaps, even, we may find, in our handling of such problems, suggestions of a better way for Europe.

The geographer Ratzel once remarked, with a characteristic German accent, that "Europe and Australia really have room enough for but one great power." He did not sufficiently consider that the one great power might be like the United States of America—a federative power. Nor is it certain that the leagues of Europe may not grow into a United States of Europe—certainly a more hopeful outlook for liberty and civilization than the triumph of a state like Imperial Germany or Russia.

In a recent book on the *Geography of History,* Brunhes and Vallaux, arguing against the League of Nations, reached the conclusion that Europe must organize in groups of leagues. "In order to form an organism as strong and rich as possible," say these French geographers, "the countries must coöperate in groups to the end that they may include within their federated territories the whole range of natural resources and manufactured products demanded by the growing complexity of social life."

The United States of America has reached a similar result, for its continental spaces, by the peaceful process of settlement of new geographic provinces in the West —a process which in Europe would be called "colonization." We have organized these new lands as territories and then admitted them as equal states in a common Union. We have no regional customs-boundaries to check interstate commerce. We have a system of free trade over an area as large as all Europe. We regulate interstate commerce from a single center, while we recognize separate sectional interests and needs. We legislate instead of going to war.

A leading French statesman, M. Tardieu, said not long ago in the French Chamber of Deputies that "it was immensely difficult for America to understand the psychological state of Europe, its national passions and the moral force of the memories which centuries of bloody struggle had left behind." "But France," he added, "knew these things." Over a century ago a French Minister to the United States said to his government, "An American is the born enemy of all European peoples."

Of course, this is not true. But it is true that an American is the born enemy of the European system of international relationships, and that he does sometimes find it hard to understand the European psychology. No small portion of the American people fled to the New World to escape the European system, and the explanation of our lack of sympathy with the methods and the fundamental assumptions of continental Europe, lies in large measure in the different course which the sections of the Union ran as compared with the nations of Europe. We substituted the system of a sectional union and legislative adjustment, for the settlement by the sword. We learned how to discuss, how to concede, and how to adjust differences, how to combine a loyalty to parties which ran across sectional lines, with loyalty to local interests. Like an elastic band, the common national feeling and party ties draw sections together, but at the same time yield in some measure to sectional interests when these are gravely threatened.

The one tragic exception in America to the unifying influence of parties and a common legislative body, lies in the Civil War, when parties did become sectional. But perhaps no more difficult test of peaceful methods of adjustment could arise than that between a slave society and a free society. After that war, peaceful

[318]

SECTIONS AND NATION

sectional relationships returned, even though an almost solid, but patriotic, South has persisted for over half a century. Nor is it certain that the Civil War was inevitable. Probably the majority of Americans, North as well as South, preferred a different solution and were astonished when secession was followed by war instead of by a reconciliation of differences.

By comparing the relations of the different nations of Europe with each other, we have the means of examining both the European and the American situation and of better understanding the real meaning of what has been in progress and what appears to be likely to influence the development of the United States.

If, for example, we describe the way in which the sections of the Atlantic seaboard have dealt with those of the interior of the United States, in such terms as "colonization," "spheres of influence," "hinterlands," American history takes on a new meaning. The formation of our great zones of population by interstate migration to the West, such as the New York-New England zone, and the Southern zone, extending from the Atlantic across the Mississippi, stands out in a clearer light. When we think of the Missouri Compromise, the Compromise of 1850, the Kansas-Nebraska Act, as steps in the marking off of spheres of influence and the assignment of mandates, we find a new meaning in the rivalry between the slaveholding and nonslaveholding sections of the United States. We see a resemblance to what has gone on in the Old World. If we express sectional contests, in national party conventions and in the federal House and Senate, in such European phrases as "diplomatic congresses," "ententes," "alliances," and attempts at "balance of

22 [319]

power," we shall not go altogether wrong in the description of what actually occurs, and we shall find that the rival sections of the United States have played parts not entirely different from those played by European states. But there was a common legislative body, as well as national parties, which brought sections together.

Is it not clear that if Europe could have followed a similar course, substituting for wars and sinister combinations between nations the American device of continental parties and legislation, "woeful Europe," as William Penn called it, would have run a course better suited to the preservation of civilization and the peace of the world? If it be said that such a solution is inconceivable in Europe, we must recall that, in spite of the sharp contrast between the American section and the European nation, there have been diplomatic congresses which attempted to deal with Europe as a whole, there have been great gatherings at The Hague to impose a system of international law, there are European international labor congresses. There is actually the League of Nations which, however imperfect, has in it the possibilities of development.

The results of the Great War have burned deeply into European consciousness the need of some better way of conducting the common enterprise of Europe than by the appeal to the sword. In spite of all the fundamental difficulties which the conferences at Genoa and The Hague have revealed, we can see in these gatherings the hopeful beginnings of a new age as well as the discouraging persistence of an old order of things. Europe might at least form an assembly, representing the people rather than the diplomats, and empowered to pass resolutions expressive of public opinion. Such recommendations and resolutions might ultimately take the form of law. However this may be, the difficulties which exhibit themselves in Europe, only emphasize the good fortune of the United States in dealing with its similar area. They help us to understand ourselves and our problems.

Bertrand Russell, in a contemporaneous article, insists that the small states of Europe will have to be forced, if necessary, to concede free trade and freedom of intercourse between one another and between neighboring great powers. "Gradually, if Europe is to survive," he says, "it will have to develop a central government controlling its international relations. If it cannot do this, it will become, and will deserve to become, the slave of the United States. . . . The time when the history of the world was made in Europe is past. America and Russia are the great independent powers of the present day." These words are, of course, the utterance of a socialist and internationalist and of a writer who, with a strange European blindness, is alarmed at the prospect of America's becoming the next great imperialistic power and mistress of the world. But they show the contrast between European and American experience.

We in America are in reality a federation of sections rather than of states. State sovereignty was never influential except as a constitutional shield for the section. In political matters the states act in groups rather than as individual members of the Union. They act in sections and are responsive to the respective interests and ideals of these sections. They have their sectional leaders, who, in Congress and in party conventions, voice the attitude of the section and confer and compromise their differences, or form sectional combinations to achieve a national policy and position. Party policy and congressional legislation emerge from a process of sectional contests and sectional bargainings. Legislation is almost never the result of purely national or purely sectional considerations. It is the result of sectional adjustments to meet national needs. For the most part, such adjustments take place in the formative stages of bills, in the committee rooms, and in the process of framing the measures by amendments. It is in these stages that the bill is most easily affected by sectional interests. The vote on the third reading of the bill affords opportunity for dissent; but after the completion of the measure, party discipline and party loyalty assert themselves and, in spite of discontent, usually furnish the necessary votes to pass the measure.

But even final votes in the Congress of the United States, both in the Senate and the House, upon important matters are, as President Lowell has demonstrated, far less frequently by parties than is ordinarily supposed. If we proceed a step further and, instead of taking account of congressional majorities by totals and reckoning the votes by party affiliation, we arrange those votes by sections and place the result on a map of the United States, we shall be astonished at how much is concealed by the mere alphabetical or party record. Under the drawing pen, as vote after vote by congressional districts is recorded on the map, they gradually arrange themselves to show the outlines of contending sections. The areas of great geographic provinces are revealed by the map of votes.

Of course, in the maps it will often be shown that

some single party dominates a whole section, as so often occurs in the case of New England or the South. But again and again, in the construction of bills and in elections, party ties are broken, and the Republicans, for example, divide into sectional wings, composed of a conservative New England and Middle State area, a divided and mediating Old Northwest (lying between the Great Lakes and the Ohio River), and a radical trans-Mississippi Middle West, voting in exact opposition to the Northeast and sometimes in alliance with the Democratic South.

From colonial days to the Civil War, the conscious and avowed policies of the leading statesmen rested on the necessity of considering the conflicting interests of the various sections and sectional wings and adjusting them by bargains, compromises, and arrangements for balance of power in congressional legislation. It is, however, impossible here even to sketch the evidences of the persistent sectionalism in party contests and congressional legislation in American history. The more the reader will probe into the distribution of votes and the utterances of statesmen and editors, the more he will see that sectionalism was the dominant influence in shaping our political history upon all important measures—not the sectionalism of North and South alone, but a much more complex thing, a sectionalism also of East and West, and of East North Central and West North Central states, shifting as economic and social conditions changed, but persistently different from the East.

Since the Civil War, although by the march of settlement to the West new sections have been added, all the important political contests have revealed the same interplay of section with section. The sectional wings of the Republican party in the seventies exhibited a New England ultraconservative; a Middle Atlantic transitional and divided; a North Central for free silver. In the later eighties the East North Central division divided and finally joined the North Atlantic States against free silver, but swung to the side of the West North Central group on the question of terminating the Silver Purchase Act. It was a mediating section with a balance of power, but responsive to party discipline.

Problems of trust regulation, free silver, banking, tariff, and devices to secure popular government have led to sectional contests. Roosevelt's "square deal" held the Eastern and Western wings of the Republicans together for a time, but when President Taft after hesitation turned to the conservative Eastern wing, insurgency followed, and the Middle West became, in his words, "enemy country." The Western programme of primary elections, popular election of United States senators, initiative, referendum, recall— all the devices for direct popular participation in government—resulted in a party rebellion which broke the power of the speakership and overthrew the rule of the elder statesmen in the Senate. All these are familiar examples of the new forces. They found their strength in the Middle West and Pacific Coast, and finally made a split in the Republican party, resulting in the formation of the Progressives under Roosevelt. It is idle to think of these events in terms of rival leaders like La Follette, Cummins, Roosevelt, and Aldrich; Bryan, Cleveland, Hill, and Parker. Such leaders really led, and some of them deeply influenced the strategy and tactics of the fighting; but their power to lead was based upon the rival sectional interests. It was not a "fight of the captains." It cannot be explained in terms of personality alone, nor even primarily.

Economic changes and the results of the Civil War had decreased the importance of the state in the nation and turned all interests towards the federal government. Some fifteen years ago, one of the most distinguished of American publicists, Elihu Root, warned the states that "our whole life was crystallizing about national centers." State soverignty, upon which the political philosopher John Taylor had once relied to avoid the collision of geographical interests, proved a broken reed. Congress was, in fact, becoming almost unconsciously "an assembly of geographical envoys," but an assembly which operated under American conceptions of the need of compromise.

Mr. Root spoke at a time when Roosevelt's strenuous assertion of national power was at its height. Little seemed to intervene between individuals and the stark power of the nation, unless it were in that twilight zone, between state and federal governments, wherein the trusts flourished. National legislation has steadily diminished the area of this "no man's land." The Great War increased the energy and scope of the federal government. But today it may fairly be asked whether all these forces of centralization of power in Washington have promoted national unity and consolidation, or on the other hand have increased sectional expression.

As the states have declined, sectional self-consciousness has risen. All those factors which were relied on to destroy sectionalism, such as the development of means of transportation, expanding domestic commerce, increase of population, have in Europe been among the most important of the forces to bring about national rivalries. If this is the result in Europe, it is certainly not clear that the opposite result must follow in the United States.

Although political sectionalism is still a term of reproach, implying unfairness and a disregard of national interests, the section reproved is seldom conscious that its action is adverse to the common good. We are so large and diversified a nation that it is almost impossible to see the situation except through sectional spectacles. The section either conceives of itself as an aggrieved and oppressed minority, suffering from the injustice of the other sections of the nation, or it thinks of its own culture, its economic policies, and well-being as best for all the nation. It thinks, in other words, of the nation in terms of itself. "I love thy rocks and rills, thy woods and templed hills," runs our American anthem. It was written by a New Englander and its scene is that of New England, not of the snow-capped mountains, the far stretches of Great Plains, or Arid America. We think sectionally and do not fully understand one another.

Underneath the party sectionalism there is, of course, a sectionalism of material interests—of business, manufacturing, mining, agriculture, transportation. To illustrate this economic sectionalism, I may point out that, of the capital invested in manufactures in the United States, nearly one-half is in the North Atlantic division, composed of New England and the Middle States; while on the other hand the great bulk of the wheat and corn, cattle and swine—the food supply for labor and the great cities—comes from the North Central States of the upper Mississippi Valley. Over half the federal income and profits tax in 1920 was paid by the North Atlantic section of the United States, which has less than one-third the population of the Union, though the appropriation of these revenues was made for the nation considered as a unit. Obviously these differences between sections in economic interests mean also differences in political interests.

Significant facts appear in the relations between sectional material interests and sectional forms of society. The group of states which has the highest ratio of automobiles to population is the region of the great wheat states west of the Mississippi—the area of the Republican wing of the "Farmers' *Bloc.*" This indicates that there is in that section a more general diffusion of prosperity. The sections which have the lowest ratio are the South and the Middle States of the Atlantic seaboard—the regions, respectively, of the negro and of the great industries. The American conscription statistics in the World War show that the regions which had the best record for physical fitness were those of the West North Central and the Mountain sections, while the lowest is again the industrial Northeast. On the other hand, a map of the reading habit, as shown by the number of books in circulation proportioned to population, reveals that the old Federalist section—New England, New York, and New Jersey—has a distinct preëminence. The statistics in the American *Who's Who* for 1916-17 show that over half of those who achieved the necessary distinction to be included in that volume, lived in the Northeastern section of the United

States, and that nearly the same number were born there. In other words, while preëminence in physical fitness and the more even distribution of wealth belong to the agricultural West, more men of talent and a larger concentration of great wealth are to be found in the Northeast. Recent inquiries show that there is a sectionalism of "wet" and "dry" areas, in public opinion on the Volstead Act. The most emphatic support of Prohibition comes from the West North Central and the South Central states—the area of the Farmers' *Bloc*.

There is a sectionalism of culture. School-teachers, historians, scientists, church associations, meet increasingly in sectional gatherings. This is in part due to the high railroad fares; but it is also due to a real consciousness of sectional solidarity. We are all aware that Kansas is not New York; nor South Carolina, New Hampshire. We have in mind a certain quality when we speak of the South, or New England, or the Pacific Coast, or the Middle West—there is in each a special flavor, social, psychological, literary, even religious.

Popular speech, likewise, reveals our sectionalism, not only in matters of pronunciation, idioms, and so on, but also in the mental attitude that underlies the expressions. When we hear that "no man in the wrong can stand up against the fellow that's in the right and keeps on a-comin'," we know that we aren't in New England, in spite of the moral flavor, and we suspect that we may be in Texas. When told that "high class swine are unknown and impossible among a low class people," that the hog of a certain state "in his sphere typifies the good, the true, and the beautiful . . . like the State that lends him as a solace to humanity," or that still another state produces the "most perfect cow that ever was by sea or land," we have little difficulty in getting our sectional bearings. It is not necessary to examine the Agricultural Atlas, for we recognize a Middle Western spiritual as well as material attitude. When we read, "We don't have to pray for rain out here, we open the irrigation ditch and stop worrying about Providence; we don't have to ask for health, we got it when we bought our railroad ticket," it is not alone the reference to the irrigation ditch that carries our thought to the exhilarating high altitudes of the Far West—the land of optimism, determination, and exaggeration. One doesn't weigh words, or cultivate restraint and the niceties, when nature is big and rough and lavish.

No one can make a sectional list of the men and women who have achieved distinction in literature, and fail to see that, whether in prose or poetry, fiction or essay, there is a special sectional quality in each, a reflection of the region's common interests and soul. Our American literature is not a single thing. It is a choral song of many sections.

We may better understand how far sectional consciousness has gone in the United States if, by way of example, we consider one of the most avowedly sectional portions of the Union—namely, New England. Her restraint, her respect for established order, for vested rights and steady habits, are traditional. As many of her discontented and disturbing elements left the section and migrated to the West, and as the interests of manufacturing and capitalism increased in sectional importance, this inheritance passed easily into an eco-

nomic conservatism. Even now, when two-thirds of
her population is either foreign-born or descended from
one or both parents foreign-born, the fundamental economic attitude of New England is still unchanged.

Historically respectful of the rights of property, this
section has been, and is, the stronghold against attacks
upon banking interests, "sound money," and the protective tariff. It opposed the federal income tax, and is
alarmed over national appropriations for roads, bills
for national educational control, and similar measures
which take from the section more than they return to
it. To New England this seems like draining the
wealthier region of its property in order to spend it
in distant and less prosperous lands—like expropria-
tion under the plea of national unity. There is a striking analogy between its attitude in this respect and the
views of the ante-bellum South as voiced by Calhoun.

Particular reasons exist for New England's sectional
discontent and alarm. She finds that the protective
tariff is so shaped by Western and Southern agricultural
interests that it increases the cost of the raw material
of her manufacture and the food for her labor population. Dependent upon transportation for the food, the
fuel, and the raw material which she uses but does not
produce in her own midst, and also dependent upon
transportation for access to her markets, she is con-
cerned over the differential railroad rates of the Interstate Commerce Commission which work to the advantage of Philadelphia, Baltimore, and the Southern
ports. In the grand strategy of railroad wars, she has
reason to apprehend the transfer of control over her
own lines, to New York, even to fear that her roads
will go into bankruptcy. She is discussing the question

of unifying and controlling the railroads of her section. Attempting to build up the port of Boston, New England is more than reluctant to see the federal government undertake the deep waterway from the Great Lakes by the St. Lawrence to the sea—a measure pressed by the North Central States. The Mayor of Boston, with a Celtic lack of restraint, recently protested that this "would obliterate New England absolutely." Evidently he forgot that Boston is not a place.

By her well-united group of twelve senators, and with the large number of votes cast in the House by New York and parts of Pennsylvania and New Jersey acting in concert with her, New England has not only had in the past a direct influence upon legislation, but a preponderating position in the councils of the Republican party. As the Middle West grew in strength, this power finally brought about a reaction. A prominent congressman broke out in 1908 with the interesting suggestion that "if New England could be ceded to Canada, the legislative difficulties of this country would be cut in half." "Let us not forget," remarked a leading Boston newspaper in 1912, "that the influence long exercised by New England in both Houses of Congress, to the great advantage of this section, has resulted in powerful combinations against us in business as well as in politics." The Boston editors denounced what they called a "Southern-Western alliance against the industrial Northeast." The Western sections in their turn demanded larger popular participation in government. Western insurgency and progressivism broke the traditional control of the Republican organization and divided the party. The victory of the Democrats under President Wilson transferred the ascendency in Congress to the South, "where once," said a Boston editor regretfully, "it belonged to New England."

Under the stress of these events and the more recent combination of the agricultural South and West, New England is becoming a little pessimistic and self-conscious. It is taking measures for more effective sectional organization. Under the heading, "All New England, the Six States Should Act as a Unit on the Issues Which Concern their Similar Interests," the *Boston Transcript* last spring voiced this conception of sectional organization, saying: "The New England States have different governments and are separate and distinct political organizations, but they are bound together by geographic, historic, political, and industrial interests. What helps one New England State in the shape of legislation originating in Washington, helps all the New England States. What injures one New England State in the shape of legislation originating at Washington, will hurt all New England States." Recently the Governor of Massachusetts said to the Vermont Press Association: "Other parts of the country regard New England as a unit and treat it accordingly. We being all one stock [!], should regard ourselves in the same light and act as a body, work towards one end." Various Boston editors endorsed the Governor's view, one of them saying that "while certain artificial limitations exist between the New England States, there are no real barriers between them; essentially they are one." Senator Lodge advanced a step farther, looking to a combination of North Atlantic states—a Northeastern *Bloc* to counteract the Farmers' *Bloc*. "The great empire State of New York," he said, "has almost identically the same interests as New England. Well, New York has forty-three members of Congress while New England has thirty-two members of Congress and twelve Senators." He added that they would make a formidable *"bloc,"* if put together. The suggestion recalls the ultra-Federalist proposals in the days of Jefferson and Madison.

Responding to these ideas, New England has developed a semi-governmental machinery for the section by means of conferences of the governors of the New England States, to consider matters reaching from railroad regulation and rates to the fuel supply and the milk question. A New England States Council, "the voice of the section," has been organized, made up of mercantile, manufacturing, financial, transportation, and agricultural (but not labor) organizations, which send delegates or reply to questionnaires from the different cities or states of the section. New England's congressional delegations consult and dine together in Washington in order to foster common action. A New England Bureau at the seat of government is a further development. From all these things it would not be a long step to the creation of a common legislative assembly and executive for the section as a whole.

I have dwelt upon the situation in New England because it shows so clearly the tendency of the time to a sectional organization of interests, to sectional feeling, and to sectional action. But New England is by no means alone. The South has long been known (somewhat inaccurately) as the "Solid South," dominated by the Democratic party, as New England is usually by the Republican party. Naturally, when the Democratic party comes into power, its leadership falls to

[333]

the South, just as, when the Republican party comes into power, its leadership is in the North and particularly, in the past at least, in the Northeast. The Middle West has also a sectionalism of its own, changing as conditions change. But on the whole its eastern half reflects its diverse economic and social interests and origins, and constitutes a divided buffer region holding the balance of power—an umpire between sections.

Leaders are reluctant to think in sectional terms. President Wilson was in origin a Southern man, proud of the political talent of the South and anxious to reveal it to the nation; but he reprobated sectionalism as such, saying in a speech in Indianapolis in 1916: "Any man who revives the issue of sectionalism in this country, is unworthy of the government of the nation; he shows himself a provincial; he shows that he himself does not know the various sections of his own country; he shows that he has shut his heart up in a little province and that those who do not see the special interests of that province are to him sectional, while he alone is national. That is the depth of unpatriotic feeling."

This is good doctrine, to be taken to heart by all Americans. But if, in Mr. Wilson's phrase, we "uncover realities," we are obliged to face the fact that sections are among these realities. Adjustments are in fact made, not between individuals in the nation, nor between states, but between sections. The whole period of Mr. Wilson's presidency emphasizes this fact, for the tariff was shaped by Southern and Western interests to the discontent of Northeastern manufacturing interests, just as the reverse had occurred when the Northeast was in power. The central-bank plan of the Northeast was replaced by the regional-bank reserve system which gives a sectional organization to credit; and before President Wilson left the White House, a plan was under way for regional administration and regional consolidation of the railroad systems. He found, moreover, that as President he was obliged to take note of the fact that the Republican agricultural West was in distinct opposition to that degree of preparedness which he supported as the World War developed. It furnished the bulk of the votes in favor of the McLemore resolution abandoning American rights on the high seas, and against the declaration of war. He had to use his party leadership to the full in order to procure the adhesion of a hesitant South to his national programme. Mr. Wilson's policy took account of the need of convincing reluctant sections, while North Atlantic leaders, in particular, were impatient and would have him proceed as though that section was itself the nation.

President Harding, in his turn, about a year ago voiced his belief that "state lines have well-nigh ceased to have more than geographical significance." "We have had," he said, "the test of disunion, the triumph of reunion, and now the end of sectionalism." But his wish was father to his thought. He illustrated the tendency of all administrations, from whatever sections they derive their power, to deny or to decry as unpatriotic any sectional dissent from the national measures of the party in power. In a few months after this funeral sermon over sectionalism, President Harding found it necessary to urge that "there is vastly greater security, immensely more of the national point of view, much larger and prompter accomplishment, where our divisions are along party lines in the broader and loftier sense, than to divide geographically or according to pursuits or personal following." The occasion for this utterance, in spirit so like that of Mr. Wilson, was the organization of the Agricultural *Bloc* in Congress, made up of Western Republicans and Southern Democrats, to secure legislation favorable to their interests. Again and again this sectional combination rejected his recommendations as the head of the Republican party and imposed its own programme in spite of the organization centered in the Northeast. The revolting Middle West conceives of the Northeast as selfishly sectional, and it thinks of the South and West, combined, as representing the really national interests. New England, on the other hand, denounces the Agricultural *Bloc* as sectional.

Last year the *Chicago Tribune* published an editorial under the title, "A Square Deal in Congress for the Middle West." This influential newspaper alleged that the Middle West had not enjoyed this square deal in the past and demanded that the section's congressmen, whom it significantly called "our Middle Western agents," should act with more effectiveness for the promotion of the interests of the section as a whole. "We have been paying long enough to enhance the prosperity of the coasts to our own disadvantage," cried the editor.

Middle Western political revolts usually occur in periods of agricultural depression, and in such times temporary third parties have formed, with their strength in the discontented sections. It is not necessary to enumerate the many illustrations of this, from the days of the Grangers, the Populists, the Insurgents, to the Progressives, the Non-Partisan League, the Farm

Bureau Federation, the Farmers' *Bloc,* and the contemporary opposition by senators from the North Central States to high protection in the textile schedules of the tariff. All of them are successive stages of the protest of the agricultural sections against the industrial North Atlantic States. They are also reflections of different social conditions and ideals.

What is the logic of all this? Does it mean the ultimate political organization of the different groups of states into sectional units for representation and administration—the formal recognition of a new federation, a replacement of the feeble states by powerful sections, each with its special economic interest? Does it mean that in the last analysis men shape their political action according to their material advantage?

This last question is not radically different from the question of the interpretation of history in general. No single factor is determinative. Men are not absolutely dictated to by climate, geography, soils, or economic interests. The influence of the stock from which they sprang, the inherited ideals, the spiritual factors, often triumph over the material interests. There is also the influence of personality. Men do follow leaders, and sometimes into paths inconsistent with the section's material interests. But in the long run the statesman must speak the language of his people on fundamentals, both of interests and ideals. Not seldom the ideals grow out of the interests. It is the statesman's duty and his great opportunity to lift his section to a higher and broader, a more far-seeing, conception of its interests as a part of the Union, to induce his section to accept the compromises and adjustments which he arranges with the leaders of other sections in the spirit of reconciliation of interests in the nation as a whole. He must be at once the section's spokesman, its negotiator, and its enlightened guide, loyal to the nation as a whole.

At the same time that we realize the danger of provincialism and sectional selfishness, we must also recognize that the sections serve as restraints upon a deadly uniformity. They are breakwaters against overwhelming surges of national emotion. They are fields for experiment in the growth of different types of society, political institutions, and ideals. They constitute an impelling force for progress along the diagonal of contending varieties; they issue a challenge to each section to prove the virtue of its own culture; and they cross-fertilize each other. They promote that reasonable competition and coöperation which is the way of a richer life. A national vision must take account of the existence of these varied sections; otherwise the national vision will be only a sectional mirage.

As the case stands, sections still, as in the past, reflect the distances and the differences of the American continent. Improvements in communication, such as the automobile, the telephone, radio, and moving pictures, have diminished localism rather than sectionalism. Class conflict and sectional conflict often coincide. The triumph of Bolshevism or of capitalism would still leave a contest of sections. But in countless ways the power of the section is conditioned largely upon its moderation. Every section is in unstable equilibrium; public opinion is often closely divided and responds to national ideals.

For, underneath all, there is a common historical inheritance, a common set of institutions, a common law, and a common language. There is an American spirit.

There are American ideals. We are members of one body, though it is a varied body. It is inconceivable that we should follow the evil path of Europe and place our reliance upon triumphant force. We shall not become cynical, and convinced that sections, like European nations, must dominate their neighbors and strike first and hardest. However profound the economic changes, we shall not give up our American ideals and our hopes for man, which had their origin in our own pioneering experience, in favor of any mechanical solution offered by doctrinaires educated in Old World grievances. Rather, we shall find strength to build from our past a nobler structure, in which each section will find its place as a fit room in a worthy house. We shall courageously maintain the American system expressed by nation-wide parties, acting under sectional and class compromises. We shall continue to present to our sister continent of Europe the underlying ideas of America as a better way of solving difficulties. We shall point to the *Pax Americana,* and seek the path of peace on earth to men of good will.

INDEX

INDEX

INDEX

INDEX

Mahan, A. T., 224
Manufacturing in West, 246-247
Maps, showing political variations of sections, 297 ff.
  of Presidential elections by county pluralities, 186
  of Presidential election of 1836, 300
  of Presidential elections of 1856-1900, 298-299
  of Presidential election of 1876, 302
  of Presidential election of 1888, 303
  of Presidential election of 1892, 304
  of Presidential election of 1904, 305
  of Southern states, 1908, Wet and Dry, 308
Marconi, 214
Mather, Cotton, 25
McCormick, Cyrus, 263
Melville, Andrew, 90
Memoire historique et politique sur la Louisiane, 141
Mendel, Gregor, 217
Metal production in West, 244-245
Michaux, André, 76
Middle West, influence of New England upon, 11
  sectionalism of, 334
Mississippi navigation, controlled by Spain, 148
Mississippi Valley, policy of France towards, 139 ff.
  physiographic areas of, 301
  sectional groupings of, 295-297
  unity of, 307
Mitchell, Thomas, 290
Monroe, James, 171
Morgan, George, 107
Morris, Gouverneur, 26, 27, 37
Moultrie, sympathetic to Genet, 72
Moving pictures, development of, 214
Murray, Gilbert, 316

Napoleon, policy of, towards Louisiana, 179 ff.
Nation, and sections, 315 ff.
National Gazette, 73
National parties, tending to compromise, 205
National tendencies in West, 138
Naval War College, 224
Navy, growth of, in U. S., 224
New England, descendants of, in West, 257 ff.
  Federalists in, 28
  history of, 10-11
  influence of, upon Middle West, 11
  sectionalism of, 329-333
New England States Council, 333
New England stock, distribution of descendants of, 187
New World, power of Spain in, 140
North Carolina, cedes land beyond Ohio, 121-122
Norton, Charles E., 266
Nouveau Voyage dans les États-Unis, 58

O'Fallon, James, 55, 56
Ordinance of 1787, 133, 135
Overpopulation, 232-233

Pacific Coast, sectional attitude of, 309
Paine, Thomas, 57, 60, 108
Parties, national, tending to compromise of, 205
Party preponderance, geography of, 203-204
Pax Americana, 203, 339
Peary, Robert E., 217
Penn, William, 320
People's party, 248
Petroleum, production of, in U. S., 219-220
  in West, 245
Philadelphia Independent Gazette, 113 n.
Phillips, U. B., 307 n.

INDEX

Physics, development of, 216
Piedmont Plateau, 292-295
Pinchot, Gifford, 202
Pinckney, C. C., 176
Pioneer, The, 282
Pioneers, children of, 256 ff.
Plymouth compact, 89
Political power of sections, disparity of, 194-196
Political rôle of West, 247 ff.
Political sectionalism, 183-185
Political variations of sections, maps of, 297 ff.
Popular government, increase of, in U. S., 227
Population contrasts, 36-37
Population of West, 236, 237
Powers, Hiram, 272
Pragmatism, 225
Presidential election of 1836, map of, 300
  of 1876, map of, 302
  of 1888, map of, 303
  of 1892, map of, 304
  of 1904, map of, 305
Presidential elections, map of, by county pluralities, 186
  of 1856-1900, maps of, 298-299
  sectionalism in, 301
Progress, results of, in U. S., 219 ff.
Progressive party, 251
Public Good, 108
Public schools, growth of, in U. S., 226

Radio, spread of, 214
Railroads, in West, 237
Randolph, John, 24
Regions, geographic, in every state, 47
Regional geography, present emphasis on, 39
Regional subdivisions, persistence of, 49
Relativity, doctrine of, 216
Research in American history, 4-5
Robertson, James, 95, 97
Rockefeller, John D., 226, 262

Roosevelt, Theodore, 222, 229, 250
Root, Elihu, 287, 325
Rosenwald, Julius, 264
Royce, Josiah, 45
Russell, Bertrand, 321

Saint Gaudens, 225
Saint Just, 58
Sargent, John S., 225
Sayre, Stephen, 61
Scotch-Irish, ascendency of, on frontier, 90-91
Scribner's Statistical Atlas, 185
Scudder, Janet, 272
Section, a fundamental factor in American history, 183 ff.
Sectionalism, American, 8-9
  antedated nationalism, 288
  appears in all Presidential elections, 301
  based on geographic regions, 45
  cultural, 328
  danger of, 338
  degrees of, 288
  factors shaping, 288
  in America, 287 ff.
  of arid region, 310
  of Middle West, 334
  of New England, 329-333
  political, 183-185
  political *vs* economic, 326
  survival of, 306-307
  test of, 288
Sections, and nation, 315 ff.
  as potential nations, 315
  blocs of, 198
  clashes of, 40-41
  conflicting interests of, 323-325
  disparity of political power of, 194-196
  influence by frontier, 23
  influenced by the West, 23
  League of, 51
  popular speech of, 328-329
  self-consciousness of, 198, 325-326
  significance of, in American history, 22
  struggles of, 291

[345]

INDEX

Shaw, Anna Howard, 282
Six Nations, ceded title to land, 91
Skyscraper, development of, in U.
S., 225
Smith, Alfred E., 202
Smith, Captain John, 221
Social origin, factors of, in elections, 187-191
"Solid South," 12, 333
Some Contemporary Americans,
276
South, history of, 12-13
South Carolina Yazoo Company,
56
Southern States, 1908, Wet and
dry, maps of, 308
Spain, anonymous draft for the
recovery of Louisiana from,
65-67
declares war against England in
1796, 175
in control of Mississippi navigation, 148
power of, in New World, 140
Spanish military strength in
Louisiana, 78-79
Speech, popular, of sections, 328-329
"Squatter Sovereignty," idea of,
135
State activity, in Western lands,
111 ff.

Taft, Lorado, 272
Taft, William H., 228
Talleyrand, 176 ff.
Tardieu, André, 317
Tate, William, 158
Taylor, John, 44, 194, 325
Telephone, spread of, in U. S.,
212-213
Tennessee, statehood claims of,
121-122
Thomas, Augustus, 274
Thwing, President of Western
Reserve University, 24

*Topographical Descriptions of the
Western Territories of Amer-
ica,* 61
Transylvania Company, formation
of, 99
Treaty of Versailles, 231
Trolley cars, changing city life of,
in U. S., 213

United States, a federation of sections, 250, 321
agrarian history of, 17
agricultural development of,
221-223
coal production in, 219
effect of immigration on, 17
growth of navy in, 224
growth of public schools in, 226
immigration to, 222
imperial in area, 289
increase of popular government
in, 227
iron production in, 219
national character of, 15
nationalizing tendencies in, 311
natural resources of, 37-38
political history of, 16
production of petroleum in, 219-220
results of progress in, 219 ff.
wealth of, 220-221

Van Buren, Martin, 199
Vandalia, new colony, 92
de Vergennes, M., 141-143 ff.
Virginia, cedes land across Ohio,
117
lands claimed by, 112-115
Vision of Columbus, 60
Voyage à la Louisiane, 142 n.

Ward, J. Q. A., 272
de Warville, Brissot, 58, 59
Washington, George, 116-117
alienated by Genet, 75
neutrality of, detrimental to
French plans, 53
Watauga settlers, 96-97

INDEX

Wealth of U. S., 220-221

West, the, 235 ff.

agricultural character of, 238 ff.

cattle raising in, 241-243

culture of, 252-254

descendants of New England in, 257 ff.

domain of, 235-236

a frontier, 237

influence of, on sections, 23

lumber production in, 243

manufacturing in, 246-247

metal production in, 244-245

national tendencies in, 138

petroleum production in, 245

political rôle of, 247 ff.

population of, 236, 237

promoted individualism, 90

railroads, 237

West, the, state activity of, 111 ff.

various meanings of, 86

Western Journal, 33

Western lands, England's policy towards, 141

Western State-making in Revolutionary Era, 86 ff.

"Western Waters," 93-94

Wet and dry map of southern states, 1908, 308

Whigs, geographical strength of, 47-48

platform of 1856, 199

Whiskey Rebellion, 133

Wilson, Woodrow, 38, 229-232, 251, 334

Wollstonecraft, Mary, 61

Wright brothers, 214

Yale Law Journal, 201